271. 509 A20 SS

ENGLAND: JESUITS: SIXTEENTH CENTURY

Campion and Parsons

By the same author:

The Field is Won: the Life and Death of Saint Thomas More (1968)
Saint John Fisher (1955, 1972)
The Roman Catholic Church in England and Wales: a Short History
(1973)
etc.

Campion and Parsons

The Jesuit Mission of 1580–1

E. E. Reynolds

Sheed and Ward
London

Contents

Preface

I first came to know of Campion and Parsons from reading Charles Kingsley's *Westward Ho!*. From it I got the impression that the two Jesuits were a couple of treacherous scoundrels. I was too young to appreciate that Kingsley was a rabid anti-Papist to whom 'Jesuit' was a term of abuse.[1] The book was published in 1855 and for half a century or more was among the most popular of boys' stories. Many thousands of adults must have been prejudiced against the Jesuits simply from having read *Westward Ho!* in their early years. It was a pity that Kingsley was writing a decade or more before his brother-in-law, James Anthony Froude, published his *Reign of Queen Elizabeth*, for the historian, strongly as he was opposed to Catholicism, gave a moving account of Campion's life (Everyman Edition, Vol. IV, pp. 278–313). Froude regarded the two Jesuits and the seminary priests as unwitting traitors, but that did not blind him to the pathos of their lives. It took me some time to overcome the effect of Kingsley's almost pathological abhorrence of the Catholic Church; it was to lead him, as we know, to his clash with John Henry Newman, and we owe the *Apologia* to the author of *Westward Ho!*

It has been customary to make a sharp distinction between Edmund Campion and Robert Parsons. For instance, Professor J. B. Black in his *The Reign of Elizabeth* (1936), wrote of Campion,

> Campion was the *beau sabreur* of spiritual gladiators – a radiant figure, whose nonchalance in the face of danger won for him imperishable renown among his followers, and a

high place in the gallery of great Elizabethans. His saintliness, transparant sincerity, and glowing rhetoric were infectuous and it was largely through his ministrations that catholicism in England rose to the heights of heroism it reached during the 'eighties.' (p. 145).

The same historian gave a very different view of Parsons.

His mind never ran on small things; and from the very first it is more likely that he felt himself irked by the limitations imposed upon him as a missionary priest in the English field. His roving, adventurous, and ambitious nature is seen to more advantage when he had fled from England after Campion's execution and became *par excellence* the politician and organizer of intrigue, plot, and invasion against his native country.

In his *The England of Elizabeth* (1950) Dr A. L. Rowse wrote of Parsons,

He was a brilliant intriguer, his hands were calloused with wire-pulling.

More recently Dr G. R. Elton has written in his *England under the Tudors* (1955),

Edmund Campion, the most saintly and most attractive of all the Jesuit missionaries, was executed in 1581 for treason committed for simple adherence to the queen's enemies (under the basic treason law of 1352); although he had done nothing except preach the faith, he had clearly adhered to the pope who was pursuing an active war against England. Parsons, a much abler and more dangerous but also much more dubious character, escaped to carry on war from Rome and Spain by pamphlets and intrigues. (p. 307).[2]

I hope that the following pages will modify these judgments on Parsons. The danger is of reading back into the Parsons of the 1580 mission, the policies that developed in later years. There is not the slightest hint in his letters and other records of his English period that he had any ulterior political motives at that time. Indeed, if I read his development aright, it was his experience in England of the almost hopeless task facing the missionary priests that led him afterwards to support William (later Cardinal) Allen's search for a political solution. Parsons' share has, I think, been exaggerated; I hope that even the brief account I give in the last few pages of this book of his later career will show that his political activities were only part, and not the major part, of his work.

There is, unfortunately, no authoritative biography of Robert Parsons. It is strange that this gap should exist in modern studies of Elizabethan notables. Whatever our judgment may be of his later activities, he was undeniably a great Englishman ('a writer of the best prose of his day'—Rowse) in an era of great Englishmen, and the Parsons myth, as it may be called, has prevented his true standing from being appreciated. He became a bogy-man, a kind of stage-Jesuit as unlike his prototype as the stage-Irishman of his. It is to be hoped that some young historian will supply a serious deficiency in our national gallery.

Edmund Campion has been more fortunate. A number of contemporary accounts of his capture, his conferences in the Tower, his imprisonment, trial and death, give us a more detailed record than we have of any other of the martyred priests of the Elizabethan period. The biography written by Richard Simpson (1867) has held the field for over a century. His documentation was sound, but some of his views were disputable (as, indeed, are mine); Newman, for instance, was angry at Simpson's treatment of St Pius V. Other material has come to light since and supplements Simpson's own researches which were thorough for his time. Evelyn Waugh published a short biography of Campion in 1935. He relied to a large extent on Simpson to whose work I also am largely indebted. Waugh's well-written short account is vitiated for the historian because it opens by accepting as true a legend of Queen Elizabeth's last days for which there is no positive evidence, but it was an opening that the novelist could not resist!

The footnotes record the sources on which I have worked. I would particularly express my indebtedness to the Catholic Record Society's volume XXXIX (1942), *Letters and Memorials of Father Robert Parsons, 1578–1588*, edited by the late Fr Leo Hicks, S.J. Unfortunately what was planned as the first of two or more

volumes has not been continued. The separate memoirs of
Parsons are printed in C.R.S. volumes II and IV.

I have not thought it useful to give the kind of bibliography
that is now customary. Several pages of lists of authors and
titles are of little help to the general reader who can get more
informative guidance from a public library; the scholar will be
familiar with detailed bibliographies of the Elizabethan period
that will meet his needs. The books I have mentioned in the
text and the footnotes will provide a foundation for further
study.

There is no authentic portrait of St Edmund Campion; two
have been claimed to be of him but they represent completely
different persons with not a feature in common; both were
seventeenth-century productions and imaginative. The only
authentic portrait of Robert Parsons shows him at the age of
sixty-five nearly thirty years after he left England.

The alternative spellings of Elizabethan names are tiresome.
Shakespeare or Shakespere? Ralegh or Raleigh? Campian or
Campion? Parsons or Persons? These variations have no
significance; all are 'correct', and it is a matter of personal
preference which is used. 'Campion' may be considered fixed
since his canonisation. I write 'Parsons' because that is the
form to which I have long been accustomed.

I am indebted to Lt-Col J. J. Dingwall for the photograph of
Lyford Grange on the jacket.

The following priests mentioned in this book were canonised
in 1970:— Alexander Briant, Edmund Campion, Luke Kirby,
Cuthbert Mayne, John Payne, Ralph Sherwin and Henry
Walpole.

E.E.R.

---

[1] Here is one example (almost comic) of Kingsley's extreme prejudice. In chapter 3
he ridiculed the clumsy efforts of the two Jesuits (disguised of course) to mount their
horses. At that period every man above the standing of labourer could ride a horse;
the only alternative was Shanks's pony.

[2] The most recent opinion is that of a Catholic author, Paul Johnson, who, on p. 161
of his *The Offshore Islanders* (1972) refers to 'the sinister Father Parsons, a professional
international conspirator,' which is nonsense.

Chapter 1

Supremacy and Uniformity

The vision of 'the spacious times of the great Elizabeth', to use Tennyson's phrase, makes it difficult for us to see her long reign of forty-four years as it was when she came to the throne in 1555 at the age of twenty-five. By the time of her death in 1603 in her seventieth year she had become as much a legend as her father had become after his reign of thirty-eight years. These legends still influence popular ideas, and, for the reign of Elizabeth, we have to make a strong effort of the imagination to get things in perspective to see the grave problems that had to be faced at the beginning of her reign. Of these the most pressing was that of religion.

Ordinary folk must have been in a confused religious state. Twenty years earlier had come the breach with Rome, the dissolution of the monasteries and uncertainty on what the people were supposed to believe. Henry VIII's vacillations had been baffling but towards the end he seemed to be tending towards some form of Protestantism. After him had come six years of pronounced Protestantism to be followed by five years of attempted return to the old ways. What was to come next?

Much would depend on the religious outlook of the queen herself, but no one then nor since has been able to give a clear account of its nature. Experience had taught her to move cautiously and not to reveal her full mind; this was to prove one of her notable characteristics which, at times, drove her councillors to distraction. She might have taken as her motto her father's saying, 'If I thought that my cap knew my counsel, I would cast it into the fire and burn it.'

Catherine Parr, Henry's last queen, made a home for his

three children, Mary, Elizabeth and Edward, and her leaning towards Protestantism influenced Elizabeth and Edward. Mary was twenty-seven years of age and proved immune, but Elizabeth at ten and Edward at six were more susceptible. Not that this meant withdrawal from the Mass; the king would never have tolerated that,[1] and, if legend is true, he was at one time alarmed at the queen's religious views. The tutors appointed for Edward and Elizabeth were Cambridge humanists, not, that is, outright rejectors of Catholic faith and practice, but having an Erasmian rather than a Lutheran outlook. Elizabeth therefore found no difficulty, as far as is known, in accepting the first Edwardian Book of Common Prayer of 1549.[2] This, apart from its use of English, was not a complete repudiation of Catholicism. There was nothing obnoxious to Catholics in Matins and Evensong. The Communion Service 'commonly called the Mass' was the touchstone for the fervent Catholic. The two Protestant notes were that the elevation of the consecrated host was forbidden, and communion was to be given in both kinds, bread and wine, instead of following the Catholic usage of in the bread alone. The second Edwardian Prayer Book of 1552 went much further. 'Matins' became 'Morning Prayer' and 'Evensong' became 'Evening Prayer.' Altars became tables standing 'in the body of the Church or in the Chancel.' Stone altars were not practicable. 'Holy Communion' was no longer said to be 'commonly called the Mass.' Ordinary bread was to be used, and was to be given 'in their hands.' In the prayers the name of Our Lady and references to saints and martyrs were omitted. At the Communion the words became, 'Take and eat (drink) this in remembrance', and the final rubric rejected the Catholic doctrine of transubstantiation in the declaration, 'For as concerning the sacramental bread and wine, they remain still in their very natural substances, and therefore may not be adored.' The term 'priest' was changed to 'minister'. The new book came into use on All Saints Day, 1st November 1552, but as the boy-king died the following summer, it did not have time to get established before the accession of Mary.

The Princess Elizabeth conformed with reluctance during the last years of Mary's reign, and when she herself was queen she continued to have Mass in her own chapel, but on Christmas Day she instructed the bishop who was celebrating not to elevate the host; as he persisted in doing so, she left the chapel. She certainly liked Catholic ceremonial and usages; thus she had lighted candles on the altar, and her lifelong aversion to a married clergy was a vestige of Catholic thinking. The title 'Supreme Head of the Church of England' was not to her liking, and in her early proclamations it was veiled by the '&c' that followed her other titles. Catholics, of course would have liked Parliament to rescind the title but even Queen Mary had not been able to get that done. Not all Protestants liked the title; it implied too much state control of religion, and some thought it incongruous for a woman to exercise such authority. We have to keep in mind that the Protestants were far from being all of one mind on church affairs. There were those who accepted the Edwardian settlement though they would have liked some changes especially as to vestments; there were others, more extreme,[3] who were highly critical of that settlement and would have liked a drastic revision of the Book of Common Prayer. These included ministers and others who had returned from exile spent in Reformist centres such as Frankfurt, Zurich and Geneva, where they had argued and even quarrelled among themselves during Mary's reign.

The first Parliament of the reign met on the 25th January 1559, and the main business put before it was a Bill on the Supremacy. The involved and far from clear proceedings that resulted in the Act of Supremacy (1 Eliz.c.1) and the subsequent Act of Uniformity (1 Eliz.c.2) cannot be followed here;[4] our concern is with the Acts themselves and how they affected Catholics. Two points may, however, be noted. The ten bishops in the Lords voted against the Supremacy; Convocation had already declared in favour of the Catholic doctrine of the eucharist, and in favour of papal primacy, and against the interference by Parliament in matters of faith and of church discipline. When the time came, all the bishops refused the oath; they were deprived and were put under constraint and some were imprisoned.[5] Among them was the venerable Bishop Cuthbert Tunstal, the friend of St Thomas More. This unanimity probably surprised the authorities; these bishops had acquiesced in previous changes, so why should they not accept yet another turn of the kaleidoscope? The second point to note is that the Acts were probably more extreme than the Bills originally presented to Parliament. Elizabeth would have been content with a reversion to the position as it was when her father died, but Protestant pressure both inside and outside Parliament forced the pace, and so what was no doubt intended as a simple reassertion of the Supremacy became more comprehensive.

The title 'Supreme Head' was changed to 'only Supreme Governor'; the application was 'as well in all spiritual or ecclesiastical things or causes as temporal.' The queen's purpose (the change would not have been made without her consent) may have been to make the supremacy more acceptable to Catholics as 'governor' implied control from outside the ecclesiastical body and carried no suggestion of sacerdotal power. Radical Protestants objected to the new title as being the old one in another guise.

The preamble of the Act, in the traditional form of a petition, declared that one purpose was 'the utter extinguishment and putting away of all usurped and foreign powers and authorities out of this your realm.' Without mentioning the pope, this meant the final rejection of his primacy. Laws affecting religion made during the previous reign were repealed and those enacted under Henry VIII were revived; these included those against appeals to Rome and the payment of annates.

Then followed a clause that seems irrelevant to the main intention of the Act. It restored the Edwardian Act (the first of the reign) against irreverence to the Eucharist; the last clause of this Act had decreed that communion should be in both kinds. The Elizabethan Act declared that this provision 'from henceforth shall and may stand, remain and be in full force.' This clause would have been more apposite in the next Bill before Parliament, that of Uniformity. Its presence in the Supremacy Act is an indication of the strength of Protestant opinion in the Commons; they would not wait to get this crucial eucharistic principle made obligatory.

The Act repealed the heresy laws enacted under Mary and then went on to repudiate yet again the claim of any 'foreign prince, person, prelate, state or potentate, spiritual or temporal' to exercise any power in England; this put into statutory form the intention given in the preamble. The next clause vested all power over the national church in the Crown.

An oath was to be exacted from every 'ecclesiastical person', from those taking university degrees, and from anyone in the state service. Those refusing the oath would be deprived of office. The oath read:

> I, A.B. do utterly testify and declare in my conscience, that the queen's highness is the only supreme governor of this realm and of all other her highness' dominions and countries, as well in all spiritual or ecclesiastical things or causes as temporal, and that no foreign prince, person, prelate, state or potentate hath or ought to have any jurisdiction, power, superiority, preeminence or authority, ecclesiastical or spiritual, within this realm; and therefore I do utterly renounce and forsake all foreign jurisdictions, powers, superiorities and authorities, and do promise that from henceforth I shall bear faith and true allegiance to the queen's highness, her heirs and lawful successors, and to my power shall assist and defend all jurisdictions, preemininences, privileges and authorities granted or belonging to the queen's highness, her heirs and successors, or united or annexed to the imperial crown of this realm: so help me God, and by the contents of this book.

'This book' was the Gospels; this was known as a 'corporal oath.'

This oath marks the beginning of the exclusion of Catholics from public life, but, in Tudor times, there was a considerable time-lag between the making of an Act and its enforcement. The administrative machinery did not exist. Thus a number of Catholic magistrates retained office, though this was also in part due to the difficulty of finding replacements. Moreover, the

oath does not seem to have been systematically applied. It
should be noted that peers were exempted from oath-taking and
some Catholic nobles, though excluded from the Council, were
employed by the queen. A good example is Viscount Montague
of Cowdray (Anthony Browne). Although he voted against the
Acts of Supremacy and Uniformity and made speeches against
these and other Protestant measures in the House of Lords, the
queen made use of his services until his death in 1591, a year
after he had entertained her for a week at Cowdray. This points
to the danger of making generalisations about the position of
Catholics during the Elizabethan period.

A clause in the Act of Supremacy penalised all who defended
any authority other than that of the queen. For the first offence,
the penalty was loss of goods; if these were worth less than £20 a
year, a year's imprisonment would be imposed; a second offence
meant the penalties of Praemunire,[6] and a third offence would
be high treason. Two further clauses attempted to circumscribe
the nature of heresy. The second of these shows how Parliament was abrogating to itself powers that had formerly been
ecclesiastical. Clause XX states that heresies would be

> . . . only such as heretofore have been determined, ordered or
> adjudged to be heresy by the authority of the canonical
> scriptures, or by the first four general councils, or any of
> them, or by any other general council wherein the same was
> declared heresy by the express and plain words of the said
> canonical scriptures, or *such as hereafter by the high court of
> Parliament* of this realm, with the assent of the clergy in their
> Convocation . . .

'The first four general councils' recognised by this Act were
Nicaea I (325), Constantinople I (381), Ephesus (431), and
Chalcedon (451).

The Act of Uniformity that followed on the heels of the Act
of Supremacy bore more hardly on Catholics. Its full title was:
'An act for the uniformity of common prayer and divine service
in the church, and the administration of the sacraments.' The
second Edwardian Book of Common Prayer was adopted with
one change in the words of the communion. They now read:

'The body (blood), which was given for thee, preserve thy body and soul unto everlasting life, and take and eat (drink) this in remembrance that Christ died for thee, and feed on him in thy heart by faith with thanksgiving.' The queen would have preferred the first Edwardian Prayer Book as this was less objectionable to Catholics. She gave way to the strongly expressed Protestant feelings of the Commons; the Radical Protestants wanted a new Prayer Book on the lines of the Geneva service book in which there were no traces of the Catholic liturgy. The wording of the litany was revised; this Litany in English goes back to Henry VIII's reign; it was the only portion of Cranmer's plan for the use of English that the king would authorise; it seems likely that, had he lived longer, he might have permitted an extension of the use of English. The chief change in the Litany made under the Act of Uniformity was the omission of the words 'from the tyranny of the Bishop of Rome and all his detestable enormities . . . Good Lord, deliver us.' The records of the debates in the Commons are so sparse that we cannot know who was responsible for this deletion. No Protestant, least of all a Radical, would have proposed it. Here we probably have an instance of how the queen as Supreme Governor exercised her prerogative; she may have been hoping that the Book of Common Prayer would in this way be less offensive to Catholics.

We must now examine the penal clauses of the Act as these directly affected Catholics.

1. 'Any person,[7] vicar or other whatsoever minister' who 'refused to use the said common prayers or to minister the sacraments', for the first offence lost his emoluments for a year and was imprisoned for six months. For a second offence the term of imprisonment was one year with the loss of the benefice; a third offence meant life imprisonment. Should the offender not be beneficed he was imprisoned for one year for his first offence, and for life for a second.

2. Anyone who spoke 'in derogation, depraving or despising the said book', or who compelled any minister to act contrary to the Book of Common Prayer, or who interrupted

the prescribed services had to pay a fine of 100 marks [say, £65] for a first offence, 400 for a second, and for a third he suffered loss of goods and life imprisonment.

3. The part of the Act enjoining attendance at Common Prayer is best quoted in full.

all and every person and persons inhabiting within this realm or any other of the queen's dominions shall diligently and faithfully, having no lawful or reasonable excuse to be absent, endeavour themselves to resort to their parish church or chapel accustomed, or upon reasonable let [hindrance] thereof to some usual place where common prayer and such service of God shall be used in such time of let, upon every Sunday and other days ordained and used to be kept as holy days, and then and there to abide orderly and soberly during the time of the common prayer, preachings or other service of God there to be used and ministered; upon pain of punishment by the censures of the church, and also upon pain that every person so offending shall forfeit for every such offence twelve pence,[8] to be levied by the churchwardens of the parish where such offence shall be done, to the use of the poor of the same parish, of the goods, lands and tenements of such offender by way of distress.

There can be little doubt that this Act went farther than the queen desired. Although she repeatedly forbade Parliament to intrude 'upon her Highness's authority ecclesiastical', it was impossible to withstand Protestant pressure. She made her own position clear on several occasions. Even after the issue of the Papal Bull of Excommunication in 1570, she could declare,

Her Majesty would have all her loving subjects to understand that as long as they shall openly continue in the observation of her laws and shall not wilfully and manifestly break them by their open acts, her Majesty's meaning is not to have any of them molested by any inquisition or examination of their consciences in causes of religion . . .; being very loth to be provoked by the overmuch boldness and wilfulness of her subjects to alter her natural clemency into a princely severity.

Such was the declaration she had made by the Lord Keeper publicly in the Star Chamber in June 1570. There is no reason to doubt her sincerity; for instance, she successfully resisted by her veto several attempts by Parliament to enforce the taking of communion as well as attendance at church. She was swimming against the tide of religious opinion; each church, Catholic or Protestant, believed itself to be the only Christian Church and wished its particular tenets and forms of worship to be imposed on the whole nation. The idea of toleration was alien to the times and, indeed, for long afterwards. Men felt so deeply and even fiercely about religion that they could not conceive how those professing different creeds could live at peace together. At the same time, it would be wrong to interpret the queen's attitude as a precocious exercise in toleration; the most likely explanation is that she herself had no deep religious convictions. She was neither a prig like her brother nor a fanatic like her sister. 'A plague o' both your houses!' may have expressed her sentiment.

[1] Henry heard two or three Masses daily, perhaps the abbreviated 'Hunting Masses'. This suggests superstition rather than true devotion.

[2] The two Edwardian Prayer Books were published in one volume of Everyman's Library (n.d.).

[3] It would be misleading, at this stage, to call them Puritans though they were among their progenitors. In these pages they will be distinguished as Radical Protestants.

[4] For the best account and discussion see, J. E. Neale, *Elizabeth I and her Parliaments*, Vol. I (1953), pp. 51–84. See also, Claire Cross, *The Royal Supremacy in the Elizabethan Church* (1969).

[5] At the beginning of the reign the archbishopric of Canterbury and five bishoprics were vacant. Four bishops died during the first year of the reign. All these sees were filled by conformists. Kitchin of Llandaff later came to terms with the government.

[6] The name given to fourteenth century statutes that forbade the reference to the papal courts of matters belonging to the king's courts.

[7] 'Person' here meant 'parson'. He held a parochial benefice in full possession of its rights and dues, i.e. a rector. He was accorded the title 'Sir'. The word 'priest' was not used in these two Acts.

[8] Suggested multipliers for giving modern money equivalents are misleading as our whole economy is so different. A rough comparison would be that in Elizabethan times a skilled carpenter could earn 10d. a day; so a 12d. fine was a day's wage for some people and more than that for many others. This fine had to be paid for each adult in a family.

Chapter 2

Catholicism on the wane

Commissioners, some of whom were laymen, were appointed in the autumn of 1559 to make visitations of all dioceses not only to see that the clergy were conforming, but to complete the work begun under Edward VI of removing all visible signs of papistry. Before he was deprived, Bishop Tunstal of Durham wrote to Sir William Cecil, the Secretary of State:

> If the same visitation shall proceed in my diocese of Durham as I do plainly see to be set forth in London, as pulling down of altars, defacing of churches, by taking away of crucifixes, I cannot in my conscience consent to it, being pastor there, because I cannot myself agree to be a sacramentary,[1] nor to have any new doctrine taught in my diocese.

Twenty years later William Harrison noted that 'all images, shrines, tabernacles, rood-lofts and monuments of idolatry are removed, taken down and defaced.'

There seems to have been little opposition to the changes. Probably up to eighty per cent of the clergy conformed. What happened to those who refused? Some would be domiciled in the houses of the Catholic gentry as chaplains or tutors or stewards; some became fugitives always on the move saying Mass in secret and bringing the sacraments to the faithful. Others fled abroad. The large number of priests who accepted the new order is an indication of their low standard of training; indeed, there had been no special training for the priesthood even in the universities. This was the biggest problem that faced the new Protestant bishops. Few of these former priests could instruct their congregations in the principles of a Protestantism of which they were ignorant. They were therefore forbidden to preach until licensed by their bishop, and for some years the number so licensed was far below the need. In place therefore of a sermon most priests read one of the Homilies published by authority. The majority of these gave uncontroversial ethical teaching, but some were directed against 'the Pope's intolerable pride' and the teaching of the Catholic Church. Others inculcated the duty of obedience to authority especially in religious practices.

The task that faced the bishops was beyond their resources. As late as 1585, Archbishop Whitgift, in answering a complaint about the ignorance of the clergy, pointed out that there were 13,000 parishes in England. Queen Elizabeth, who was present when Burghley (Cecil) raised the matter exclaimed, 'Jesus! 13,000! It is not to be looked for. My meaning is not that you should make choice of learned ministers only, for they are not to be found, but of honest, sober and wise men and such as can read the scriptures and homilies well to the people.'

There was nothing new in this situation; the Archbishop was, of course, greatly disturbed at the lack of a teaching clergy, but when England was Catholic there was also a lack of priests who could preach; many were simple, devout men, not greatly advanced in learning above some of their parishioners, but competent to say Mass and administer the sacraments. The Protestant ministers put little emphasis on the sacraments; they concentrated on doctrine. This want of an understanding beyond the catechism of the underlying truths of the faith was one reason for the comparative ease with which the majority of ordinary folk accepted the new services. No doubt they were bewildered by the changes; we, in our time, have had a parallel experience; most would not have been able to argue on the doctrinal issues just as to-day the ordinary Catholic cannot go deeply into the doctrinal basis of his faith.

We must bear in mind that out of a population of some four and a half millions, only half a million lived in the larger towns, including London. The other four millions lived in small market towns, villages and hamlets and would be out of reach of Protestant propaganda, though garbled versions of the Lutheran and other heretical tenets might come from chance travellers. It was in London and Norwich and a few other towns that Protestantism had taken a firm hold; the south-eastern part of the country was the most affected; the rest of the country, especially the north and west, was relatively free from such influences. To this it should be added that firm Tudor rule had become acceptable as the only alternative to the former anarchy and the habit of obedience to the government had been strengthened.

All this was true of those whose religious practices had hitherto been an unquestioned part of their lives, passing from parents to children for generations; there were also many who were deeply devoted to their religion; it was they who used the primers and other devotional aids that had become so common since the spread of printing. How many were there of these convinced Catholics? No answer can be given as there are no statistics and any attempt to suggest numbers would be guess-work. All one can say is that the number of convinced Catholics was not great enough to influence general opinion. What we can examine is the problem that Catholics had to face and how they dealt with it. But, first, it should be noticed that they were given neither guidance nor encouragement save from the handful of priests who chose to go out into the wilderness. The Catholic bishops were under restraint or in prison. Rome remained unhelpfully silent for some years.

It would be difficult to exaggerate the work of those priests who refused to conform. They were comparatively few in numbers but dauntless in their determination to preserve at least a remnant of the Church. Without their labours, Catholicism would have died out in England as it did in the Scandinavian countries. Their achievement has been over-shadowed by the missionary work of the seminary priests but they did not begin to enter the country, and at first only in small numbers, until 1574, sixteen years after the passing of the Act of Uniformity.

There is an account of what was probably the normal reaction in the autobiography (though written in the third person) of Fr Augustine Baker, O.S.B. (1575–1641). His father was William Baker a magistrate of Abergavenny. The extract is long but it will repay careful reading and pondering. Some key sentences are italicised.

His parents were of honest condition for the world, and were for their birth and education in their youth of the time of King Henry VIII, his father having been born in the twenty-first year (1529–30) of the said king's reign. The which king, though afterward in the twenty-sixth of his reign he became injurious to Holy Church, to arrogate to himself and to his regal condition ecclesiastical supremacy for all England, and thereby became at least schismatical, yet in all other respects Catholic religion was the legal and common external religion of the kingdom until the death of the same king. By means whereof the parents (especially the father) of the person whose life we are to describe, knew and for that space exercised the manner of Catholic rites in religion. But the said king dying, upon the succeeding of his young son, being King Edward VI, Catholic religion was publicly abandoned and heretical services introduced in lieu of it, which continued till the seventh year of the same child king's reign. And he then dying, there succeeded the good and most Catholic and pious Queen Mary, who restored religion to the whole land. And in the midst or nearer the beginning of her reign were those parents married and so then with others were in exercise of the Catholic religion to which they were both as it were naturally inclined and affected.

But the said Queen Mary in the fifth year of her reign dying, and Queen Elizabeth succeeding, she being affected by heresy soon brought it to the public and universal profession of the land, the Catholic religion being, as to all public use, clean suppressed. And those parents accommodated themselves *at least exteriorly* to the common though schismatical service of the land. And indeed at the first, and for some years after, the said change made by Queen Elizabeth, *the greatest part even of those who in their judgments and affections had before been Catholics, did not well discern any great fault, novelty or difference from the former religion that was Catholic* in this new set up by Queen Elizabeth, save only the change of language, bringing in service in the English tongue, in lieu of that

which had been in Latin, in the which difference they
conceived nothing of substance or essence to be. . . .

By these means and occasions those parents, with
thousands of others that likewise had been professors of the
Catholic religion (besides those that proved enemies thereto,
as being Protestants) *in tract of time and gradually, and indeed as
it were unawares to themselves, became neutrals in religion*, viz.,
neither indeed true Catholics, for perfect knowledge, belief
and practice, nor yet mere Protestants or otherwise heretics
in their belief though schismatical, by their external
accommodation to the schismatical service of the English
Church. Of the number or quality of those kind of neutrals,
the said parents, in the said later condition of theirs, to have
been and remained. . . . *They gave no education at all as to any
religion to their children*, but regarded only in them a good
moral external carriage to which through nature they were
even of their own selves disposed. But what their children's
belief or practice should be, in matter of religion, they
heeded not.

Fr Baker went on to describe his father's private devotions
which lingered from his Catholic days.

Yet did he for all that daily at least, whensoever and so far
as possibly he could get vacancy from his employments and
solicitudes, spend much time in recital of vocal prayers and
that out of Latin Catholic authors, whereof by some means
or other he had gotten some variety. In the English tongue
were then no prayer books save some few Catholic ones
whereof he had also gotten some. And of these books, one
after another, walking in the garden and in his way to and
fro thither, he would recite to himself, yet so audibly that
others could not but hear somewhat. And so his manner in
this kind, viz., such his much praying, was somewhat
notorious, though imitated by none, no, not by his own
children. And indeed he was even naturally so devout and
affected to Catholic religion, both as to belief and practice,
that he having been married in Queen Mary's days, and
Queen Elizabeth succeeding her and changing the religion
of the land, turning it from Catholic to become heretical or
schismatical, he was in his mind and affection so much
troubled and offended thereat, that *if he had not been in the
state of a married man and a father of children living, he would upon*

*such change made by Queen Elizabeth for Catholic religion's sake,
have forsaken the kingdom, and gone overseas and lived there in some
Catholic condition.* But in time *he came to lose all sense of Catholic
religion,* accommodating himself exteriorly to the schismatical service of England, and nothing troubled his mind
either one way or other concerning Catholic and Protestant
beliefs, but yet still persevered in daily use of vocal prayer.[2]

It seemed worthwhile giving this testimony in some detail as it
helps us to appreciate the situation in which Catholics found
themselves. The choice that a father of a family had to make
must often have been agonizing. William Baker's decision not
to bring up his children on either Catholic nor Protestant lines
must have been followed by many who managed to keep within
the law, giving the minimum of adherence to the new teachings.
So it was inevitable that the rising generation accepted the
Anglican form of religion. At the same time it should be noted
that one of William Baker's sons, David (Augustine), became
a Benedictine monk and a spiritual guide whose influence has
been lasting. William Baker returned to the faith of his fathers
before his death in 1606.

The many Catholics who conformed may have had in mind
the possibility of yet another turn of the wheel should the
queen marry a foreign Catholic prince, or should she die. And
who would be her successor? The law was by no means clear.
Strict heredity would mean that the Catholic Mary Queen of
Scots would come to the throne. Indeed when she married the
Dauphin of France in 1558, she quartered the arms of England
with those of France. As the years passed, this hope of another
reversion of religion grew fainter.

There is much we should like to know about the early years
of the enforcement of the Act of Uniformity, but we lack the
necessary information. It must have taken some time for knowledge of the Act to reach the remoter villages; there was,
too, the practical problem of supplying copies of the Book of
Common Prayer and of the Homilies. For a longish period
there must have been confusion and even bewilderment among
priests and people before the new order could get stabilised.

The rubrics of the Book of Common Prayer were not as precise as they might have been; this was probably intentional in the first place; this affected, for instance, what vestments were to be used. Another detail that is not made clear was how frequently the new Communion Service was to be said. This had sufficient resemblances to the Mass for some Catholics to accept it as a substitute. It may be that at first the Communion Service followed Morning Prayers each Sunday but this was not explicitly laid down. We do know, however, that, later in the reign, it became customary to have the Service only once a quarter. Thus Church Papists, as those who conformed came to be called, were deprived of even a semblance of regular Sunday Mass and their children could not have known what the Mass meant in the Catholic Church.

Some conforming priests said Mass privately for those who persevered in the faith, and they secretly administered the sacraments of baptism, matrimony and penance, and it seems that some Church Papists took Communion according to the Prayer Book rite. There were no doubt many variations in the degrees of conformity from those who did the minimum to satisfy the law to those who strove to save as much of their Catholic practices as possible behind closed doors. Much might depend on the presence locally of a lord of the manor or one of the landed gentry who remained a convinced Catholic; he could shelter the priest and allow neighbours to come to his house for Mass. The country gentry were in fact the key to Catholic survival.

We do not know how far the 12d. fine was exacted as it was collected by the churchwardens and used for local poor relief and therefore did not come under exchequer control for record. The implementation of the Act of Uniformity was the business of 'archbishops, bishops and all other their officers exercising ecclesiastical jurisdiction' in the church courts. The magistrates had a watching brief and could report defaulters to the bishop or bring them to the Assizes. It has been pointed out that the administrative machinery in those times was sketchy and the sheer physical problem of supervision defeated the full application of the Act. There was also the human factor. One M.P. in 1571 complained that the 12d. fine was not being exacted. The churchwardens, he said, were 'simple, mean men' who 'would rather commit perjury than give their neighbours cause for offence.' This would particularly apply to small communities where everyone knew everyone else, where there was much inter-marrying and where all had been brought up together from childhood. The churchwarden was one of themselves and, after his year of office, unless reappointed, would find himself again an ordinary parishioner, so 'live and let live' would be the prudent policy. No doubt personal spite was at times active and perhaps some mild blackmail was extorted, but the general picture would be one of neighbourly tolerance. The intrusion of a Protestant fanatic could, of course, upset the whole village and much bitterness and strife would follow. The same kindly feeling would be found also among the magistrates and landowners, some of whom, it has been noted, were Catholics until replacements could be appointed. A magistrate would not be anxious to persecute someone with whom he had gone to school, hunted, and enjoyed social relations.

During the early years of the reign Catholics were not unduly molested. They had to decide how far they could comply with the new regulations and every year that passed meant that more and more of them yielded, first just sufficiently to escape paying fines and then by an inevitable process of little by little to become so accustomed to the new services that they accepted them as normal and forgot their old ways. By 1570 it could be said that the government policy of letting Catholicism fade out was within sight of being accomplished. There had been no organised opposition, nor had there been any local still less national uprisings. As the old priests died out, so the argument went, so Catholicism would die out with them. The young generation, brought up under the new dispensation, would not hanker after the religious practices that their parents had known in their earlier days. At the same time the Radical Protestants had been kept in check and the queen's determination that there should be no further changes was unshaken.

She and William Cecil must have been well satisfied with the way things were going.

The puzzle remains of the failure of Rome to give Catholics in England any guidance. The explanation lies paradoxically in the anti-papal policy of Philip II of Spain who for four years had been King of England. When, on two occasions, the pope wished at the beginning of Elizabeth's reign, to send envoys in the hope of effecting some kind of rapprochement, Philip prevented them from leaving the Netherlands. For his own political purposes he wanted to remain on good terms with the new queen; he did not want to see England making overtures to his enemy France. The Spanish ambassador assured King Philip that he had advised Catholics not to offend the queen. 'Rather let them treat matters which are not against their conscience with moderation and reserve, since respect for superiors is a duty they owe to God.' This avoided the awkward problem of deciding what was a matter of conscience. Is it surprising that Catholics in England felt they were abandoned and must depend on their own individual judgements?

---

[1] One who denied the Real Presence.
[2] C.R.S. Vol. XXXIII, pp. 15–19.

Chapter 3

Douay

March 1563 saw the publication of John Foxe's *Actes and Monuments of these latter and perillous dayes, touching matters of the Church, wherein are comprehended and described the great persecutions and horrible troubles, that have bene wrought and practised by the Romishe Prelates, specillye in this Realme of England and Scotlande, from the year of our Lorde a thousande, unto the tyme nowe present.* This book became commonly known as Foxe's *Book of Martyrs.* It has been said, 'It is impossible to exaggerate its influence on English feeling and opinion. The Catholics angrily named it "Foxe's Golden Legend", but the nickname defines very accurately the place taken by the book in the minds of the common people of England.' Another scholar has declared that 'Foxe's *Book* counted in English history as much as Drake's Drum.'[1] Convocation in 1571 ordered that a copy should be made available for public use in every cathedral (it cost £2.2s.6d) and copies were also widely bought for parish churches; some of these copies, with the old chains, are still to be seen. A reader would gather people around him to listen to these accounts of the Protestant martyrs,[2] and, those who could not read, could turn the pages and study the lurid illustrations. Five editions of the book were printed during the reign of Elizabeth, and it continued to be in steady demand for more than two centuries. It became a second book to the Bible in many households, though, later on, Bunyan's *Pilgrim's Progress* (1678) took its place in popularity. Many, many thousands of children and adults received their impressions of Catholicism from this book, and became imbued with dread and horror of the Catholic Church.

At the time of the publication of Foxe's *Book*, Parliament was busy extending the application of the Act of Supremacy. The enforcement of the oath seems to have been largely confined to the parish clergy and, even so, was demanded rather haphazardly. Refusal to take the oath now meant loss of goods and life imprisonment; a second refusal entailed the death penalty. Not only ecclesiastics were now to take the oath but lawyers, public officials, schoolmasters and members of the House of Commons. The Parliament of 1566 was the first in which there were no Catholics in the Commons; peers were specifically excluded from taking the oath. The queen was evidently reluctant to accept this new law but Protestant opinion in the Commons was too strong for her; she got round it by giving instructions through the Archbishop that the oath was not to be proferred a second time without his written consent.

The action of the Commons in framing this new law was partly due to the frustrating knowledge that the queen would not allow the Radical Protestants to transform the Book of Comon Prayer into something more in keeping with the forms of worship recommended by 'the best reformed Churches of Europe.' In later years the extremists went so far as to describe the Prayer Book as 'an unperfect book, culled and picked out of the Popish dunghill, the Mass book, full of abominations.'[3] The queen remained unshakenly resolved to have no more changes made in the prescribed services; she was aware that in its existing form the Prayer Book was not wholly unacceptable to lukewarm Catholics, and she wanted things to remain that way. The Radicals deceived themselves in thinking that the populace was anxious to imitate 'the best reformed Churches of Europe.' The fact was that most of them became apathetic as a result of being pushed this way and that during the past twenty years in the observance of religion. It was to take many years for Radical Protestantism and, later, Puritanism, to become dominant and even then it was far from being generally accepted. More and more former Catholics were becoming gradually habituated to the Prayer Book services. How many remained defiantly faithful is not known but it was certainly a dwindling number and this was a matter of grave concern to those who, in spite of all, clung to the Old Faith. Some could get to the manor houses of the Catholic gentry where priests were sheltered; others would be known to itinerant priests who risked imprisonment to keep in touch with Catholics of whom they had knowledge. The more isolated Catholics, of whom there may have been many, would be the first to fall away. As the years passed, so the outlook became more bleak; the 1563 Act brought more pressure to bear on men of position and some, like William Baker, conformed for the sake of family and property. The old priests were dying and there were none to take their places. There was not a bishop in England to ordain young men.

That the Catholic decline was checked was largely due to the work of one man – William Allen. He was born in 1532 at Rossall in the Lancashire Fylde of a gentle family related to many of the great landowners of that strongly Catholic county.  In 1547 he entered Oriel College, Oxford, and was elected a fellow in 1550. He became principal of St Mary's Hall six years later. It was possible, even during the reign of Edward VI for Catholics, provided they remained quiet, to continue their studies. The position was less favourable when Elizabeth came to the throne but it was not until 1561 that Allen's religious convictions led him to leave the country for Louvain which had become a centre for Catholics who chose exile rather than conform. Allen returned to Lancashire about 1563 for his health's sake. There he could live with his family in security. Of the religious position in that county a few years later, Strype wrote, 'religion, in Lancashire and parts thereabouts, went backwards, papists about this time showing themselves to be numerous, Mass commonly said, priests harboured, the Book of Common Prayer and the church established by law laid aside, many churches shut up and cures unsupplied, unless with such popish priests as had been ejected.' William Allen did not remain in Lancashire for the whole of his stay in England; he was in the Midlands and in East Anglia, and he found that the position there was far different from that in his home county; conformity was common among Catholics who were steadily losing their faith. He returned to the Low Countries in 1565 with the intention of being ordained to the priesthood; this took place at Mechlin in 1567.

A number of scholar-exiles as well as members of the Thomas More circle had settled at Louvain;[4] their leader was Nicholas Sander (Winchester and New College, Oxford), who had been among the theologians at the Council of Trent (1545–1563). With him were Thomas Harding and Thomas Stapleton, both of Winchester and New College, as well as other scholars. Their work was apologetical and controversial and the books and pamphlets they produced were an important weapon in the war against Protestantism. For several years they were engaged in refuting Bishop John Jewel's *Apologia Ecclesiae Anglicanae* (1562), the most effective statement of the Anglican position. The book was translated into English by Lady Bacon, mother of Francis, in 1564. Devotional books were also printed, such as Lawrence Vaux's Catechism, the title of which was *A Cateschisme, or a Christian Doctrine, necessarie for Children & ignorant people*. The author had been a fellow of Corpus Christi, Oxford. He returned to England in 1580 and was almost immediately arrested and spent the remainder of his life in prison. Between 1559 and 1570 nearly sixty books were published. Among them was Stapleton's translation of Bede's *Ecclesiastical History*. This was published in 1565 and dedicated to the queen to show her 'what faith your noble Realm was Christened.' The considerable cost was met by donations from Catholics in England and in exile.

The distribution of these books was full of risks. Many proclamations were issued against importing Catholic books as well as against reading them or even possessing them. Special precautions were taken at the ports to search for and examine all books brought in by traders and travellers. The considerable trade between England and the Low Countries presented countless opportunities for smuggling books especially by way of the lesser ports and harbours. Sometimes the carriers were put ashore on lonely parts of the coast. In spite of all these difficulties the books were widely distributed by paid agents (a costly business), by private colporteurs and, later, by the incoming missionary priests. It was a dangerous business and could land the bearer of the books in prison for life.

While William Allen was studying theology at Louvain, he wrote two books. The first, published in 1565, was *A Defense and Declaration of the Catholike Doctrine of Purgatory*. His name headed a writ sent in February 1567 to the High Sheriff of Lancashire for the arrest of priests who 'were justly deprived of their offices for their contempt and obstinacy.' Allen is there described as the man 'who wrote the late booke of Purgatory.' The second book was entitled *A Treatise made in defence of the lauful power and authoritie of Priesthood to remitte sins*. This was published in 1567 and in that year Allen went to Rome with his friend Jean Vendeville who was professor of canon law at Douai university. On their journey they discussed the possibilities of reviving Catholicism in those countries where Protestantism was established. One outcome of their discussions was the decision to establish a college at Douai where young English Catholics could receive the education they could no longer get at Oxford or Cambridge. So Douay[5] came to be founded in 1568. Allen had clear objectives in mind; in summary they were these,

1. the training of English youths in the Low Countries in 'common conference and public exercise,' so that if, or when, they returned to England they would be faithful to their religion. 'Our aim,' Allen later wrote, 'is and has always been, to train Catholics to be plainly and openly Catholics; to be men who will always refuse every kind of spiritual commerce with heretics';
2. to attract young men from England who wished to have a 'more exact education than is in these days in either the Universities';
3. to train those who have vocations for the priesthood to replace the diminishing number of priests in England.

Allen set his great project on foot in full trust that somehow or other the necessary funds would be forthcoming. English Catholics in the Low Countries and friends in England sent donations. We know, for instance, that William Roper, son-in-law of St Thomas More, was fined for sending money abroad for this purpose. Later on the popes and Philip II gave regular support, but, even so, the college always had a difficulty in making two ends meet. There was a quick response when the college opened; the numbers soon reached a hundred and at times a hundred and fifty. The emphasis soon came to be put on training for the priesthood but the general education of youths continued.

The three-year course of training for the priesthood which followed the general education, was very thorough and was designed with the practical needs of England in mind. Allen's purpose was not to produce learned scholars and controversialists; the Douai university could supply that need. Allen wanted to train men who could meet the actual situation of the times. Primary importance was placed on the study of the Scriptures since this was the basis of Protestant teaching. With this can be linked the translation of the New Testament, though this was not published until 1582 when the College had temporarily moved to Reims (1578–93) owing to disturbances in the Low Countries. There were regular disputations on those texts on which Protestants put so much emphasis, and every week the students had to practise preaching in English. Great care was taken to train them as catechists and confessors.

The first priests were ordained in 1573 and four went to England in 1575. By 1578 seventy-five priests were ordained and fifty-two were 'on the mission'; 'mission,' because England was no longer a Catholic country.

Four months before William Allen founded Douay, Mary Queen of Scots took refuge in England. In January 1567 her husband, Henry Darnley, had been murdered; within five months she married James Hepburn, Earl of Bothwell, who had just divorced his wife. As he was a Protestant, the marriage was according to the Protestant rite. All this shocked Catholics, and Pope Pius V declared that there was little to choose between Mary and Elizabeth. The events of the following twelve months are well known – the imprisonment on Loch Leven, her abdication, her escape, and her desperate attempt to win back the throne. Her arrival in England presented Elizabeth with a dilemma that for nineteen years was to bedevil English politics. Mary inevitably became the centre of plots; she was, after all, on strict hereditary principle, the heiress to the throne. Some Catholics, but not all by any means, were prepared to forget her murky past and to see her as the Catholic supplanter of Elizabeth. As the years went by, a romantic mist enshrouded 'this fascinating, artful and dangerous young woman.'[6] Many went to the gallows or the block on her behalf. One of the purposes of the Rising in the North in November 1569, when Mass was again said in Durham cathedral, was to set Mary free. It was put down ruthlessly; Thomas Percy, Earl of Northumberland was beheaded and eight hundred of his followers were hanged; they were, for the most part, artisans and rustics. Then in 1571 came the grotesque Ridolfi plot. He was a Florentine banker resident in London. Like so many conspirators he imagined that he had only to stamp his foot and armed bands would spring up; a general uprising would be supported by an invading Spanish army. Part of the scheme was that the Duke of Norfolk should marry Mary of Scots, a proposal she approved. He was a Protestant, if he was anything so distinctive, and not too stupid to realise what was involved. His execution in June 1572 closed the episode.

Meanwhile, Rome had at last acted. A Dominican friar became pope as Pius V in 1565. He was a man of strict, holy living and in his seven years as pope, he did much to clean up the curia and to make bishops and clergy attend to their pastoral duties. He was in no sense a politician; his religion came first and last. So it was that in February 1570 he issued the Bull *Regnans in Excelsis* excommunicating Queen Elizabeth and thereby freeing her subjects from their allegiance. He did this without consulting any of the kings or princes whose duty it was, in his view, to enforce the Bull. Philip of Spain was affronted for he thought he had the pope in his pocket; his political plans did not include a break with England, and so, as far as he was concerned, the Bull was a dead letter, as it was for other princes. Rome had yet to realise that in a Europe divided into Catholic and Protestant states, the pope had little influence in a world of power politics. There has been much discussion on the wisdom or folly of the pope's action. It seems clear that few Catholics were likely to renounce their allegiance to the queen, though it must have taken a long time for the news of the excommunication to reach most of them as the Bull was not published in England. A daring layman, John Felton, fixed a copy of the Bull to the door of the Bishop of London's palace, and for this he was hanged in St Paul's Churchyard on the 8th August 1570. The most serious objection to the Bull was that it put into the hands of the government an additional weapon. Catholics could now be charged with being traitors, and they could be faced with 'the bloody question,' as it was called, 'If a Catholic army invaded the country, would you support the queen or the pope?' It is, however, unrealistic to argue that the Bull was responsible for the subsequent persecution; that would have come in any case for the queen and her councillors, especially William Cecil and Francis Walsingham, were determined to suppress residual Catholicism; the Bull happened to be a welcome and extra means for doing so.

It did not create the conflict of loyalties for Catholics; the dilemma was the result of the Act of Uniformity. The 'bloody question' itself was an obvious one to put to suspects, whether priests or laymen; Cecil and Walsingham did not need the pope to suggest it to them.

One result of the crisis set by the arrival of the Queen of Scots in the country, and to a lesser extent by the papal Bull, was that a new penal law was passed in 1571. It now became treason to question the sovereignty of the queen of her religion, to reconcile anyone to the Catholic Church, to bring or receive papal Bulls, crucifixes, rosaries, or an Agnus Dei. Abettors and harbourers were liable to loss of goods and life imprisonment.

Two events outside England during these years added to the growing hostility to Catholicism. The Massacre of St Bartholomew on the 24th August 1572, horrified Protestants and made many Catholics recoil. The *Te Deum* was sung in St Peter's and a special papal medal was issued. Soon French Protestant refugees were arriving in England. Then in 1576, Spanish troops sacked Antwerp in what became known as the 'Spanish Fury.'

So we see how fears and suspicions of Catholics were mounting during the early years of the establishment of Douay. The priests who came on the mission now had to face stronger opposition and run graver personal risks than when the college was founded. It was not long, of course, before the government was being kept well informed of what was going on. Spies were soon at work ferreting out any scrap of news that would put the government on its guard. No doubt the awareness of the purpose of Douay was one of the reasons for the passing of the 1571 Act.

[1] Ronald Bayne in *Shakespeare's England* (1917), I, p. 70. Gordon Rupp, *The English Protestant Tradition* (1949), p. 209. It was typical that the East India Company provided their ships with copies of the Bible and of Foxe.

[2] A martyr for religion is one who submits to death rather than renounce his faith, however mistaken we may regard his faith to have been.

[3] *An Admonition to Parliament* (1572).

[4] For a full survey see A. C. Southern, *Elizabethan Recusant Prose, 1559–1582* (1950); of the thirty-two writers there catalogued, eleven were Wykehamists and fellows of New College. Nine others were Oxford scholars.

[5] 'Douai' is here used for the town and university; the traditional 'Douay' is used for the college; 'Doway' was also used.

[6] Neale, *op. cit.*, I, p. 177.

Chapter 4

The Mission is agreed upon

St Pius V died in 1572 and was succeeded by Gregory XIII. He called William Allen to Rome in February 1576 to consult on a scheme for an invasion of England. The relations between that country and Spain were becoming strained and England was making overtures to France. King Philip was therefore more favourable to action against the country of which he had been king. The leader of the projected expedition was Thomas Stukeley, once a Protestant pirate and now a Catholic adventurer. The pope was to supply shipping and men. Allen approved the scheme, the outcome of which can be briefly given. After all the delays inevitable in such an enterprise, Stukeley left in 1578 in one ill-founded ship with a crew and men-at-arms most of whom had been press-ganged. He got to Lisbon only to learn that King Philip now needed all his troops to deal with a rising in the Spanish Netherlands. Sebastian, King of Portugal, persuaded Stukeley to join him in an attack on the Moors, and both were killed at the battle of Alcazar in August 1578.

A more important aspect of Allen's visit to Rome than this fiasco was the possibility of the medieval English Hospice becoming a seminary. Allen had more applicants to enter Douay than he could accommodate. The pope accepted the suggestion and the English College (the Venerabile) was established in February 1577. Its early years were marred by those internal squabbles and personal animosities that were, unhappily, a feature of English Catholic affairs both at that period and for some years to come and, indeed, are not unknown today. The problem of the control of the College was at last resolved when the pope put it under the direction of the General of the Society of Jesus. For a few weeks Fr Robert Parsons took charge until the new Rector, Alphonsus Agazzari, could arrive. William Allen had returned to Rome on account of these troubles in 1579 and he was well satisfied that the Jesuits, for whom he had much admiration, should be put in charge of the new English College. It was probably on this occasion that he and Robert Parsons met for the first time; they were to remain close allies until Allen's death in 1594.

Robert Parsons was born at Nether Stowey, Somersetshire, in 1546; he was thus fourteen years younger than William Allen. The father is said to have been a blacksmith.[1] The parish priest, who must have conformed, helped to get the boy a sound education at the free school at Taunton. From there he went to St Mary's Hall, Oxford, in 1564. He passed on to Balliol College of which he became a fellow in 1568 when he took his degree; he was bursar and dean in 1574. Quite clearly he had capabilities that his college recognised and used. He left soon after becoming bursar; his own account suggests a leaning towards Catholicism though this was not openly declared; he had twice taken the oath required by the Act of Supremacy; he was not ordained. The Master and some of the fellows brought pressure to bear on him on account of his Catholic inclinations. The reason for his change may be seen in the following passage he wrote in later years.

Whatever we had heard or conceived in the whole day for pulling out this thorn of conscience, and for smoothing the way to be Protestant, either by good fellowship and conversation with Protestants themselves, or by hearing their sermons or reading their books, all this was dashed by one hour's reading of the old holy doctors, and the wound of conscience was made green again, and as grievous as ever, by every page which spake of virtue and austerity, or of questions of controversy, which were settled there as clearly as if the Fathers had distinctly foreseen the tumults of these days.

From Oxford Parsons went to London with the intention of
studying medicine, but on the advice of Thomas Sackville,
Lord Buckhurst, he set out for Padua, the leading medical
school of the day. Nothing is known of the connection with
Sackville who was firmly Protestant.[2] Parsons broke his journey
at Louvain where he made the Spiritual Exercises of St
Ignatius Loyola; his director was Fr William Good, and it may
be presumed that it was then that Parsons was reconciled to
the Church; that would be in the summer of 1574. We do not
know how he came to take such a definite step as making the
Exercises; it may be that companions on the journey from
London persuaded him to make his decision on a vital question
that had been troubling him for some time. We have no
account of his spiritual progress. He continued his way to
Padua but visited Rome at the beginning of the Holy Year. He
reached Padua in the spring of 1575 but after two or three
months his sense of vocation to the priesthood became
irresistible and he returned to Rome where he was received
into the Society of Jesus on the 4th July. After his novitiate, he
began his theological studies at the Roman College and was
ordained, it is thought, in 1578. How quickly he impressed his
superiors is shown by his appointment as English penitentiary
at St Peter's before he had completed his theological course.
He replaced Dr Nicholas Morton.

   No simple explanation in human terms can be given for the
phenomenal success of the Jesuits within a generation of their
foundation in 1534. The Society became the spear-head of the
Counter Reformation. St Ignatius and his six companions had
decided 'to offer themselves to the pope to be employed in the
service of God in what manner he judged best.' Their rigorous
organisation, their strict and unquestioning obedience to their
superiors as well as their thorough training formed the frame-
work within which they worked with total dedication. When
St Ignatius died in 1556, the year after the accession of Queen
Elizabeth, there were a thousand members at work in nine
European countries as well as in India and Brazil. Numbers
continued to increase and their missionary labours expanded

rapidly. They became particularly notable in the field of education where they pioneered improved methods of teaching. Such a dynamic, single-purposed society inevitably attracted young men who were anxious to give their lives and devote all their abilities to the cause of a Church that was no longer on the defensive but was going out to combat its opponents vigorously.

One of William Allen's purposes in colonising Rome from Douay had been to get more recruits for the English mission. Some of his students had gone over to the Jesuits with his blessing though, as he realised, this meant, in keeping with current Jesuit policy, that they would not be available for England. Could the Society be persuaded to change this policy? In a letter to Fr William Good written in 1579, perhaps at the end of March, Robert Parsons raised this very question.

> Thus much I can assure you not only of the Englishmen, but also of all others who abide in the English College, so great and marvellous is the affection they bear England, and to the English Catholics, that if our Superiors would but once give a sign of consent to set open the College gates towards the enterprise[3] of England, they would all run out, even from the Rector himself to the lowest scholar in the College, and this I well perceived in the handling of this matter past, for albeit none of them knew of the matter, yet suspecting some such thing by my often recourse to the General, it was a thing wonderful to see, how many, and they who were of the best, made suits and insinuations to me, that if any such matter should fall out, that they might be named in the enterprise.[4]

This passage raises an interesting point. The students at the English College were not Jesuits, yet it seems that, being under Jesuit control, they felt they were being kept back from the 'enterprise' of England. Perhaps Allen not only wanted to persuade the General to allow Jesuit priests to go to England, but to remove the impression that the students at the College were being hindered from the work they most desired to do.

The General of the Society at this time was a Belgian, Everard Mercurian, who must have known Allen in the Low Countries.

When he went to Rome in 1579, Allen urged that some Jesuit priests should be allowed to go to England. The matter was discussed with Mercurian, Claudius Acquaviva (who succeeded Mercurian as General in the following year) and some of the other Jesuit fathers. The fact that Parsons was also present is another indication of the standing in the Society he had already gained. The Jesuits put forward several cogent objections. The English government would announce that the Jesuits had come for political as well as religious purposes; the priests would have to be disguised and would not be able to meet for retreats to renew their spiritual fervour; such retreats were an integral part of the Jesuit life; they would be in such a rush of business that there would be few opportunities for quiet meditation. Moreover there would be the risk of clashing with the secular priests on the mission who for many years had no bishop over them to maintain discipline and prevent discord. In the event these objections proved only too prophetic of what was to happen. Allen put the question of the need for a bishop to the pope who at once decided that Thomas Goldwell, Bishop of St Asalph, should go with the missioners. He was the only English bishop in exile and had been living at the English Hospice since 1560. He gladly accepted the pope's mandate although he was in poor health and must have been in his late seventies. With this problem of a bishop overcome, the General, strongly urged by Acquaviva, gave way and agreed to send some Jesuits to England.

At the time, and even by recent historians, a distorted impression of this mission has been popularised. It was not a 'Jesuit invasion'; of the fifteen who left Rome, only two were Jesuit priests. The list is as follows:

THOMAS GOLDWELL

We have already noted him.

NICHOLAS MORTON

He preceded Parsons as English penitentiary at St Peter's. He had been sent to England by the pope in 1569 and, after landing in Lincolnshire, had got into touch with the leaders of the Northern Rising. It is not known when he left England.

EDWARD BROMBOROUGH
WILLIAM GIBLET
THOMAS CRAYNE
WILLIAM KEMP

The six priests so far mentioned had all had rooms for some years in the English Hospice before it became the English College. Apart from Bishop Goldwell, it is not clear why they were included in the party; they were aging men and hardly suited to the hazardous life of a priest on the run; they do not appear to have entered England.

RALPH SHERWIN
LUKE KIRBY
EDWARD RISHTON

These three priests had been transferred from Douay to Rome. Sherwin, the proto-martyr of the English College, was hanged at Tyburn on the 1st December 1581, and Kirby on the 28th May 1582. Both have been canonized. Rishton was imprisoned in 1581 and banished four years later.

THOMAS BRISCO
JOHN PASCHALL

Both were students at the English College. John Paschall crossed to England; he was arrested and, under torture, broke down and apostatized.

LAWRENCE VAUX

He has already been noted. He died in the Clink in 1585.

ROBERT PARSONS, S.J.
EDMUND CAMPION, S.J.

With them was a lay-brother,

RALPH EMERSON

It may be noted that eight of the party were Oxford men and one of Cambridge. At least four of them were converts.

William Allen returned to Reims before the mission left Rome. It is surprising that he had not been told of the parallel action being taken by the pope that could, and indeed was bound to, prejudice the work of the missionary priests. Pope Gregory was still intent on taking military action against Elizabeth using Ireland as a spring-board. The Stukeley fiasco did not deter the pope from a fresh scheme; and he may have decided that this time, the fewer in the secret, the better. He was beguiled by James Fitzmaurice Fitzgerald (who earned for himself the cognomen of 'the arch traitor') into supporting another wild Irish venture. King Philip gave it half-hearted support but inadequate practical assistance. Dr Nicolas Sander accompanied Fitzgerald as papal nuncio in the summer of 1579. The invaders were defeated and Fitzgerald killed. Additional Italian and Spanish troops were sent in September 1580; they were too few to be effective and were soon overcome. Sander became a fugitive and died of exposure in the spring of 1581. The Church in exile thereby lost one of its leading apologists. While it is strange that Allen gave no warning of this renewed Irish venture to the mission, it is as strange that reports of what was happening in Ireland had not become public knowledge in Rome where it was almost impossible to keep a secret. Yet Parsons was quite emphatic in stating that all this came as a shock when Allen told them about it on their arrival at Reims at the end of May 1580.

Dr Allen also told us that he had heard from Spain that Dr Sander was just gone into Ireland to comfort and assist the Earl of Desmond, Viscount Ballinglas, and others that had taken arms in defence of their religion, and had asked the pope's help, counsel and comfort in that cause. Though it belonged not to us to mislike this journey of Dr Sander because it was made by order of his superiors, yet were we heartily sorry, partly because we feared that which really happened, the destruction of so rare and worthy a man, and partly because we plainly foresaw that this would be laid against us and other priests, if we should be taken in England, as though we had been privy or partakers thereof, as in very truth we were not, *nor ever heard or suspected the same until this day*. But as we could not remedy the matter, and as our consciences were clear, we resolved through evil report or good report to go on with the purely spiritual action we had in hand.

We are presented with another puzzle in this matter when dates are taken into account. Nicolas Sander landed in Ireland in June 1579, nearly a year before the mission reached Reims. The Irish venture was not a hole-and-corner business and knowledge of it spread about as soon as hostilities began. Whatever the explanation may be, and none offers itself, the effect of this two-fold policy of a mission to England concurrent with war in Ireland had grave repercussions as Parsons rightly pointed out; any priests arrested in England could now be charged with having been 'privy or partakers thereof.'

We have given an account of the early career of Robert Parsons as far as it is known; that of Edmund Campion is more fully documented and now calls for our consideration.

---

[1] All kinds of accusations were made against him in later years – illegitimacy, expulsion from the university, incontinence, even incest, and embezzlement. No evidence was produced to support these charges which were in accordance with the controversial manners of the day.

[2] While on an Italian tour in 1564, Sackville had been arrested as a dangerous heretic, but the chaplains of the English Hospice (where he was a guest) intervened successfully. He is best known as a poet who contributed to the *Mirror for Magistrates* (1559), and was part author of *Gosbuduc* (1565). His fellow author was Thomas Norton, later known as the rack-master of Catholic priests. Sackville had a distinguished career as a statesman and was created Earl of Dorset by James I. For some years Sackville lived in St Thomas More's former house at Chelsea.

[3] This does not refer to the proposed military expedition but to the mission to England.

[4] C.R.S., Vol XXXIX, p. 7.

Chapter 5

Edmund Campion: i. Protestant years

Edmund Campion was born on the 25th January 1540 in
London of which his father was citizen and bookseller. Nothing
is known of the mother. There were three sons and a daughter;
only Edmund's sister is mentioned in the records; she was
allowed to see him in the Tower shortly before his death.[1] The
boy's intelligence attracted the interest of members of the
Grocers' Company of which his father may have been a
member, and they sent him first to one of London's grammar
schools and then to Christ's Hospital which had been established in 1552 in the buildings of the Grey Friars in Newgate
Street, so Edmund Campion may have been among the earliest
pupils. As the school was intended for orphans or other poor
children, it may be presumed that his father, and perhaps his
mother, had died before his admission. There were over three
hundred boys at Christ's Hospital. Stow in his *Survey* (he was
born about 1525), recalled the annual contests between the
City schools when the best scholars 'were rewarded with bows
and arrows of silver.' During Edward VI's reign, he says, the
contests were held in the cloisters of Christ's Hospital, and the
prize scholar received a silver pen. Edmund Campion is said
'ever to have borne away the game in all contentions of learning
proposed by the schools of London.' He liked in later years to
recall the prizes he gained. He was so outstanding that he was
chosen to make the scholars' address to Queen Mary when she
rode through the City to the Tower on the evening of the 3rd
August 1553.[2]

What were a boy's thoughts on religion at that time? Perhaps he was too young to wonder why, after the Protestant teaching of Edward's reign, he had now to learn all about the Mass and go to confession. He would have faint memories of his earliest years in a Catholic home while the old king was alive. He probably accepted what came without question, but surely an intelligent boy must have had some questions to ask.

Edmund Campion's success at school led the Grocers' Company to solicit of Sir Thomas White a place for the boy in the college he was founding at Oxford. This was the college of St John the Baptist for which the royal license was granted in May 1555. Sir Thomas was Lord Mayor of London when Edward VI died and he played an important part in keeping the City loyal at the time of Wyatt's rebellion (1554). He had no need to turn his coat when Mary became queen for he was a devout Catholic; no doubt his high standing as a leading merchant kept him out of trouble during the Protestant interlude. He naturally desired that his college should be a stronghold of Catholicism and it must have broken his heart before his death in 1567 to see his hopes frustrated. The first president was Dr Alexander Belsire who had to resign in 1559 because he would not take the oath to the Supremacy. His successor Dr William Ely managed to evade commitment until 1563 when he too had to go. William Stocke followed as president for about a year when he too refused the oath. Then came a conformist, John Robinson who resigned in 1572 to follow a successful career as a popular preacher and the holder of many benefices.

In his account of Campion, Allen noted that he was 'very much beloved for his excellent qualifications by Sir Thomas White.' Campion was at St John's during the reigns of the first four presidents of whom only the last, as we have seen was a conformist; thus for some nine years there must have been a tolerance of Catholicism in the college even though the first three presidents had to walk warily. There is, however, no evidence that they had any direct influence on Campion who was for some years content to take things as they were. It would indeed have been surprising if a boy of fifteen or so had taken a different line from that which was expected of him. His popularity and public successes probably delayed his religious development. A charm of manner combined with physical attractiveness won him a wide circle of admirers and when he became a tutor in his college, his students imitated his dress and mannerisms, a sure sign of a magnetic personality that could lead to passionate attachment. This is always dangerous to character and may encourage vainglory; perhaps Campion's brilliant intellect saved him from this. His first tutor was John Bavand, a foundation fellow. He left the country in 1559 rather than submit to the Elizabethan Church order.

Campion's first public oration at Oxford was at the re-burial of Lady Amy Dudley (Robsart), the wife of Sir Robert Dudley, in St Mary's Church in September 1560.[3] The chief funeral oration was given by Dr Francis Babington, Master of Balliol and chaplain to Sir Robert, who was not present at the funeral. Campion took his degree in 1564 and became a fellow of his college. He summed up his course of study in the words, 'First I learned grammar in my native place; I went to Oxford where I studied philosophy for seven years and theology for about six — Aristotle, Positive Theology, and the Fathers.'

Queen Elizabeth visited Oxford University in the summer of 1566; she was accompanied by Sir William Cecil (later Lord Burghley), and by the Earl of Leicester. Sir Robert Dudley had been created an Earl and appointed University Chancellor two years previously. For six days the queen was entertained with academic and dramatic displays. Many Latin and Greek orations were delivered and there were set disputations on carefully chosen subjects that would evade religious differences. Campion was given the task of arguing with four disputants on two subjects, one was about the cause of the tides and the other, 'Whether the lower bodies of the universe are regulated by the higher?' Formal scholastic methods were followed in such disputations. We may think that a succession of prepared displays of this kind must have been very boring, but, to the listeners of those days, they were probably no more tedious than similar broadcast discussions in our days. It was part of the convention that speakers seized the occasion to lavish flattery on the queen and Campion showed that he was apt at doing so. 'The only thing,' he said, 'that reconciles me to the unequal task which I have to maintain single-handed against four argumentative scholars, is the thought that I am speaking in the name of philosophy, the princess of letters before a lettered princess whose blessed ancestors were proficient in science, who set her an example of visiting us poor scholars.' Leicester too must have his meed of praise for having wakened the university from its lethargy. 'May God preserve these benefits to us; may He preserve your Majesty, your Honour; you, our mother; you, our protector; you, who do these things; you who advise them; you, who preserve us; you, who honour us; you, who give us security; you, who give us happiness.' After which the tides and the heavenly bodies were briefly noticed.

This personable and eloquent young man pleased the queen, and when the Spanish ambassador hinted that the speeches had been carefully rehearsed beforehand under supervision, she decided to test the congenital ability of the disputants by an impromptu debate. Again Campion won the laurels. He was summoned to Woodstock, and, although momentarily thrown off his balance by the splendour of the court, he for the third time showed that his eloquence was a natural gift. The queen commended Campion to Leicester and Cecil and they both promised him their patronage. There was an urgent need in the new Church for sound scholars with the power of speech such as Campion had proved himself to have, and had he accepted the golden opportunity offered him, he could have risen to high office. The promises made to him were not empty ones; Leicester soon showed that he was prepared to foster Campion's advancement. Had Campion at that time given any overt signs of a leaning towards Catholicism, he would not have been taken up by the queen's two leading councillors. What led to his turning away from this alluring prospect?

There were a number of fellow-scholars of Campion's age

who were already being drawn towards Catholicism; perhaps we can see here the influence of John Bavand. Two in particular were notable. Gregory Martin, who had entered St John's at the same time as Campion, was his close companion for thirteen years and was tutored by Bavand. Richard Bristow of Exeter College who had also disputed before the queen, was another friend. Both were moving towards the Catholic Church more quickly than Campion, and they, and similarly minded scholars, must have had many a long talk over their religious problems.

Edmund Campion's friendship with an older man, almost twice his age, was another influence of importance. Richard Cheyney had been appointed Bishop of Gloucester in 1562 at Cecil's suggestion. It is not recorded how Cheyney and Campion came to know one another; perhaps they met when they were both waiting on Cecil. Be that as it may, the older man welcomed the association with the brilliant Oxford scholar. It is difficult to define Cheyney's religious position. He was a convinced Protestant but far from rabid; perhaps 'unattached' would best describe his attitude. He had not conformed under Mary Tudor but had lived in seclusion. The wordy warfare among the Protestant factions was not to his liking and he kept aloof. His sermons in his diocese raised doubts as to his doctrinal soundness especially on the subject of the Eucharist, and the Council rebuked him for his reluctance to search out Catholic recusants. In 1571 he was excommunicated for his refusal to sign the Thirty-nine Articles but he later submitted and was absolved. From then he lived quietly at Gloucester where he died in 1579 and was buried in an unmarked grave in his cathedral. It may be hazarded that Cheyney's position was more common than the records show; many would share his dislike for extreme opinions in controversial matters and wish that the state would be more accommodating in its religious policy especially as it became more radically Protestant. His belief that the true faith was to be found in the writings of the Early Fathers and in the decisions of the ecumenical councils from which, in his view, the medieval church had diverged, points to him as a forerunner of the Tractarians and Anglo-Catholics. In 1572 Campion wrote a letter to the bishop from Douay. From it we can glean a few facts about their association. 'So often was I with you at Gloucester,' he wrote, 'so often in your private chamber, so many hours have I spent in your study and library, with no one near us, when I could have done this business and I did it not.' By 'this business' he meant the duty of persuading his host to become a Catholic. He went on,

> And although you were superior to me in your counterfeited dignity, in wealth, age and learning; and although I was not bound to look after the physicing or dieting of your soul, yet since you were of so easy and sweet a temper as in spite of your gray hairs to admit me, young as I was, to familiar intercourse with you, to say whatever I chose in all security and secrecy, while you imparted to me your sorrows and all the calumnies of the other heretics against you; and since like a father you exhorted me to walk straight and upright in the royal road, to follow the steps of the Church, the councils and the fathers, and to believe that where there was a consensus of these there could be no spot of falsehood, I am very angry with myself that I neglected such a beautiful opportunity of recommending the faith through false modesty or culpable negligence, that I did not address with boldness one who was near the kingdom of God, but that while I enjoyed your favour and renown I promoted rather the shadowy notion of my own honour than your eternal good.

The self-righteous tone is not attractive, but the letter was probably written in the first flush of Campion's eventual submission to the Church. One implication of the letter is that Campion was himself an unavowed Catholic while he was enjoying the bishop's hospitality. Against this is the fact that Cheyney persuaded Campion to be ordained deacon in the Church of England, and at the same time (March 1569) gave him the living of Sherborne (Gloucestershire). This act was ever afterwards a matter of bitter regret to Campion, and 'he took a remorse of conscience and a detestation of mind' whenever he recalled his ordination.

Another glimpse of the past:

Do you remember the sober and solemn answer which you gave me, when three years ago [i.e. 1569] we met in the house of Thomas Dutton[4] of Sherborne where we were to dine? We were talking of St Cyprian. I objected to you, in order to discover your real opinions, that synod of Carthage which erred about the baptism of infants.[5] You answered truly, that the Holy Spirit was not promised to one province, but to the Church and that the universal Church is represented in a full council, and that no doctrine can be pointed out about which such a council ever erred.

He went on to point out that the Council of Trent was just such a council; why then did not the bishop accept its decisions?

It is difficult to pardon the main part of the letter which was an attempt to frighten the aging bishop with the fear of hell fire if he died a heretic. Here is a specimen.

Then those hands which have conferred spurious orders shall for very pain scratch and tear your sulphureous body; that impure mouth, defiled with falsehood and schism, shall be filled with fire and worms and the breath of tempests.[6]

Paul Bombinus, S.J., who wrote a life of Campion published in 1618, said that Cheyney preserved this letter as his chief treasure. It is difficult to accept the reason for keeping such a letter, but it may be the basis of the unconfirmed rumour that Cheyney was reconciled to the Church before his death.

There seems little doubt that the study of the Early Fathers was one cause, perhaps the effective one, of Campion's conversion. A conversation he had with a contemporary at Oxford bears this out. He asked Tobie Mathew how he, an assiduous student of the Fathers, could take the Protestant position. The reply was, 'If I believed them as well as read them, you would have good reason to ask me.' Tobie Mathew vehemently denied that he had ever said so. He went on to gather benefice upon benefice until ultimately he became Archbishop of York, and, to his horror, the father of Sir Tobie Mathew, the Jesuit.

Sir Thomas White died in 1567 and Edmund Campion gave the funeral oration when the founder was buried in the college chapel. The speaker recalled his own association with Sir Thomas.

> As soon as his last fatal paralysis attacked him, he immediatly sent off for one of us. Our president was away, and I was sent instead. As soon as he saw me, the old man embraced me, and with tears spoke words that I could not hear with dry eyes, and cannot repeat without weeping. The sum was, that we should take every care that the college was not harmed, that we should be in charity among ourselves, and educate the youth entrusted to us liberally and piously. He begged that we would not pray for his recovery, but for faith and patience in his last moments.

Did Sir Thomas say anything about the preservation of the Catholic faith? If he did so, and it would seem to have been likely, Campion tactfully refrained from saying so, but the admonition of the dying man may have been another factor in Campion's religious progress.

He does not seem to have hidden the intellectual and spiritual problems that beset him, and he discussed them, not only with such intimates as Martin and Bristow, but with anyone who might be helpful in resolving his crisis of conscience. Rumours of his tendencies reached the Grocers' Company which was still supporting him. The record for 1568 of their court of assistants reads:

> to accord and clear the suspicions conceived of Edmund Campion, one of the Company's scholars, and that he utter his mind in favouring the religion now authorised, it is agreed that between this and Candlemas [February] next he shall come and preach at Paul's Cross in London or else the Company's exhibition cease, and be appointed to another; and that he shall have warning from Mr Warden.

He asked for a postponement and it was agreed that he should be given until Michaelmas [September]. Campion attended the court and begged for a further delay; to this the court agreed and also that a less public pulpit should be chosen, such as St Stephen's, Walbrook. Once more Campion raised objections on the grounds that he was tutor to 'divers worshipful men's children.' The Company thought this a poor excuse.

Campion then resigned his studentship. It was about this time that he spent several months at Harrowden as tutor to Lord Vaux's eldest son Henry.

Pressure at Oxford on suspected Catholics became more relentless. Campion was proctor during 1568–9 and was thus in a vulnerable position. He was not yet prepared to declare himself a Catholic but he found a way out of his predicament when he was invited to go to Dublin by James Stanyhurst who was recorder of the city and speaker of the Irish House of Commons. He was an advocate of extending the educational opportunities in Ireland by increasing the number of schools and by the foundation of a university in Dublin.[7] His invitation to Campion may have been in connection with these projects; and he had heard of him and his outstanding abilities from his son Richard who was a favourite pupil of Campion. James Stanyhurst had been mainly responsible for getting the Act of Uniformity through the Irish Parliament in 1560. At the same time there was no strong anti-Catholic feeling in the English Pale, but it is unlikely that James Stanyhurst would have tolerated an avowed Catholic in his household which Campion joined late in 1570.[8] The Earl of Leicester gave his approval; his brother-in-law, Sir Henry Sidney (father of Philip) was lord-deputy and a close friend of James Stanyhurst. Campion very soon became a welcome member of Dublin society; indeed, it is noticeable that, throughout his life he made friends wherever he went. This was the more unusual as, at that period, social distinctions were rigidly observed, yet Campion came of the tradesman class and was without influential family connections.

While with the Stanyhursts he wrote *De Homine Academico* in which he set down what seemed to him to be the desirable qualities and duties of a student. This may have been written to support James Stanyhurst's scheme for a Dublin University. A more interesting composition was his *History of Ireland* which, in a garbled form, was included in Holinshed's *Chronicles* of 1578. Richard Stanyhurst had a share in the writing; but it is impossible to separate his work from Campion's. There are

many notable passages in the book, but its chief interest for
our purpose lies in the dedicatory epistle to the Earl of Leicester;
it reveals how close was the patronage the earl bestowed on
the Oxford student.

> There is none that knoweth me familiarly, but he knoweth
> withal how many ways I have been beholden to your lord-
> ship. . . . How often at Oxford, how often at Court, how at
> Rycote,[9] how at Windsor, how by letters, how by reports
> you have not ceased to further with advice, and to counte-
> nance with authority, the hope and expectation of me, a
> single student.

When this was written Leicester had become a leader of the
Protestant party, and the tone of Campion's tribute, making
all allowance for convention, is puzzling. It suggests that even
when he was in Ireland, he was still undecided as to his future
course. We must not forget how alluring, almost irresistible to
a young man, must have been the prospect opened up by
being favoured by one of the most powerful men in the country,
and one who had the ear of the queen who herself had shown
an interest in the Oxford student; 'how often at Court' suggests
frequent attendances on Leicester and that would mean to the
knowledge of the queen herself. Here we may see what must
have been Campion's greatest temptation, one that few of his
contemporaries could have resisted.

Meanwhile Richard Bristow and Gregory Martin had left
Oxford. The former went to Douay and became the right-
hand man of William Allen. Gregory Martin had accepted the
position of tutor to the sons of Thomas Howard, fourth Duke
of Norfolk, who was a conformist for political rather than for
religious reasons. Martin later wrote, 'As long as his grace did
prosper, I lived in his house without trouble to my conscience;
when he was in the Tower [Oct 1569–August 1570] and other
men ruled his house, I was willed to receive the communion or
depart. If I would have yielded, I had very large offers. It
pleased God to stay me so with his grace, that I chose rather to
foresake all, than go against my belief. For a time I lay secretly
in England; afterwards I came beyond the seas.' He too joined

Allen at Douay and he is chiefly known now as the translator of the Reims-Douay version of the Bible. From Douay he wrote to his old companion urging him to make the great decision. We learn this from a letter to Martin written by Campion from Prague in July 1577.

> I remember too how earnestly you called me from Ireland to Douay, and how effective were your words. Before that, I remember how from the Duke of Norfolk's house you dealt with me to keep me from ecclesiastical dignity, which, as a friend, you feared might betray me into serving these wretched times. In these words, as I consider, you were even prompted by the Holy Ghost – 'If we two can live together, we can live for nothing; if this is too little, I have money; but if this also fails, one thing remains – they that sow in tears shall reap in joy.'

The Northern Rising in November 1569 inevitably led to a closer watch on suspected Catholics especially in Ireland on which Philip II had designs. The Stanyhursts thought it prudent for their guest to leave Dublin. It is said that Sir Henry Sidney had dropped a hint to James Stanyhurst that Campion was in danger. He was taken during the night by Richard[10] and his brother Walter to Turvey, eight miles from Dublin, and was there received by Sir Christopher and Lady Barnewall. Campion wrote on the 19th March 1570 to James Stanyhurst to thank him for his hospitality; the letter continues,

> As soon as I saw you heard the first rustlings of the storm which was sure to blow to a hurricane if I stayed longer in sight of the heretics of Dublin, you opened to me this secret hiding-place among your country friends. . . . Your friend Barnewall is profuse in his promises. When he had read your letter, he was sorry for the hardness of the times, but was as glad of my coming as if I had done him a great favour. As he had to go to Dublin, he commended me to his wife who treated me most kindly. I was shut up in a convenient place within an inner chamber, where I was reconciled to my books. With these companions I lie concealed in my cell.

The search for Campion was not relaxed and he dared not

remain at Turvey. By June he was at Drogheda after paying a quick visit to Dublin probably to arrange for a ship. He eventually got away from a small harbour south of Dublin; he was disguised as the servant of Melchior Hussey, steward to the Earl of Kildare, who had business in England. The ship was searched for Edmund Campion by name, but as he was using the name of Patrick he escaped their notice, but the manuscript of his history of Ireland was seized.[11]

He found the situation in England so menacing that he decided to go to Douay as quickly as possible. Parsons said that Campion was present at the trial of Dr John Storey, formerly professor of Civil Law at Oxford. He had been active with Bishop Bonner in the persecution of Protestants under Queen Mary. In May 1563 he had escaped from prison and went to the Low Countries, whence he was kidnapped and brought back to England. He was tried at the end of May 1571 and hanged at Tyburn on the 1st June. Campion's first attempt to cross the Channel was frustrated. An English frigate stopped his ship and, as he had no licence to travel, took him to Dover. The captain confiscated Campion's money which his friends had contributed for his support, and set out with him for London. On the way they agreed to part on the understanding that the captain kept the money. So Campion went east and, having got further help from friends in Kent, at last succeeded in crossing to Calais and from thence he went to Douay.

It is not possible to say exactly when it was that Campion was reconciled to the Church. Perhaps it was just before he went to Dublin for there he was certainly regarded as a Catholic. Yet against this must be put his fulsome dedicatory letter to Leicester and a curious phrase in his letter of thanks to James Stanyhurst – 'in sight of the heretics.' He was writing to one who, in Catholic eyes, was a heretic. We get the impression that for some considerable time, perhaps two years, he was 'halting between two opinions.' The golden prospects open before him under the patronage of Leicester pulled him in one direction; the doctrines of the Early Fathers pulled him in another. We cannot know how or when he made his great decision; all we can be sure of is that, when he arrived at Douay in June 1571, he knew that his vocation was to be a priest.

[1] See below, p. 199.

[2] So the record goes, but had there been time to make the necessary arrangements? I suspect the incident occurred during the coronation procession from the Tower to Westminster on the 25th September.

[3] She had been hastily buried at Cumnor. Readers of Scott's *Kenilworth* will know the story of her death; it is still disputed whether it was murder or suicide or accident. Elizabeth must have known of the marriage which Edward VI attended (1550). It is said that Babington 'tript once or twice by recommending his auditors the virtues of that lady so pitifully murdered' instead of 'so pitifully slain' by accident. Later he was suspected of being a concealed papist and in 1565 he left England.

[4] Thomas Dutton (d. 1581) bought the manor of Sherborne in 1551; it had been part of the Winchcomb Abbey lands. He was the ancestor of the present Lord Sherborne.

[5] That heretical and schismatical baptisms were invalid and that the sacrament depended on the full faith of the baptiser and the baptised.

[6] I find it impossible to accept the eulogy bestowed on this letter by Richard Simpson and Evelyn Waugh.

[7] Eventually in 1591, Trinity College was founded.

[8] See *Early History at St John's College*, ed. Stevenson & Salter.

[9] Rycote was the seat of Lord Williams of Thame; Leicester was a close friend who, presumably, invited Campion to Rycote when he visited there.

[10] Richard went to the Low Countries about 1580 and some years later became a Catholic priest. See, *D.N.B.*

[11] There may be some confusion here. In a letter to Martin from Prague in 1577, Campion asked him to send him 'those writings of mine about Irish history which you have.' No doubt Richard Stanyhurst had contrived to send him a copy. Holinshed must have got his copy from Stanyhurst, to whom the history was ascribed as the name of Campion was officially execrated.

Chapter 6

Edmund Campion: ii. The Jesuit

The reunion at Douay of the three friends, Edmund Campion, Gregory Martin and Richard Bristow, must have been a joyous occasion. They were much of an age; Bristow was thirty-three, Campion thirty-one and Martin a bit younger. There were several other Oxford men at Douay who had known Campion. William Allen would also welcome this brilliant scholar who had the gift of eloquence and was a skilled dialectician. His leaving England had not gone unnoticed. William Cecil said to Richard Stanyhurst, 'It is a great pity to see so notable a man leave this country, for indeed he was one of the diamonds of England.' There is no record of Leicester's feelings.

There would be no need for Campion to follow the preliminary course of studies at Douay, but his knowledge of Catholic doctrine would be insecure, so he went to the university for his theological formation and there he took his degree in divinity on the 21st January 1572. He also had his share in the work of the seminary as professor of rhetoric. One of his students was Cuthbert Mayne who, six years later, was to be the protomartyr of Douay. Campion not only had to teach rhetoric but he was called upon to exercise his own talent as an orator. One complete specimen has survived; this was his *Oratio de Juvene Academico*, probably based on his *De Homine Academico* of his Dublin days which is not extant. One passage will serve as a specimen.

Listen to our heavenly Father asking back His talents with usury; listen to the Church, the mother that bore us and nursed us, imploring our help; listen to the pitiful cries of our neighbours in danger of spiritual starvation; listen to the howlings of the wolves that are spoiling the flock. The glory of your Father, the preservation of your mother, your own salvation, the safety of your brethren, are in jeopardy, and can you stand idle? If this house were blazing before your eyes, what would you think of the young reprobate who sang, who grinned, or snapped his fingers, or rose cock-horse on his cane in the common crisis? Behold, by the wickedness of the wicked the house of God is given over to flames and destruction; numberless souls are being deceived, are being shaken, are being lost; any one of which is worth more than the empire of the whole world.

He could not settle down at Douay. Unfortunately he did not record why this was so; it is not possible to do more than speculate. He decided to go to Rome and seek admission to the Society of Jesus. Did he feel the need for submitting himself to the stricter discipline of an Order where personal decisions on what to do would be subordinated to direction from authority? He may have felt that it was in a moment of weakness that he had accepted ordination in the Church of England, and we have seen how for several years he had hesitated and compromised himself before submitting to the Church. He seems to have been the kind of man who finds it difficult to make up his mind; his keen intelligence, practised in disputa-tion, showed him more than one side of any problem. This may have been the line of thought that led him to put himself under the discipline of the Jesuits.

So he set out for Rome on foot, perhaps imposing this hard way as a penance for his past vacillations. He had the good will of Allen, and some of his friends accompanied him for the first day; after that he was alone. Only one incident has been recorded of that pilgrimage. An old Oxford acquaintance riding on his return from Rome passed Campion on the way and did not at first recognise him; then something familiar in the style of the pilgrim struck the traveller and he turned back and presently found himself greeting Edmund Campion whom he had last seen as a leading light of their university. He did his best to persuade Campion to give up his foolish notion and offered him money, but Campion 'made such a speech of the contempt of this world, and the eminent dignity of serving Christ in poverty, as greatly moved the man, and us also his acquaintance that remained yet in Oxford when the report came to our ears.' Such was Parson's record of the incident. About a year later, he too left Oxford; perhaps this report had its influence on him.

Early in 1573 Campion reached Rome. He arrived during an interregnum in Jesuit affairs. The third General of the Order, Francis Borgia, had died in October 1572 and it was not until six months later that his successor, Everard Mercurian, was elected. No decision could therefore be made on Campion's application to join the Society, but he was not friendless. His old tutor, John Bavand, was one of the chaplains at the English Hospice. He had been a foundation fellow of St John's and tutor of Campion and Martin. As he could not accept the new religious regime, Bavand left the country in 1559 and eventually made his way to Rome.[1] A letter to him from Campion written from Prague about 1577 tells us something of their association. The opening sentence refers to Gregory Martin who was in Rome in connection with the founding of the English College.

> Thanks to our good Martin, who in his last letter to me enlarged on your goodness and kindness to him, I am reminded, not by his precept but by his example, not to shirk my duty, or to loosen any of those old links by which your undying care of both of us has bound us to you. I must own that, if I had thought frequent letter-writing the sum of fidelity and gratitude, I had been too neglectful of what my respect for you, and your fatherly care and provision for me, required. But there are other tokens of love and friendship beside letters, and my sentiments from my earliest childhood have been so well known to you that they can never be clouded over either by my epistolary neglect, or by our separation in place. I should be a mere knave and unworthy of the liberal education which you gave me, if, while I have any memory at all, I forgot you, instead of bearing witness, by all sorts of observance, to the care, the prudence, the sympathy, and the purity you displayed in teaching and

educating me. To these I must add the clear proofs of your favour and affection since bestowed on me, and they the more pleasant because they so plainly manifested in uncommon benevolence. For though in my youth I was but an indifferent subject, yet, since I was entrusted to you and clung to your side, hung upon your looks and lived in your society, I do not much wonder that a good man like you, so diligent in your duties, took such care of me. But that in after years, you undertook to feed me and polish me, as it was from your free choice, so does it more redound to the credit of your virtue and kindness. And what is your last favour? When I was in Rome, did you not altogether spend yourself upon me? Did you not give me introductions, help, and money? And that to one who, as you knew, not only could never repay you, but who was on the point of leaving the world, and so to speak, of death. One of the greatest works of mercy is to bury the dead, for they help those towards whom neither flesh, blood, nor goods, nor hope, nor favour, nor any thought of earthly convenience attracts them. You were munificent to me when I was going to enter the sepulchral rest of religion. Add one further kindness, my dear father; pray for me, that in this seclusion, far from the noise of all vanity, I may be buried really and meritoriously. For it was the Apostle's declaration, 'You are dead, and your life is hidden with Christ in God.' I remember how, on the eve of your leaving England, you bade me farewell with the words, 'I go to die.' For you had determined to let death overtake you any where rather than in Egypt.

Egypt stood for England, the land of oppression. In spite of its rhetorical flavour, this letter is revealing.

In a letter to Gregory Martin written about the same time, Campion said, 'Though I have many greetings for John Bavand, our old tutor, of whom it would be too long to write all I might and ought to say, yet, as I am writing to him, I will send him a very brief message.'

The Jesuit training was the most thorough-going of all those devised for the formation of priests in the implementation of the Council of Trent's instruction that all dioceses should establish seminaries. The Jesuit novitiate was for two years; the spiritual *Exercises* of St Ignatius was the foundation. During this period the novice worked in the kitchen and had spells in the hospitals doing the most menial tasks. The catechetical instruction of children was another task for the novices. The novitiate was followed by the scholasticate of several years but the length depended on the director's appraisal; this was the educational period and included the humanities, philosophy and theology; in addition there would be training in rhetoric, preaching and disputation. Charitable works were a duty at all times. At the end of this stage would normally come ordination. This was followed by the tertianship of one year during which it was decided how best the new Jesuit could be employed. On paper this appears to be a rigid scheme, but one characteristic of the Jesuit system has always been its adaptability to the spiritual needs and mental calibre of the individual.

Soon after the election of the new General on the 23rd April 1573, Edmund Campion was accepted as a novice after assenting to the following series of questions.

Are you willing to renounce the world, all possessions and all hope of temporal goods? Are you ready if necessary to beg your bread from door to door for the love of Jesus Christ? Are you ready to reside in any country and to embrace any employment where your superior may think you to be most useful to the glory of God and the good of souls? Are you willing to obey in all things in which there is evidently no sin, the superiors who hold towards you the place of God? Do you feel resolved generally to renounce without reserve all those things which men in general love and embrace, and will you attempt and desire with all your strength what our Lord Jesus Christ loved and embraced? Do you consent to put on the livery of humiliation worn by Him, to suffer as He did and for love of Him, contempt, calumnies and insults?

Campion was assigned to the Austrian Province and in June he went with a party of Jesuits to Prague; from there he went to Brunn in Moravia for a year, and then returned to Prague where he remained for six years. Bohemia was as much a missionary country as England and the Jesuits had to face what was in the main a hostile population. Bohemia was the land of Hus who had been martyred in 1415; subsequently a religious war raged through the country which became predominantly Protestant; a compromise had at last been reached which gave an uneasy measure of toleration. An archbishop had been appointed to Prague in 1561 and he looked to the Jesuits to lead the attack on the schismatics. The emperor, Maximilian II (1564–76) maintained the equilibrium. The Jesuits opened a school in Prague in 1574 and it was here that Edmund Campion found his work while going through his own training. His various employments, lecturing, teaching, the writing of plays, and so on, do not concern us here.

Philip Sidney, son of Sir Henry Sidney and nephew of the Earl of Leicester, was in Prague in 1576 to offer Queen Elizabeth's congratulations to the new Emperor Rudolph. Sidney was at Oxford during Campion's last year but they had probably already met when Campion was waiting on Leicester. Two years earlier at Venice Philip had been much in the company of his cousin Sir Richard Shelley, Grand Prior of the Knights of St John. This association led to rumours that Philip was about to become a Catholic. He naturally wished to meet Campion at Prague, but, in view of these rumours, discretion was necessary in making arrangements. Here is Campion's account of what happened; it comes from the letter to John Bavant already quoted.

A few months ago Philip Sidney came from England to Prague as ambassador, magnificently provided. He had much conversation with me, I hope not in vain, for to all appearance he was most eager. I commend him to your sacrifices, for he asked the prayers of all good men, and at the same time put into my hands some alms to be distributed to the poor for him, which I have done. Tell this to Dr Nicolas Sander, because if any one of the labourers sent into the vineyard from Douay seminary has an opportunity of watering this plant, he may watch the occasion for helping a poor wavering soul. If this young man, so wonderfully beloved and admired by his countrymen, chances to be converted, he will astonish his noble father, the Deputy of Ireland, his uncles the Dudleys, and all the young courtiers and Cecil himself.

A number of Campion's letters from Prague were carefully preserved; they throw light not only on his personality but on the Jesuit outlook. Some passages have been given in previous pages. A few further extracts are of interest.

In a letter to Robert Parsons dated the 25th June 1577, Campion refers to their efforts to get Gregory Martin to enter the Society.

> Do let us conspire to deliver that good soul; it is good fishing. I love him on many accounts; I congratulate him with all my heart upon making the acquaintance of so many of you; my part shall not be wanting.

However, William Allen called Martin back to Reims where the Douay students had had to withdraw. There are no indications that Martin would have preferred to remain in Rome.

Reports in Rome suggested that Campion's health was suffering from the work he was doing – and he certainly seems to have been kept at full stretch. This he contradicted in a letter to Parsons.

> About myself I would only have you know that from the day I arrived here, I have been extremely well, in a perpetual bloom of health, and that I was never at any age less upset by literary work than now when I work hardest. We know the reason. But, indeed, I have no time to be sick, if any illness wanted to take me. So you may unhesitatingly contradict those reports.

In August 1577 he wrote to Fr Robert Arden, S.J.

> If you are the Arden I fancy, this is not our first acquaintance; for we were members of neighbouring colleges, I of St John's, you of Trinity. If you are not the man, you need no more be ashamed of being taken for him than of being yourself.

Parsons wrote in November 1578 telling him of the failure of Stukeley's enterprise and giving him news of the progress of the English Jesuits in Rome.

> We are here at Rome now twenty-four Englishmen of the Society, whereof five have entered within this month; one

named Mr Holt which was once of Oriel College, Master of Arts, and the other four came hither from Paris, all excellent towardly youths and all have ended the course of philosophy. Two of them are your countrymen born in Paternoster Row, one named Harwood and the other Smith. One Englishman of good learning is presently from herehence sent towards Japan. I hope ere it be long we shall find a vent another way. Father Darbyshire is come hither from Paris and it may be that I shall go ere it be long in his place thither. Mr Lane as I wrote you before is gone to Alcala in Spain and arrived thither hath written your commendations in a letter to me. And this is as much as I have to write to you at this time. Mr Martin was called away herehence by Mr Dr Allen his letters. I think they were half afraid of him what might become of him, but Mr Holt's entering the Society of late, hath much amazed them. I pray you, Mr Campion pray for me for I have great need of it; all our countrymen here do commend themselves heartily to you. From Rome this xxviii of November 1578.

This passage is typical of the writer; there are no rhetorical flourishes; it is all matter-of-fact; a budget of news. It is so packed with material that it calls for comment.

'Mr Holt' was William Holt who later became involved in Scottish affairs. He was at Douay and, after ordination, had come to Rome to help establish the English College; his decision to enter the Society of Jesus was unexpected by Allen. His later career was as controversial as Parson's. The two students named, Edward Harwood and Nicholas Smith, were described as 'your countrymen born in Paternoster Row.' Here 'countrymen' is used in the contemporary sense of 'born in the same place.' This is a unique reference to Campion's birthplace. Stow tells us that Paternoster Row was so called as many of its inhabitants were makers of paternoster beads or rosaries; he adds that others were sellers of devotional books. We know that Campion's father was a bookseller, so it may be inferred that Edmund was born in Paternoster Row. Parsons did not give the names of the two other students. One was Matthew Marshall who died in Rome of consumption in 1584. The second was Robert Southwell who was to become only second to Campion in fame. The Jesuit who was going to Japan was Thomas Stephens; actually he went to India and laboured at Goa for forty years. 'We shall find a vent another way' shows that Parson's thoughts were on England. Fr Thomas Darbyshire, a nephew of Bishop Bonner, was one of the earliest of English Jesuits; he had been attached to the Jesuit College of Clermont near Paris and had been the director of Robert Southwell and his companions. John Lane, a former fellow of Corpus Christi College, Oxford, entered the Society in February 1576; he died three years later in Spain. Parsons himself was the novice-master of the new arrivals; he became greatly attached to Robert Southwell.

When Parsons wrote this letter, he may not have been aware that Edmund Campion had been ordained deacon and priest by the Archbishop of Prague; he said his first Mass on the 8th September 1578. He was then thirty-eight years of age; this was unusually late in life for ordination.

A letter from him to Gregory Martin in August 1579 tells us that Campion had now heard of the martyrdom of his former pupil Cuthbert Mayne (29th November 1577).

> We all thank you much for your account of Cuthbert's martyrdom; it gave many of us a real religious joy. Wretch that I am, how has that novice distanced me! May he be favourable to his old friend and tutor! I shall now boast of these titles more than ever.

Then at the end of 1579 came an ecstatic letter from William Allen; it called Campion to a more dangerous service. The letter is worth giving in full.

> My father, brother, son, Edmund Campion, for to you I use every expression of the tenderest ties of love. Since the General of your Order, who to you is Christ Himself, calls you from Prague to Rome, and thence to our own England; since your brethren after the flesh call upon you (for though you hear not their words, God has heard their prayers), I who am so closely connected with them, with you, and with our common country both in the world and in the Lord, must not be the only one to keep silence, when I should be the first to desire you, to call you, to cry for you. Make all haste and

come, my dearest Campion; you have done enough at Prague towards remedying the evils that our countrymen inflicted upon Bohemia.² It will be dutiful, religious, and Christian in you to devote the rest of your life and some part of your extraordinary gifts to our beloved country, which has the greatest need of your labours in Christ.

I do not stay to enquire what your own wish and inclination may be, since it is your happiness to live, not by your own will, but by others', and you would not shrink from the greatest perils or the furthest Indies if your superiors bade you go. Our harvest is already great in England; ordinary labourers are not enough; more practised men are wanted but chiefly you and others of your Order. The General has yielded to all our prayers; the Pope, the true father of our country, has consented; and God, in whose hands are the issues, has at last granted that our own Campion, with his extraordinary gifts of wisdom and grace, should be restored to us. Prepare yourself then for a journey, for a work, for a trial. You will have an excellent Colleague [Parsons]. It is not I that am preparing for you and your Order the place in England that your soul presaged, but it is you, I hope, who will procure for me and mine the power of returning.

We will talk over the rest, my dear Edmund, and I hope you will be here as soon as may be, for I know not how long I can stay in Rome; and as soon as the winter is past, I mean to go to Reims or Douay, where our common friends Bristow and Martin now live. You will be astonished to see our Belgian and Roman Colleges, and will easily understand why we have at last such hopes of our country.

In the mean time let us pray the Lord of the harvest to make us worthy of His mercy and visitation, and do you, by your prayers and sacrifices, wash away my sins before Jesus Christ. May He send you to us as soon as may be.

Entirely thine,
William Allen.

Rome, the English College, 9th Dec. 1579.³

The official call did not come until March 1580. A curious incident is related in connection with the summons to Rome and England. One of the Jesuit fathers felt impelled the night before the departure to write over Campion's door, 'P. Edmundus Campianus, Martyr.' He left Prague on the 25th March 1580 in the train of Ferdinand, son of the Duke of

Bavaria, as far as Munich where he was persuaded to preach to the students. He was escorted to Innsbruck and from there made his way on foot over the Alps to Padua where he was instructed to proceed by horse. He arrived in Rome on Holy Saturday, the 5th April 1580.

[1] He returned to England in June 1581 a month before Campion's capture. He was in prison 1585–6, and thereafter managed to evade trouble until his death in 1613. He was greatly respected and exercised a steadying influence during the inter-clerical squabbles.

[2] John Hus had derived his teaching from John Wycliffe.

[3] See, T. F. Knox, *Letters and Memorials of Cardinal Allen* (1882).

Chapter 7

Rome to Reims

The instructions[1] drawn up by the General for the guidance of Parsons and Campion are important; it should be kept in mind that any deviation from these would be against the strict rule of obedience that every Jesuit accepted without question.

The purpose of the mission was defined in the first paragraph.

> The object aimed at by this mission is, firstly, to preserve, if God is propitious, and to advance in the faith and in our Catholic religion, all who are found to be Catholics in England; and, secondly, to bring back to it whoever may have strayed from it either through ignorance or at the instigation of others.

It will be noted that the conversion of Protestants was not included in the purposes of the mission; Catholics and lapsed Catholics or Church-Papists were to be their primary care.

Two 'weapons' were essential: 'firstly, with virtue and piety out of the ordinary; and, secondly, with prudence.' They were to be temperate in their eating, and, as far as practicable, have their meals in private. Of necessity they would have to dress as laymen but in a 'modest and sober' style.

> They are not to be in possession, however, when they are permanently stationed, of clothes of the sort customary in the Society, unless it is evident that they can have them perfectly safely; and in that case they are only to be used for the purpose of holding services, hearing confessions and carrying out other duties of this kind.

> If it is out of the question for them to live in community, let them at least take care to visit one another as often as

possible and have intercourse, so that they may console one another and also help one another with advice and assistance as has been our custom.

'Fr Roberts will be in charge of all who are now sent . . . and all are to obey him as they would ourselves.'

Then follow two important paragraphs on their dealings with laymen.

As regards intercourse with strangers, this should at first be with the upper classes rather than with the common people, both on account of the greater fruit to be gathered and because the former will be able to protect them against violence of all sorts. Then, in the case of Catholics, let it be with the reconciled rather than with schismatics; with heretics they should have no direct dealings. . . . If necessity forces them to dispute with heretics, they should refrain from biting and intemperate words and give evidence of their modesty and charity not less than of their learning, and let them make use of solid arguments in preference to bitter wrangling.

They were warned against 'familiar conversation with women, even the best of them.'

In view of the 1571 Act, under which Cuthbert Mayne had been condemned, they were 'to take with them none of those articles which have been proscribed under pain of death.' And they should observe the same prudence in carrying letters about with them.

Then comes a crucial paragraph which is here italicised.

They are not to mix themselves in the affairs of States, nor should they recount news about political matters in their letters to this place [i.e. Rome], or to that [i.e. England]; and there also they are to refrain from talk against the Queen and not allow it in others.

The rest of the instructions concerned means of maintaining correspondence with Rome. A number of such letters from Parsons are extant, but we have no knowledge of the way in which they were sent; it seems that he sometimes sent two or three copies of a letter by several routes to ensure receipt. This regular communication with the General was part of the Society's system; the secular priests were less favourably situated as they had no bishop to whom they could report. Occasional letters to Douay or to one of the other English seminaries partly filled the gap, but it means that we know far less of the day to day affairs of these priests than of the Jesuit mission itself.

In addition to these instructions the Jesuits were given a papal declaration to be passed on to all Catholics. This concerned the application of the Bull *Regnans in excelsis*. The Bull could not be withdrawn, but the official ruling was that, until it could be carried out, and as things then stood, *rebus sic stantibus*, it did not bind Catholics. This relieved the more scrupulous of them from the dilemma in which the Bull had placed them, facing them with conflicting loyalties; but it also provided the government with the telling objection that all it meant was that Catholic loyalty was conditional until a favourable opportunity came for throwing it off.

In their instructions the priests were advised to keep their mission secret even on their journey, but their departure from Rome was anything but secret. When they set off from the Flaminian Gate on the 18th April 1580 they were accompanied by most of the Englishmen in Rome, headed by Sir Richard Shelley, as far as the Ponte Molle where they took a solemn farewell. Not that there was anything really indiscreet in such a public leave taking. They would be aware that spies in Rome would have already sent reports of the mission with the names and descriptions of the members. Indeed news of the possibility of such a mission had reached Walsingham more than a year earlier. His informant was Charles Sledd, a servant at the English College, professing to be Catholic, who turned spy. Here is his description of Parsons.

> Sometimes a student of physic, and at finding [now] about forty years of age. Tall and big of stature. Full faced and smooth of countenance; his beard thick of a brown colour and cut short.

Unfortunately the spy could not give a description of Campion as he had arrived in Rome only a few days before the mission left. Another spy in Rome about this time was Anthony

Munday, the future playwright. Both he and Sledd were to play a part in the trial of Campion and his fellows.

The party had only two or three horses; Bishop Goldwell and Dr Morton, being too aged to walk, rode on ahead and were not seen again until Reims. The main party followed on foot. In his unfinished life of Campion,[2] Parsons wrote,

> It was thought convenient that each priest should change his long apparel, both for better travelling on foot, as also not so easily to be discerned in Germany and some other places of Protestants, where priests are little favoured. And when some new apparel was offered to Campion, he would in no wise take it, but only covered himself with certain old buckram under an old cloak, and passed with that attire throughout his long journey . . . for, he said, that to him that went to be hanged in England any apparel was sufficient . . . And to prove the blessed man more, God sent continual rain for the first eight or ten days after our leaving Rome, so as from morning to night he travelled in the wet with that evil apparel, and oftentimes stuck so fast in the mire in those deep and foul ways that he was scarce able to get out again.

It was Campion's custom to say Mass as early in the morning as he could and then to push on alone and make his meditation and read his breviary.

Their first considerable halt was at Bologna, and, judging by the description of the weather conditions just quoted from Parsons, they must have been in need of a few days to recover. The archbishop welcomed them and provided for them. From Bologna Campion wrote to one of his colleagues at Prague.

> I am now at Bologna on my return from Rome and on my way to my warfare in England. . . . In this expedition there are two Fathers of the Society, Robert Parsons and myself, seven other priests, and three laymen, one of whom is also of us [i.e. Ralph Emerson]. I see them all so prodigal of blood and life that I am ashamed of my backwardness. I hope to be with Allen at Reims in the beginning of June. We all travel at the pope's cost. Though we should fall at the first onset, yet our army is full of fresh recruits, but by whose victory our ghosts will be pacified. . . . Here I am reminded of my pupils, and of my companions, whom I often think of.

There are so many to whom I wished to write severally, and
I was so overwhelmed with their number and my other
business, that I have hitherto written to none of them. I am
tired when I reach our colleges; in the inns I can scarcely
breathe. I was at Rome about eight days, cramped for time,
more than during all the rest of my journey. I must ask them
therefore, and especially my fathers and brothers at Prague,
to pardon what I cannot help. The rest I reserve for a fourth
letter. I shall be very glad if I find one from you before I pass
over into England. You may send to Reims, Paris or Douay,
for I suppose I shall visit those places. But, anyhow, if they
are sent to Allen they will be delivered to me. In uncertainty
whether we shall ever see one another again, I write my will,
and I leave to you and all of them the kiss of charity and the
bond of peace. Farewell. Bologna, the last of April, 1580.

Reverend Father, again and again, and for ever, farewell.

From Bologna they went to Milan where Cardinal Charles
Borromeo persuaded them to remain a week. Later he wrote to
Alfonso Agazzari, s.j., rector of the English College.

I saw and willingly received those English who departed
hence the other day, as their goodness deserved, and the
cause for which they had undertaken that voyage. If in
future, your Reverence shall send any other, to me, be
assured that I will take care to receive them with all charity
and that it will be most pleasing to me to have occasion to
perform the duties of hospitality, so proper for a bishop,
towards the Catholics of that nation. Milan, the last of June,
1580.

At Bologna and Milan both Edmund Campion and Ralph
Sherwin gave discourses which were highly appreciated.

They crossed the Alps by the Mont Cenis Pass and, in order
to avoid marauding bands of Spanish soldiers, went by way of
Geneva. They took the precaution of further disguising themselves before entering the Calvinist city. Campion took the role
of an Irish servant to Fr Paschall. They resolved to declare
themselves to be Catholics if challenged; this they did when
brought before the magistrates who expressed surprise that
Englishmen were not of the same religion as Queen Elizabeth
which was the same as that of Genevans. One of the priests
(his name is not given) answered,

As for our Queen, we cannot tell whether she is of your religion or no, considering the variety of opinions this age has brought forth, but we are sure she is not of ours. Though for the realm, you must understand, that all are not of her religion, nor of yours, but many are good Christian Catholics, and do suffer losses both at home and banishment abroad for the same, of which number are we who have lived divers years in Italy and are now going towards the English seminary in Reims.

The magistrates gave the travellers the usual permission to stay three days. On their way to their inn, they had to submit to some mild barracking.

The missioners decided, somewhat imprudently one would think, to seek a meeting with Theodore Beza, Calvin's successor and a notable theologian. He received them in the courtyard of his house, but was not eager to argue with these Catholics. They discussed the government of the Church in Geneva and the episcopal form in England. Campion, forgetting his rôle of servant, tried to open a discussion on more fundamental questions but Beza was not to be drawn. That evening a group of Englishmen who were resident in or visiting Geneva called on the Catholic travellers. One was named Powell and he had known Campion, Parsons and Sherwin at Oxford. There was a warm discussion but Powell warned them that they would run serious risk of imprisonment, especially if, as they proposed, they challenged Beza to a public debate. Parsons wisely decided to leave next morning. As was his custom Campion went ahead and he met a Genevan minister with whom he could not refrain from arguing; fortunately the main party arrived in time to prevent the angry minister from denouncing Campion to the magistrates. Powell was with them and now recognised Campion who had kept out of sight the previous evening. Powell managed to pacify the minister.

We may note here Campion's impulsiveness even recklessness and his love of argument; it was in a good cause but it meant grave risks for his companions as well as himself. No further incidents are recorded of the remainder of the journey to Reims which they reached on the 31st May 1580; here they rejoined Bishop Goldwell and Dr Morton. It was disconcerting to learn on their arrival of the Fitzgerald-Sander expedition to Ireland.[3]

They also learned of a fresh royal proclamation against suspected Catholic adherents of this latest attack on the state. Vigilance at the ports of entry had been sharpened and it was becoming more and more difficult to infiltrate priests into the country. In view of these difficulties it was decided to break up the party of priests waiting to cross to England into twos and threes and for them to use different points of departure – Dieppe, Rouen, Boulogne and Dunkirk. There were three newcomers: Dr Humphrey Ely (alias Havard),[4] brother of the William Ely who had been third president of St John's, a Douay priest named John Hart, and Thomas Cottam who had had to cut short his Jesuit training on account of poor health.

Meanwhile Bishop Goldwell had decided to give up the attempt to enter England. In a letter dated the 13th July 1580 he explained his reasons to the Pope.

Beatissimo Padre. If I could have crossed over into England before my coming was known there, as I hoped to do, I think that my going thither would have been a comfort to the Catholics and a satisfaction to your Holiness; whereas now I fear the contrary, for there are so many spies in this kingdom, and my long tarrying here has made my going to England so bruited there, that now I doubt it will be difficult for me to enter that kingdom without some danger. Nevertheless, if your Holiness thinks differently, I will make the trial, though it should cost me my life. Still it would be impossible for me alone to supply the wants of the Catholics who are more than many thousands than I thought and scattered over the whole kingdom. The most that I can hope to do is to supply for the city of London and some miles round. And therefore, in my ignorance, I cannot but marvel how it is that, after God has given your Holiness grace, as it were, to plant anew and support the Catholic faith in that kingdom, you make so many difficulties about creating three or four titular bishops to preserve and propagate it, a thing that might be done with as little expense as your Holiness pleases; for God has so inclined the minds of the priests to spend their lives in promoting the reduction of that kingdom to the Catholic faith, that, after being made bishops, they would be content to live as poorly as they do now, like the bishops of the primitive Church. God inspire your Holiness to that which shall be most to His honour, and prosper you many years.

I humbly kiss your feet.

Your Holiness's most devoted servant,

The Bishop of St Asaph.

This was a sensible letter and presumably the pope agreed to Bishop Goldwell withdrawing from the mission as he returned to Rome and with him went Dr Nicholas Morton, whose exact age is not known but he had taken his degree at Cambridge in 1542. It would have put an unwarrantable strain on the missionary priests in England to have to safeguard an aged and frail bishop who was being sought by the authorities.

Parsons and Campion with Ralph Emerson went to St Omer, where they were again warned of the close surveillance being kept on all travellers entering England. Moreover they were all conscious of the fact that their names and descriptions were in the hands of the government. An Englishman in exile for the faith, George Chamberlain,[5] admitted the risks were grave but thought they had been exaggerated. It was therefore decided that Parsons should make the first attempt by way of Calais and Dover, and, should that be successful, he would somehow get a message sent back to Campion so that he could follow.

[1] C.R.S., Vol. xxxix, pp. 316–321.

[2] Published by the Manresa Press with the title *On the Life and Martyrdom of Father Edmund Campion*. It is really a collection of notes rather than a biography and is incomplete. Paul Bombinus learned some details from Parsons, and used this in his life of Campion (1618).

[3] See above, p. 34.

[4] He was not then a priest; this was probably the reason why, after his arrest in England, he was soon released. He returned to Reims and was ordained in 1582.

[5] He was the son of Sir Leonard Chamberlain, governor of Guernsey. His own son, also George, went to the English College, Rome, and eventually became Bishop of Ypres.

Chapter 8

London: 16th June–18th July 1580

Robert Parsons was disguised as an army captain in a uniform of buff trimmed with gold braid, and a hat with a feather in it. His companion, George,[1] was also suitably dressed for the part he had to play. They landed at Dover on the 16th June 1580. The official searcher at the customs saw no reason to question their identities; he even got them horses for the journey to Gravesend, which they would do by way of Canterbury and Rochester. As the searcher was well-disposed, Parsons told him that a friend of his named Edmunds, now at St Omer, would be coming over in a few days' time, and the searcher promised to forward a letter, which he read, to this jewel-merchant as Campion was supposed to be. Campion received the letter which urged him to come quickly as the writer had heard of a good opportunity for selling the jewels.

Parsons and George reached Gravesend in the evening without further incident and disposed of the horses. They boarded a tilt-boat[2] to row them up the river. Parsons was worried as the boat was crowded with a company of young lawyers and court gallants with their musicians; they might, he felt get inquisitive about two strangers. However, they kept up their merry-making far into the night and may have been half-seas-over. Parsons decided to take no risks and, at dawn, he and his companion called a wherry and were put ashore in Southwark about four o'clock. They found it impossible to get a lodging; the inn-keepers were suspicious of two men on foot whose dress was outlandish; a recent proclamation against receiving strangers made them especially cautious. In desperation Parsons went to the Marshalsea prison[3] and asked for Thomas Pound.

This seems a strange proceeding to us; we should not go, say, to Pentonville to get into touch with friends. The prison system – if it can be called such – of Elizabethan times was both more harsh and more humane than ours. The key to understanding much that happened to priests and others is that the prisons were not run by the state but were leased to gaolers who were out to get as much return on their investments as possible. So prisoners who had funds were almost like paying guests, and they were even allowed out on occasions; there is no record of this permission being abused. Prisoners without money or friends were almost starved and kept in foul conditions. One of the great demands on Catholics for years to come was to provide funds for the support of their co-religionists, who were in prison and without resources. The power of what was known as 'the silver key' explains why Catholics could lead a club-like life and priests could say Mass which outsiders, for a fee, could attend. What we call bribery, often under the guise of fees, was a normal practice from the Court downwards.

Thomas Pound, who was about forty years of age, had been educated at Winchester and in the law; for a time he had been a court favourite. He was converted about 1570 and was arrested three years later when trying to leave the country; his intention had been to seek entrance to the Society of Jesus. He was moved from prison to prison until his release in 1604; he died in 1615.

Pound told Parsons that they already knew that he and Campion were coming on the mission. A friend, Edward Brookesby,[4] happened to be visiting Pound and, after the imprisoned Catholics had given them dinner, he took Parsons to a house in Chancery Lane where several priests and laymen were gathered. This was the house of George Gilbert who was already well-known to Parsons. He was a wealthy young man who had been drawn to Catholicism by Fr Thomas Darbyshire when in Paris; his conversion was completed by Fr Parsons in Rome. Gilbert had thought of making a pilgrimage to the Holy

Land, but Parsons suggested he should return to England and put himself and his resources at the service of the missionary priests. Gilbert did this and gathered round him other young Catholics to organise the care of newly arrived priests and to put them in touch with Catholics. Among these companions were bearers of the names of leading Catholic families, such as Vaux, Throgmorton, Titchborne and Stonor. Douay had not been able to set up even a rudimentary system of supervision in England; in consequence, some priests not knowing the ropes were seized and imprisoned soon after arrival. As we have seen, Parsons himself experienced this problem of arriving in England without preparation for lodging. George Gilbert's activities soon attracted the attention of the government and the pursuivants got on his trail. A year later Parsons advised Gilbert to leave the country rather than risk imprisonment and, probably, death. So Gilbert set off for Rome bearing a letter from Parsons to the pope.

> Though he was of ample fortune,' wrote Parsons, 'and in great favour at Court, he has dedicated himself and all his possessions to the defence of the Catholic religion. When we first entered this island, whilst others were either afraid or hesitant, he was the only one who took us in, comforted us, clothed and fed us; with his horses, money and servants he gave us aid; later at his own expense he took us round the island; he himself travelled with us; he gave us books and other necessaries; he contrived a printing press for us; he sold some of his property and from the proceeds assigned us a good sum of money for all the purposes whereby the Catholic cause can be promoted; nor was this all, for he continually relieved by his alms all those who are imprisoned for the Catholic faith.[5]

This has taken us somewhat ahead chronologically, so we must return to Parsons' early days in London. The Catholics who met him advised him to move out of London and this they arranged. Some of them agreed to look out for 'Mr Edmunds' and his servant.

Meanwhile Edmund Campion was getting rather restless at St Omer and from there he wrote a letter to the General,

Everard Mercurian. The following extracts show the mood of the waiting Jesuit.

Father Robert, with Brother George his companion, had sailed from Calais after midnight, on the day before I began writing this; the wind was very good, so we hope that he reached Dover some time yesterday morning, the sixteenth of June. He was dressed up like a soldier – such a peacock, such a swaggerer, that a man needs must have very sharp eyes to catch a glimpse of any holiness and modesty shrouded beneath such a garb, such a look, such a strut. Yet our minds cannot but misgive us when we hear all men, I will not say whispering, but crying the news of our coming. It is a venture which only the wisdom of God can bring to good, and to His wisdom we lovingly resign ourselves. According to orders, I have stayed behind for a time to try, if possible, to fish some news about Father Robert's success out of the carriers, or out of certain merchants who are to come to these parts before I sail across. If I hear anything, I will advise upon it; but in any case I will go over and take part in the fight, though I die for it. . . . On the twentieth of June I mean to go to Calais; in the mean time I live in the College at St Omer, where I am dressing myself and my companion Ralph. You may imagine the expense, especially as none of our old things can be henceforth used. As we want to disguise our persons, and to cheat the madness of the world, we are obliged to buy several little things which seem to us altogether absurd. Our journey, these clothes, and four horses, which we must buy as soon as we reach England, may possibly square with our money; but only with the help of Providence which multiplied the loaves in the wilderness. . . . To-day the wind is falling, so I will make haste to the sea. I have been thoroughly well treated in St Omer College and helped with all things needful. Indeed, in our whole journey we received incredible comfort in all the residences of our fathers. . . . We purposely avoided Paris and Douay. I think we are safe unless we are betrayed in these sea-side places. I have stayed a day longer than I meant, and as I hear nothing good or bad of Father Robert, I persuade myself that he has got through safely.

Parsons' letter from Dover must have reached Campion shortly after he had written this letter. He at once went to Calais but was delayed for want of a fair wind; then on the

evening of the 24th June he and Ralph Emerson crossed to
Dover. Campion's first impulse was to fall on his knees and
commend his cause and himself anew to God. No doubt he
would recall his previous unfortunate experience of Dover and
hope for better luck. Unfortunately for him instructions had
been sent to the searchers to look out for Gabriel Allen, the
brother of William, who was known to be going to visit relatives
in Lancashire. It is indeed remarkable how every movement of
these Catholic exiles was reported; but that did not deter them.
So Campion had to submit to a more thorough interrogation
than Parsons had had to face. The description of Gabriel Allen
tallied in some respects with Campion's appearance. He was
therefore taken before the mayor who charged him with being
Allen; this Campion denied but the mayor decided to send
him to London. While they were waiting for the guard and the
horses, the mayor changed his mind and dismissed Campion.
No explanation has been given for this; it may be that the
searcher (no doubt bribed) who had dealt with Parsons came
along and explained all about 'Mr Edmunds.'

Campion and Emerson, encouraged by their escape,
hastened to London, and like Parsons, finished their journey
by boat up the Thames. They were more fortunate than he
had been; Gilbert had posted men at likely landing places,
and, as Campion stepped ashore, he was greeted by a Thomas
James who must have had a description of Campion from
Parsons, but the fact that Campion was tall and Emerson very
short must have helped. They were at once taken to Gilbert's
house. A well-bribed pursuivant actually lived in the house
and this was a useful, though precarious, safeguard. Campion's
reputation as an orator was so widespread that Gilbert and his
companions persuaded him to preach to them and other
Catholics. Such a reputation could be a snare and it eventually
led to Campion's capture. Parsons was still out of London; had
he been available, he would surely have vetoed such a rash
suggestion, for it was most imprudent to arrange such an
occasion when the magistrates and pursuivants had been put
on the alert. The place for the meeting was arranged by

Thomas, Lord Paget,[6] himself an avowed Catholic but protected
by his peerage. How many attended is not known, perhaps a
dozen or so. They were deeply affected by Campion's sermon
and as a consequence he was beset by those who wanted to
consult him or to make their confessions. Someone with a cooler
head, must have realised the mounting risks of the constant
visits, and he 'retired for his more safety into a certain poor
man's house in Southwark near the Thames, where men might
repair without great show of suspicion both by land and water.'

The search for priests was intensified. Among the most active
spies was Charles Sledd who, on one occasion, narrowly missed
taking both Parsons and Campion, but he secured a priest,
Robert Johnson, and a layman, Henry Orton. Parsons must
have been worried at the turn of events and at Campion's too
easy acquiescence on demands on him; within a few weeks five
priests were imprisoned. It was decided that the sooner the two
Jesuit priests left London, the better, but before they went
Parsons decided that they ought to meet such of the priests as
were accessible in or near London. This was a wise move. He
knew that doubts had been raised of the prudence of their
mission, as there had been so much publicity. Parsons had, of
course, no authority over the secular priests, but as he came
from Rome where he was esteemed, and had had much talk
with William Allen, what he had to say carried its own
authority.

A place of meeting was found in Southwark and those present
included some of the oldest and most experienced priests as well
as some new-comers. The first point discussed was the popular
belief that the Jesuits were engaged on a political mission.
Parsons assured them 'that their coming only was apostolical to
treat of matters of religion in truth and simplicity, and to attend
to the gaining of souls without knowledge or intention in the
world of matters of state.' He then read to the priests the
instructions given to him and Campion. He added that it was
not until they reached Reims that they heard of the Fitzgerald–
Sander expedition to Ireland. One priest suggested that in view
of the outcry the Jesuits should leave England. To this Parsons

replied that they were there by command of the pope; they
would, however, go nowhere without being invited by Catholics,
an undertaking that, as far as can be judged, was observed.
Next came the crucial matter of Catholics attending their parish
Churches to satisfy the law; they were present in body but not
in spirit; could they not be granted dispensations? Parsons
stated that the pope had made it clear that no dispensations
could be granted for attendance at Protestant services, 'a
Catholic cannot without great impiety bind himself to be
present at those acts'.

[1] Campion refers to him as 'Brother George'; he was in fact Parsons' brother and
was later with him in Rome and elsewhere. It is not known if he was ever ordained; he
may have been a Jesuit lay-brother.
[2] A tilt-boat was a large rowing-boat with a tilt or awning and seems to have been
peculiar to the Gravesend–London stretch of the Thames. A wherry was a light
rowing-boat plying for passengers.
[3] At that period the Marshalsea was immediately south of our Guy's Hospital,
between Newcomen Street and Mermaid Court. The Marshalsea of Dickens was a
later building just north of the present St George's Cathedral.
[4] Edward Brookesby of Shoby (Leics.) was the husband of Eleanor Vaux, the sister
of Henry Vaux, Campion's former pupil. Edward Brookesby died in 1581.
[5] C.R.S., Vol. XXXIX, p. 67.
[6] He was later involved in the Throgmorton plot and left the country in 1583. He
was attainted in 1587, and died three years later, a pensioner of King Philip.

Chapter 9

The Challenge

Parsons and Campion decided to leave London immediately after this synod at Southwark; as they were living in separate lodgings, they arranged a meeting place and went there by night. George Gilbert was Parsons's companion; Campion was guided by either Charles Basset or Gervase Pierpont,[1] both members of Gilbert's group; there is a conflict of evidence as to which it was; Charles Basset's mother was Mary Roper, granddaughter of St Thomas More. Gervase Pierpont was of a leading Catholic family of Nottinghamshire. There is no mention of Ralph Emerson at this period but he would be with them. The meeting place was at Hoxton, then a village ('a large street', according to Stow) a mile or so north of the City. Several Catholic families had houses there, notably Sir Thomas Tresham and Sir William Catesby,[2] who were both brought before the Privy Council in November 1581 for habouring Campion. At his examination Sir Thomas asked to speak with Campion to see if he was the man who stayed in his house. 'For this Mr Campion and I,' he said, 'were never of much familiarity, so that in thirteen years [i.e. the time Campion was abroad] he might grow out of my knowledge, who never saw him in the university but once, before his departure beyond the seas, who, as your lordship did say, stayed little with me, came much disguised in apparel, and altering his name.' He was not allowed to see Campion. Sir William Catesby denied that Campion had been at his house. Both Tresham and Catesby were fined a thousand marks and committed to the Fleet prison. One significant fact about this examination was that Parsons' name was not mentioned, yet he was certainly at Hoxton.

While the two priests were planning their next movements, Thomas Pound arrived having bought a few hours of liberty from his gaoler. The question arises, how did he know where they were? Perhaps Gilbert had given him the information, but it seems to have been imprudent. Other records show that Catholics were not too careful in passing on news of the whereabouts of the priests; they must have known that spies, a few of them renegade priests or seminary students, were very active and eager to pick up every scrap of news.

The Catholics in the Marshalsea had sent Pound to put before the priests a suggestion for meeting what they felt was a great need. It was the problem of the true purposes of the Jesuit mission. They felt that, as a safeguard, the two priests should draw up declarations of their intentions; these should be sealed and deposited with friends, so that should the need arise, such as capture and trial, they could be made public and so vindicate the cause of the priests. It was naïve to think that any judges or other officials would have taken the least notice of such documents.

Curiously enough it was Campion, usually so impulsive, who was hesitant until persuaded by Parsons. Once he had agreed, Campion worked quickly and within half an hour produced a thousand word address to the Privy Council; this became known as his 'Challenge' and by his enemies as his 'Brag.' Parsons produced a more carefully thought-out statement of five times the length to which Campion had gone. This was a Confession of Faith[3] addressed to the magistrates of the City. Campion and Parsons kept the originals but gave Pound signed copies; Parsons took the precaution of sealing his, but Campion's was left open.

Pound rode back to London delighted with the success of his mission, but in his exultation, as Parsons wrote to Rome, he 'for some reason or other handed a copy of these documents to another man, and he to a second; so that in a few days' time the thing reached the hands of a countless number of men, including the Queen's Councillors themselves.' Parsons may have been wrong in writing 'documents' as there is no evidence that his own became known; had it been, there would have been replies as there were to Campion's 'Challenge'. Pound no doubt respected the seal on Parsons' statement, but thought that as Campion had left his unsealed it could be communicated to others; Campion may indeed have given permission for it to be shown to other prisoners. The dissemination of the 'Challenge' was traced to Pound; he was at once transferred from the comparatively easy-going Marshalsea to the Bishop of London's[4] prison at Bishop's Stortford where he was put in solitary confinement. A number of those who were found to have copies were also imprisoned.

Two replies to Campion were at once published, one by William Charke, sometime fellow of Peterhouse, Cambridge, and the second by Meredith Hanmer, formerly of Corpus Christi College, Oxford, where he had been a chaplain during Campion's time. Charke's pamphlet was entitled *An Answer to a seditious Pamphlet lately cast abroad by a Jesuit, with a discovery of that blasphemous sect*. Hanmer's title was *The greate Bragge and Challenge of M. Campion, a Jesuite, confuted and answered*. Hanmer did Campion a service by printing the 'Challenge' as the text of his book. Hitherto it had circulated in written copies only; how many of these were made is not known but, judging from the response, the number must have been considerable. Parsons at once replied with *A brief Censure upon two books in answer to M. Edmund Campion's offer of disputation.*[5] The inevitable replies came. Charke wrote *A Reply to a Censure written against the two Answers to a Jesuit's seditious pamphlet*. Hanmer produced *The Jesuites' Banner: displaying their origin and success; their vow and oath; their hypocrisy and superstitions*. This was not the end of the controversy. After he had withdrawn to Rouen, Parsons replied with *A Defence of the Censure*. Charke, however, was not to be silenced. He issued a brief *Answer* in 1583, and three years later a more substantial work entitled *A Treatise against the Defence of Censure given upon the books of Wm. Charke and Mer. Hanmer by an unknown Popish traitor, in maintenance of the seditious challenge of*

Edm. Campion, lately condemned and executed for high treason. In which the reader shall wonder to see the impudent falsehood of the Popish defender in abusing the names and writings of the doctors old and new to blind the ignorant. These titles are suffient evidence not only of the impact made by Campion's 'Challenge' but of the growing animosity to the Jesuits. One result of this uproar was that Edmund Campion became the main quarry of pursuivants and spies.

'The Challenge' is brief enough to be given here in full. The spelling has been modernised.

TO THE RIGHT HONOURABLE, THE LORDS OF HER MAJESTY'S PRIVY COUNCIL

RIGHT HONOURABLE:

Whereas I have come out of Germany and Bohemia, being sent by my superiors, and adventured myself into this noble realm, my dear country, for the glory of God and benefit of souls, I thought it like enough that, in this busy, watchful and suspicious world, I should either sooner or later be intercepted and stopped of my course. Wherefore, providing for all events, and uncertain what may become of me, when God shall haply deliver my body into durance, I supposed it needful to put this in writing in a readiness, desiring your good lordships to give it your reading, for to know my cause. This doing, I trust I shall ease you of some labour. For that which otherwise you must have sought for by practice of wit, I do now lay into your hands by plain confession. And to the intent that the whole matter may be conceived in order, and so the better both understood and remembered, I make thereof these nine points or articles, directly, truly and resolutely opening my full enterprise and purpose.

i. I confess that I am (albeit unworthy) a priest of the Catholic Church, and through the great mercy of God vowed now these eight years into the religion of the Society of Jesus. Hereby I have taken upon me a special kind of warfare under the banner of obedience, and also resigned all my interest or possibility of wealth, honour, pleasure, and other worldly felicity.

ii. At the voice of our General, which is to me a warrant from heaven, and oracle of Christ, I took my voyage from Prague to Rome (where our General Father is

always resident) and from Rome to England, as I might
and would have done joyously into any part of Christendom or Heatheness, had I been thereto assigned.

iii. My charge is, of free cost to preach the Gospel, to
minister the Sacraments, to instruct the simple, to
reform sinners, to confute errors – in brief, to cry alarm
spiritual against foul vice and proud ignorance, wherewith many of my dear countrymen are abused.

iv. I never had mind, and am strictly forbidden by our
Father that sent me, to deal in any respect with matter
of state or policy of this realm, as things which appertain
not to my vocation, and from which I gladly restrain
and sequester my thoughts.

v. I do ask, to the glory of God, with all humility, and
under your correction, three sorts of indifferent and
quiet audiences: *the first,* before your Honours, wherein
I will discourse of religion, so far as it toucheth the
common weal and your nobilities: *the second,* whereof I
make more account, before the Doctors and Masters
and chosen men of both universities, wherein I undertake to avow the faith of our Catholic Church by proofs
innumerable – scriptures, councils, fathers, history,
natural and moral reasons: *the third,* before the lawyers,
spiritual and temporal, wherein I will justify the said
faith by the common wisdom of the laws standing yet
in force and practice.

vi. I would be loath to speak anything that might sound of
any insolent brag or challenge, especially being now as
a dead man to this world and willing to put my head
under every man's foot, and to kiss the ground they
tread upon. Yet I have such courage in avouching the
majesty of Jesus my King, and such affiance in his
gracious favour, and such assurance in my quarrel, and
my evidence so impregnable, and because I know
perfectly that no one Protestant, nor all the Protestants
living, nor any sect of our adversaries (howsoever they
face men down in pulpits, and overrule us in their
kingdom of grammarians and unlearned ears) can
maintain their doctrine in disputation. I am to sue
most humbly and instantly for combat with all and
every of them, and the most principal that may be
found: protesting that in this trial the better furnished
they come, the better welcome they shall be.

vii. And because it hath pleased God to enrich the Queen my Sovereign Lady with notable gifts of nature, learning, and princely education, I do verily trust that – if her Highness would vouchsafe her royal person and good attention to such a conference as, in the second part of my fifth article I have motioned, or to a few sermons, which in her or your hearing I am to utter – such manifest and fair light by good method and plain dealing may be cast upon these controversies, that possibly her zeal of truth and love of her people shall incline her noble Grace to disfavour some proceedings hurtful to the realm, and procure towards us oppressed more equity.

viii. Moreover I doubt not but you her Highness' Council being of such wisdom and discreet in cases most important, when you shall have heard these questions of religion opened faithfully, which many times by our adversaries are huddled up and confounded, will see upon what substantial grounds our Catholic Faith is builded, how feeble that side is which by sway of the time prevaileth against us, and so at last for your own souls, and for many thousand souls that depend upon your government, will discountenance error when it is bewrayed [revealed], and hearken to those who would spend the best blood in their bodies for your salvation. Many innocent hands are lifted up to heaven for you daily by those English students, whose posterity shall never die, which beyond seas, gathering virtue and sufficient knowledge for the purpose, are determined never to give you over, but either to win you heaven, or to die upon your pikes. And touching our Society, be it known to you that we have made a league – all the Jesuits in the world, whose succession and multitude must overreach all the practice of England – cheerfully to carry the cross you shall lay upon us, and never to despair your recovery, while we have a man left to enjoy your Tyburn, or to be racked with your torments, or consumed with your prisons. The expense is reckoned, the enterprise is begun; it is of God; it cannot be withstood. So the faith was planted: so it must be restored.

ix. If these my offers be refused, and my endeavours can take no place, and I, having run thousands of miles to do you good, shall be rewarded with rigour, I have no more to say but to recommend your case and mine to Almighty God, the Searcher of Hearts, who send us his grace, and see us at accord before the day of payment, to the end we may at last be friends in heaven, when all injuries shall be forgotten.

Robert Parsons' 'Confessio Fidei' is too long to print here, but a summary and a few extracts will show his line of approach; he gave more thought to the composition than Campion had done when he dashed off his 'Challenge', yet it must have been written with a sense of urgency as Pound had to get back to the Marshalsea to meet his obligations to the gaoler.

Parsons began by pointing out that he was aware that Catholic prisoners were given no opportunity to defend their faith.

Nay, that *anyone thus imprisoned was not only refused permission to speak again, but that even the words and arguments he had previously used* were all suppressed or were reproduced in an entirely changed form, sayings of his slyly quoted in a distorted sense, or certain monstrous crimes being falsely attributed to him, such as conspiracy, rebellion, or the crime of high treason or such like.

He had therefore decided to state his own case while he was at liberty. After a eulogy of the Jesuits, 'this most blessed Society,' he gave a review of how he was brought to submit himself to the Church. While at Oxford,

I desired to accept the attitude newly adopted by my country and by degrees to reconcile my conscience which was very opposed to it; for I perceived that all promotion in the service of the kingdom had been made to depend on this.

He was turned from these worldly considerations by his study of the Early Fathers and by talks with Catholics. Then he gave a brief account of the Jesuit system and policy. At length he turned to the question of the attitude of the Jesuits to secular or state affairs,

For we are proposing to do here nothing more than our comrades are doing in other parts of the world, viz. to teach those Christians who shall receive us, the rudiments of the

Catholic faith and to make their habits conform to the most holy commandments of God. And that obedience which they owe to their Sovereign we inculcate not less but truly much more than does any of the Protestants. For we preach that Princes should be obeyed not merely for fear of punishment or for the sake of avoiding scandal but for conscience's sake as well; and that he may be condemned who does not obey his Prince even in the utmost secrecy of his closet, where no fear of punishment or scandal exists. . . . We preach to the people that a salutary observance of the commandments of God is so essential that, lacking it, bare faith will be of little value. And so whosoever has not determined from his heart to amend both in word and deed the irregularities of his life, who is not willing to put away once for all stealing, licentiousness, bribery and other sins of that kind, such a one can nowise live a healthy life in our Church or obtain any absolution (which the Catholic Church has power to give by reason of that authority to bind and loose left her by Christ). We restore to you your friends and servants instilled with much higher principles of conduct than when they first approached us.

It was an ingenious argument, but little likely to win acceptance of the City magistrates.

Then he issued his challenge.

I beg most earnestly that either here or elsewhere at your pleasure I may join battle in some kind of disputation with some of your ministers or prelates. I bar none of them, but in this cause I challenge the lot of them, knowing full well that when they have been stripped of a certain sort of parade and pretence, they make no defence of their perversions of the truth. For I have no doubt that, when a few small withered flowers of oratory have been lopped off, Your Worships will perceive clearer than light the complete nakedness of these men and the fullness of their ignomy. And if you shall not consent to allow me this contest, still by the fact of the petition we shall give abundant testimony of confidence on our part and on theirs of exceeding incompetence. Finally I ask, with all the earnestness I am capable of, that you will not atribute my petition to arrogance or obstinacy or any suchlike humour, for it proceeds from obedience, and a certain conscientious zeal.

He ended by assuring the magistrates that 'if your intentions are bloodthirsty' then whatever might be the fate of the captured priests, others would take their places 'for you are persecuting a corporation that will never die.'

Although this appeal could hardly be called placatory, indeed it might be rather be called provocative, it was a pity that it did not get circulated in the same way as Campion's briefer 'Challenge'; it would have given a more developed idea of what the Jesuits hoped to achieve, and, at the same time, it might have served to modify some of the bitter attacks on Parsons as it reveals his burning sincerity and zeal.

[1]Charles Basset left the country with Gilbert for the English College, Rome. He died at Rouen in 1584. Gervase Pierpont was arrested on the 14th August 1581, but his subsequent fate is not known.

[2]Tresham as a minor was brought up as a Protestant, but was reconciled by Fr Parsons. He spent much of his life from 1581 in prison or under house arrest. Catesby was also harried as a recusant. Their sons, Francis Tresham and Robert Catesby, were implicated in the Gunpowder Plot. For this group of Catholics, see Godfrey Anstruther, O.P., *Vaux of Harrowden* (1953).

[3]C.R.S., XXXIX, pp. 28–41. It was written in Latin.

[4]This was John Aylmer noted for his exceptional severity towards Catholics and others who refused to conform.

[5]'Imprinted at Douay by John Lyon, 1581.' This was a false imprint; the book was printed secretly at the Greenstreet House press; see below p. 88.

Chapter 10

The Secret Press

Parsons and Campion separated at Hoxton; Parsons visited Catholics in Gloucestershire, Herefordshire, Worcestershire and Derbyshire, while Campion kept to Berkshire, Oxfordshire and Northamptonshire. Their exact itineraries are not known and in their letters and reports to Rome they of course gave no place names. Parsons wrote to the Rector of The English College at Rome in August 1580.[1] A few extracts from his letter help to set the scene.

> We are encountering many dangers – greater than those which are likely to be met with by those who come after us, seeing that they will have the benefit of many habitations arranged by us, and also because the enemy have a special hatred for us who are the first to come as precursors and they are planning every sort of evil for us. But the dangers are not such as we cannot escape from during many years, or at any rate months; and I hope we shall avoid them, although indeed we are not certain of a single day.

One may note here a suggestion of an attitude that was eventually to cause some friction with the seminary priests; Parsons seems to underrate the work of these pioneers and also the steady apostolate of the Marian priests some of whom were still active, though there is no way of estimating their numbers. By 1580 there were probably at least one hundred and fifty Douay priests on the mission, as well as a few already coming from Rome.

> As long, then, as our Lord shall leave us to enjoy this free-dom, the hope of a harvest is excellent, for we are so spoilt

by the Catholics and kept so busy that we have neither time nor strength sufficient. I am forced two or three times every day on this my tour to give discourses to men of rank, and they are touched by the spirit of God and are most ready for any distinguished service. More often than not they put at my disposal their persons and all their chattels, and their zeal and fervour is worthy of astonishment principally in these three matters: first in hearing Mass, at which they assist with such sighs and such a flood of tears that they move even me, dry as I am, to weep against my will. The second thing is the devotion and reverence they have for the Supreme Pontiff. . . . The third thing is that wonderful fortitude of soul that makes them ready to undergo any labour in the cause of religion.

This was too optimistic a picture of the actual situation. The letter ended,

I beg your Reverence to get for me from his Holiness and from our Fr General the help of men of the Society, men of learning, not fewer than three or four. And let one of them be a Spaniard, another an Italian if possible; but let them be of suitable education, so that they may stop in London, where they will be quite safe, and solve the cases of conscience and of doubt that are brought to them. I should like them to be sent separately from the priests of the English College, so that they may come more secretly and their arrival hardly known.

This seems a strange request unless the Spaniard and the Italian could speak English; this would be unusual at a period when English was a language that foreigners did not think worth learning. Presumably Parsons hoped they would be protected by the embassies, but this may be doubted.

A letter from Campion of a later date tells us how his days were spent.

I ride about some piece of the country every day. The harvest is wonderfully great. On horseback I meditate my sermon; when I come to the house, I polish it. Then I talk with such as come to speak with me; they hear with exceeding greediness, and very often receive the Sacrament, for the ministration whereof we are ever well assisted by priests, whom we find in every place, whereby both the people is well served and we much eased in our charge. The priests of our country themselves being most excellent for virtue and learning, yet have raised so great an opinion of our Society, that I dare scarcely touch the exceeding reverence of all Catholics do unto us. How much more is it requisite that such as hereafter are to be sent to supply, whereof we have great need, be such as may answer all men's expectation of them. Specially let them be well trained for the pulpit. I cannot long escape the hands of the heretics; the enemies have so many eyes, so many tongues, so many scouts and crafts. I am in apparel to myself very ridiculous; I often change it, and my name also. I read letters sometimes myself that in the first front tell news that Campion is taken, which noised in every place where I come, so filleth my ears with the sound thereof that fear itself hath taken away all fear.

It may be noted that Campion appreciated the work of the priests who were already on the mission. He wrote too of the new measures taken against Catholics. 'They have filled all the old prisons with Catholics, and now make new.' This was the result of the apprehensions of the government of concerted action under King Philip, as in Ireland, being imminent. It was decided to round-up the Catholic gentry. A number of castles or suitable buildings were selected throughout the country as special prisons, or what we should call, internment camps. Parsons gave a list of some of the notable Catholics who had been taken in charge – Paget, Arundel, Culpepper, Talbot, Shelley, Southworth, Throckmorton, Giffard and Gage; it reads like a roll-call of the old Catholic families. He added, 'Thus it comes about that not only the old prisons of England, but even the many new ones do not suffice now to harbour the Catholics. The very pursuivants are wearied out.' At first the regulations were very strict; visitors were not allowed though servants were permitted. Not the least of the sufferings of these detainees was that they had to listen to the discourses of visiting Protestant ministers, but the results of these 'conferences,' as they were called, were so meagre that they were faded out. Gradually the gentry were sent back to their estates and were restricted in their movements; their arms and horses were taken away.

Parsons' account of the experiences of this first foray was perhaps over-confident.[2]

Although public decrees forbid all intercourse with us, yet everywhere we are sought out most eagerly, and wheresoever we go we are received with the utmost pleasure. Many people undertake long journeys in order merely to talk with us, and they place themselves and all their possessions at our disposal; clothes, horses and all other equipment they press on us in abundance everywhere; the secular priests co-operate with us, or rather I should say obey us in all things with the greatest goodwill; in fine the reputation of the Society with everybody is so great that we are in fear as to how we can preserve it, especially as we are very far from that perfection which they suppose us to have; and so we need your prayers all the more. We have spent our time hitherto in this way: all last summer we spent very usefully preaching in the country, being escorted in each county by a number of young men of gentle birth, of whom there are quite a lot here who volunteer to be our servants (as they themselves term it). Very generously they pay our expenses as well as their own. When summer was over we withdrew to London, assembling in places that had been agreed, and as soon as we had carried out our duties which the Society imposes,[3] we separated again, and yesterday Fr Edmund set out with Ralph for the counties assigned him. I am left here with the burden of much business, which I cannot easily support without fresh help. Therefore I implore your Reverence to press by every means for a new draft of men of our Society.

Once more he urged the need for a bishop; a subject on which his views were to change.

There is a crying need for a bishop of some sort, to supply us with holy oil for baptism and extreme unction. For lack of this we are reduced to the greatest straits and unless his Holiness soon gives us relief in this matter we do not know what in a short time we shall have to do. Would that the Reverend Bishop of St Asaph had succeeded in reaching us here as he wished. For I had procured everything necessary for him, and found places that were safe and secure. But his efforts did not meet with success. We are hoping that his Holiness will very soon supply us with someone else of more vigorous body. It is certainly in the interests of the common cause that we get someone soon.

Meanwhile he had realised a long-contemplated project: this was the setting-up of a printing press. In anticipation of this the two Jesuits had been given a faculty to publish Catholic books anonymously, notwithstanding the decree of the Council of Trent forbidding the publication of such books without the author's name on the title-page. Parsons shared with William Allen a belief that much could be achieved by books and pamphlets, both controversial and devotional. The leading priests were in full agreement on this matter. The utmost secrecy was necessary. Edward Brookesby and his brother William persuaded their father Robert to allow his unoccupied house at Greenstreet[4] to be used. Stephen Brinkley undertook the provision of the equipment and the management. Very little is known of him; Parsons referred to him as 'a virtuous gentleman'; he was a man of culture for he had adapted and published a book by an Italian, Gasper Louarte, entitled *The Exercise of a Christian Life*. George Gilbert provided the necessary funds for the press. The first two books[5] may have been Thomas Hide's *A Consolatorie Epistle to the afflicted Catholikes*, and Richard Bristow's *A Reply to Fulke*. The latter was a defence of Allen's book on purgatory.

The third book (or some believe the first) was Parsons' *A brief discours contayning certayne reasons why Catholikes refuse to goe to Church. Written by a learned and vertuous man, to a friend of his in England And dedicated by I.H. to the Queenes most excellent maiestie.* I.H. stood for John Howlet who signed the address to the queen; it was the pseudonym of Robert Parsons. The imprint was *Doway by John Lyon 1580*. This too was intended to throw the authorities off the scent. Parsons set down nine reasons why Catholics refused to go to church and showed that 'conscience and not obstinacy or other evil meaning was the true cause of Catholics refusing to go to Protestant churches.' Three answers were published in 1581. The first was *A briefe Confutation of a Popish Discourse*. The author was Dr William Fulke, a puritan divine, formerly of St John's College,

Cambridge, and Master of Pembroke Hall; he had already crossed swords with William Allen and was to meet Campion in 'conference.' The second reply was entitled *A Caueat for Parsons Howlet,* and was by John Field one of the younger puritan ministers who produced the famous Admonition to Parliament of 1572 which advocated a Presbyterian form of church order. The third reply was anonymous but had an attractive title, *A Checke or reproofe of M. Howlets untimely shreeching in her Maiesties eares.* Such speedy replies not only show how effective Parson's book was, but they served to advertise it.

There was a fourth reply to *A brief discours* that has a special inerest as it illustrates the anomalies of the religious situation. This pamphlet, circulated in manuscript, was by Dr Alban Langdale. He had been archdeacon of Chichester and was deprived for refusing to take the oath under the Act of Uniformity; he had been ordered to reside in Lord Montague's household. Lord Montague, we have seen, was one of the Catholic lords whose religion was, as it were, overlooked by the queen as their services were needed. Lord Montague allowed English prayers to be said in his house for those who conformed while he himself went to Mass. Langdale's position was that Catholics could attend the statutory services, as a mark of respect to the queen, provided they did not give interior consent; they could silently say their own prayers. This was a not uncommon attitude among the more easygoing Catholics and had the support of some priests; it almost inevitably led to eventual conformity.

Parsons described some of the difficulties they had in running the press.

Everything had to be brought from London and the press had to be worked so that Mr [Robert] Brookesby should not know what was going on. Then the parish officials began to cause trouble by wanting us to go to their church. There were rumours too that the press was suspected, and that owing to an incautious purchase of paper we should certainly be taken. In truth Catholics were daily being arrested in London and one day Brinkley's man was captured and hauled off to be tortured. That night Gilbert and I fled. Next day, as we had nowhere to go to, we returned and sent my servant, Robert Alfield,[6] to explore. He did not come back which increased our suspicions, especially as his father was a Protestant minister. So we fled again. However, he returned the next day, but I was never quite free from fear in his regard. At last, by God's favour, we completed the impression amid great difficulties and dangers, and Brinkley dismantled the press.

The next call on Parsons' pen was the publication of the two books already mentioned by William Charke and Meredith Hanmer in reply to Campion's 'Challenge.' Stephen Brinley offered to set up the press again, but where? An offer came from Francis Browne, brother of Lord Montague, of his house in the parish of St Saviour's (now the Cathedral), Southwark. Here it was that Parsons brought out his *Brief Censure* to which reference has already been made.

He then turned his attention to the case of John Nichols. He had been a Protestant minister and had gone to the Low Countries in 1577 where he had an interview with William Allen; he then made his way to Rome where he recanted his Protestantism and entered the English College where he stayed for two years but was not ordained. On his return to England, he was arrested and committed to the Tower; this was probably a put-up job. Once more he recanted, this time of his pretended Catholicism, and preached in the Tower church of St Peter-ad-Vincula to Catholic prisoners, who openly showed their contempt; the special congregations of nobles and courtiers were invited to hear him. The authorities built up Nichols as a leading authority on Catholicism and on the Roman system. Parsons at once went into action. The following passage is taken from an anonymous letter published in Rome in 1586 but probably written in 1581. There can be little doubt that the writer was Robert Parsons.

I have written before about the relapse and apostasy of John Nichols who, after being a Calvinist minister, had at one time masqueraded as a scholar of your College. This man sometimes preached in the Tower of London to the priests imprisoned there, who were dragged forcibly to the church in the presence of a large crowd of courtiers assembled to grace the comedy. It is almost unbelievable how this fellow is everywhere talked in terms of the highest praise. He is held to be the most learned of all Jesuits, a Pope's scholar,[7] a preacher to the Cardinals, a theologian, a philosopher, a scholar of Greek, Hebrew, Chaldean, most skilled in all languages and sciences. He published a printed recantation of his faith, and in it are an infinity of lies about Rome, the Pope, the Cardinals, your College, the Jesuits, the scholars, about every kind of monk and priest. The pamphlet was hailed as a signal success by the heretics and distributed abroad; but almost within a month a second book entitled *A discoverie of J. Nichols* [i.e. by Parsons] in which it was proved on the clearest grounds that he was neither a Jesuit nor a priest, nor a theologian or philosopher, and that he had never made an address to the Pope or Cardinals (except once or twice in Rome in the presence of the Inquisitors when he abjured the Calvinist heresy) and that he had no knowledge of any learned tongue nor of any science, but was only a relapsed minister, a very unskilled grammarian, a wandering vagabond, and a most deceitful fellow.[8]

Once more there was anxiety about the location of the press; anywhere near London was exposed to risk; there were too many prying eyes about and the authorities were doing all they could to track down these Popish printers. 'Imprinted at Doway' did not deceive the experts. When one of Brinkley's men was arrested, taken to the Tower and tortured, it was decided to dismantle the press once again and seek safer quarters. A new place was found with the help of John Stonor, one of the Gilbert group. He was the younger son of Lady Cecily Stonor, a widow, and she offered a refuge at Stonor Park[9] on the southern Chilterns about forty miles west of London and five miles north of the Thames. She herself was living at the Lodge in the village. The manor house was surrounded by beech woods; the rambling buildings offered many out-of-the-way rooms and attics where priests could enjoy some security. At that time a Marian priest, William Morris was chaplain, and a seminary priest, William Hartley, used Stonor as the base for his missionary work. Stephen Brinkley organised

the transfer of the press with the type and paper to Stonor.
This was about March 1581.

This account of the adventures of the secret press has taken
us ahead; we must return to October 1580 when Parsons and
Campion met to concert future plans. Their original intention
had been to meet in London, but the intensification of the
search for priests made it unwise for the much-sought-after
Campion to risk such a rendezvous, so Parsons arranged for
him to stop at Uxbridge at the house of a William Griffiths
where several other priests joined them. They talked over their
experiences and compared notes. In the letter from which an
extract has just been given Parsons summed up their
impressions.

I should never come to an end if I began to talk about the
zeal and fervour of the Catholics. When a priest comes to
lodge with them, they greet him in the first instance as if he
were a stranger and unknown to them; then they conduct
him to an inner chamber where an oratory has been set up.
There they all kneel down and very humbly beg the priest's
blessing. Next they enquire how long he is going to stay with
them and this they would like to be as long as possible. If he
says he will be leaving the following day (which is the
common practice in order to avoid risk from a longer stay)
on that same evening they all prepare themselves for the
confession of their sins and the next morning they hear
Mass and fortify themselves with the most holy Sacrament
of the Eucharist; after that an address is given and they
again beg the priest's blessing and he departs; and almost
invariably some young men of birth accompany him on his
journey.

The Catholics in various parts of their houses have a
number of secret places in which to hide the priests from the
violence of the officials, who make sudden incursions. But
now, owing to their being in use for a long time and also by
reason of the treachery of some false brethren, for the most
part they have come to the knowledge of the pursuivants. It
is the custom of the Catholics themselves to take to the
woods and thickets, to ditches and holes even, for conceal-
ment when their houses are broken into at night. Sometimes
when we are sitting at table quite cheerfully, conversing
familiarly about matters of faith and piety (for this is the

most frequent subject of conversation of all) if it happens
that someone rings at the front door a little more insistently
than usual so that he can be put down as an official,
immediately, like deer that have heard the voices of hunters
and prick their ears and become alert, all stand to attention,
stop eating, and commend themselves to God in the briefest
of prayers; no work or sound of any sort is heard until the
servants report what is the matter; and if it turns out that
there is no danger, after the scare they have had, they
become still more cheerful. It can truly be said that they
carry their lives always in their hands.[10]

It will be noted 'that the contacts made by the Jesuits were
with the Catholic gentry. This was sound strategy. The future
of Catholicism in England lay in their hands; if they were to
lapse, there would be no rallying centres for secret Masses and
fewer places where priests could minister in comparative
safety. During the succeeding centuries, many did lapse so
that by the end of the eighteenth century, the government
could ignore Catholics as they no longer presented any threat
to national stability.

It was decided at the Uxbridge meeting that Parsons should
remain in or near London and that Campion should go north
towards Lancashire. He was also urged to write a more
extended defence of the faith to follow up his 'Challenge',
which had excited so much interest not only in England but in
France according to a report from the English ambassador to
Walsingham. This second defence, it was suggested, should be
in Latin as Campion's prestige was high in the universities,
especially at Oxford where many had warm memories of him.
Several topics were suggested such as 'Consolation to Catholics
in this time of persecution', and 'To reprove this manner of the
Protestants' proceedings [i.e. by persecution] contrary to their
own doctrine and protestations in time past.' When Campion
suggested 'Heresy in despair', they objected that the present
persecution showed that heresy was getting the upper hand.
To this he replied that the heretics were so despairing that
they had to resort to terror because they dared not argue their
case. One wonders if the priests realised how powerful a threat

Puritanism was now becoming to the established religion which had to face muted opposition from the Catholics on the one hand and open opposition from Puritanism on the other. It was left to Campion to work out his own ideas as he rode about the countryside.

Parsons returned to London. He later wrote to the Rector of the English College in Rome an account of the kind of life he had to live.

> Though I have many places in London where I can stay, yet in none of them do I remain beyond two days owing to the extremely careful searches that have been made to capture me. I think, however, that by the Grace of God I am sufficiently safe from them owing to the precautions I take, and am going to take, of being in different places from early morning till late at night. After divine service has been performed and sermons preached – I am compelled to preach twice on the same day sometimes – I struggle with almost unending business. This consists mainly in solving cases of conscience which occur, in directing other priests to suitable places and occupations, in reconciling schismatics to the Church, in writing letters to those who are tempted at times in the course of this persecution, in trying to arrange temporal aid for the support of those who are in prison and in want.

He added,

> Get ready for us fresh reserves from the College of his Holiness of numerous soldiers, courageous for the battle; there is need for them to be courageous to undertake the contest that must be waged here, bringing labours, ill report, prison, poverty and ignominious death; they must be numerous, not only because the vineyard is large and cannot be cultivated by a few missioners, except in a long period of time, but also because some of those who are sent necessarily fall into the hands of the heretics.[11]

Writing in November 1580 to Agazzari, Parsons gave the names of some of those who had fallen into the hands of heretics: Ralph Sherwin, Luke Kirby, Robert Johnson, William Hart, John Paschall, Henry Orton, Thomas Cottam and Thomas Clifton. Of these only John Paschall, one of the mission from Rome, gave way and recanted. It seems that the following month saw the beginning of the odious torturing of priests. Torture had not been used in England except in cases of suspected treason, and then only by royal warrant. Two members of the Council had to be present.

At length Parsons felt that it was too dangerous for him to rely on the shelter of Catholic homes which were being brought under closer surveillance and could bring the owners into trouble. So he took a house near the Bridewell[12] where he kept vestments, books and devotional objects; it also gave priests a haven where they could relax for a day or so.

Edmund Campion's exact itinerary after leaving Uxbridge cannot be determined. All we have to guide us is a list of names compiled by Burghley of Catholic gentry who later admitted having entertained him or were suspected of doing so. The period up to Christmas 1580 is a blank. He was then with the Pierponts at Thoresby in Nottinghamshire, from there he went into Derbyshire. Then 'a certain Mr Tempest guided him into Yorkshire. He was certainly at Yafforth in the North Riding on January 28th, then at the houses of Mr William Hawksworth, Asculph Cleasby and Mr Grimston between the 28th and mid-Lent, still with Tempest. In mid-lent he passed to Mount St John, an isolated house in the parish of Felixkirk, now in the North Riding but then part of the Archbishop's Liberty of Ripon. There he passed the third week of Lent and was taken over by a new guide. This was an ex-pupil of his at Oxford, a married man "Mr More living near Sheffield." More was taken on as Campion's guide to Lancashire which they reached by Easter and whence Campion passed directly to the south. On the whole it seems likely that the bulk of Campion's stay in Yorkshire was passed discreetly in a few very remote houses in Allertonshire and Mount St John, organised by the North Riding priest, Richard Holtby.'[13]

Campion went south to Stonor to see to the printing of his *Rationes Decem*, the little book he had written at the suggestion of the priests at the Uxbridge meeting.

[1] C.R.S. XXXIX, pp. 41–6.

[2] C.R.S. XXXIX, pp. 47–62.

[3] Confession one to another and renewal of vows.

[4] Green Street, East Ham, south of Wanstead Flats, may record the site.

[5] For discussion see, A. C. Southern, *Elizabethan Recusant Prose* (1950), pp. 356–8.

[6] Robert Alfield was the brother of the Martyr Thomas Alfield. Robert did eventually become an informer but not while Parsons was in England.

[7] A 'Pope's scholar' was one supported financially by the Pope.

[8] C.R.S. XXXIX, p. 85.

[9] See *Stonor* by R. J. Stonor, O.S.B., (1951) for the Stonor associations of Parsons.

[10] C.R.S. XXXIX, pp. 85–6.

[11] C.R.S. XXXIX, p. 61.

[12] Formerly the palace of Henry VIII; Bridewell Place, New Bridge Street, marks the site.

[13] Quoted from Dom. Hugh Aveling, O.S.B., *The Catholic Recusants of the West Riding of Yorkshire* (1963), p. 204.

Chapter 11

Rationes Decem

A Royal Proclamation was issued on the 15th July 1580 calling for the loyalty of all Englishmen and denouncing traitors living abroad. This was occasioned by the unfounded report of a league having been made between Rome, Spain and Tuscany[1] directed against England. A second Proclamation was made on 1st January 1581 'for revocation of students from beyond the seas and against the retaining of Jesuits.' Students abroad were given three months in which to return and their parents were forbidden to send them money. These Proclamations prompted William Allen to write his *Apologie and true declaration of the institution of two English Colleges, one in Rome, the other now resident in Reims: against certain sinister informations given up against the same.* It was printed at Reims by John Fogny and was issued by June 1581.

In the following paragraphs, Allen explained the Catholic position, and, however much his and Parsons' views changed in later years, this was certainly an authentic statement of how they regarded matters in 1581.

The universal lack then of the sovereign Sacrifice and Sacraments catholicly ministered, without which the soul of man dieth, as the body doth without corporal food: this constraint to the contrary services, whereby men perish everlastingly: this intolerable oath repugnant to God, the Church, your Majesty's honour, and all men's consciences: and the daily dangers, disgraces, vexations, fears, imprisonments, impoverishments, despites, which they must suffer: and the railings and blasphemies against God's Sacraments, Saints and Ministers, and all things holy which they are forced to hear in our Country: are the only causes, most dear Sirs, or (if we may be so bold and if our Lord permit this declaration to come to her Majesty's reading) most gracious Sovereign, why so many of us are departed out of our natural country, and do absent ourselves so long from that place where we had our being, birth and bringing up through God, and which we desire to serve with all the offices of our life and death: only craving correspondence of the same, as true and natural children of their parents.

From which we are not fugitives, as sometimes uncourteously we are called, nor are fled for following any factions or differences of noble families, nor for any crimes or disloyalties done against the Prince or Commonwealth, nor for any disorder in our lives, or worldly discontentment or disagreement with the present civil state and polity, or for mislike of any her Majesty's ministers, whose persons, wisdoms, moderation and prudence in government, and manifold graces, we do honour with all our heart in all things; excepting matters incident to Religion, wherein their honours cannot be offended if we prefer the judgement of God's Church before their human counsel. Acknowledging that her Majesty's reign and their regiment had been most glorious and renowned to the world abroad, and most secure and happy to the subjects at home, if it had not been contaminated by the fatal calamities (so to call God's provident justice for our sins) of alteration in Religion and the things thereon depending. Which not consisting (as we have declared) with any Christian Catholic man's conscience, such as we profess ourselves to be, nor with liberty of mind, nor safety of body, we were constrained to flee and forsake our Country, parents, friends, and whatsoever by nature is there dear unto us, by the warrant and example of Christ, his Apostles, St Athanasius, St Hilary, and other our forefathers in faith, in the like persecution.

In a letter dated the 23rd June 1581 to Agazzari,[2] Allen referred to his *Apologie*.

Our Apology, as I hear, is read both by adversaries and friends, and the chief of the French mission has given it to the queen to read.

Whether or no a copy reached the queen, one certainly came into the hands of Walsingham. From this same letter we can glean some other pieces of news. 'Fr Robert,' Allen wrote, 'wants three or four thousand or more of the Testaments, for many persons desire to have them.' The translation from the Vulgate of the New Testament was not yet ready, but its publication was eagerly awaited as this reference testifies. It was mainly the work of Gregory Martin; his draft was checked by Allen and Richard Bristow; it was not finished until the end of 1581 and was printed the following March. Perhaps as many as five thousand copies were issued. We do not know how the considerable cost had been covered but the donations from Catholics in England were important.

In his letter Allen pleaded for more help in providing missionaries; apparently there were some who questioned the prudence, even the morality, of sending young men to what was almost certain death now that the persecution had been so intensified; this was a view neither Allen nor Parsons could share. They regarded the need as imperative, a duty that must be accepted.

> I write also that the dangers are not so great as to make it expedient to relinquish this duty, seeing that of the fifty priests (at least) who have this year been sent from the two colleges, not more than ten have fallen into the enemies' hands, and up to this time the Fathers [i.e. Parsons and Campion] are altogether free and labouring fruitfully.

Within a month Campion was in the Tower.

Allen next reported the arrival at Reims of George Gilbert.

> I have with me at present the generous companion and benefactor of the priests in England, Mr George Gilbert, who on their account has suffered the confiscation of almost all his goods and estates and whom the heretics have personally persecuted more than the rest, knowing that the Fathers of the Society were kept and sustained by him. He has come hither into France by the advice of Fr Robert and others. . . . He tells me that more Fathers are very much wanted, if it were only to assist Father Robert who, he says, has an incredible burden to bear. . . . He has seven men continually at work at a press outside of London (where the noise of the machine is less likely to betray it). He is

Rationes Decem:
QVIBVS FRETVS, CERTA-
men aduersarijs obtulit in
causa FIDEI, Edmun-
dus Campianus,

E Societate Nominis IESV Presbyter:
ALLEGATÆ
Ad clarissimos viros, nostrates Academicos.

Ego dabo vobis os & sapientiam

aduersarij vestri. Luc.cap.21.

cui non poterunt resistere

& contradicere omnes
Psal.63.
Sagittæ paruulorum factæ sunt plagæ eorum.

Title-page of *Rationes Decem*

continually appealed to by gentlemen and by some of the council for necessary advice; so this Mr Gilbert tells me, who has been his inseparable companion for this whole year and who at his departure left Father Robert seven horses for the necessary journeys and affairs of the Fathers and priests, and a large sum of money to procure needful things, paper, types, ink and the like.

Edmund Campion sent the manuscript of *Rationes Decem* to Parsons at the end of March 1581. The work contained a number of quotations and Parsons saw the need for checking these as opponents would leap at the chance of accusing Campion of inaccuracy. This task was undertaken by Thomas Fitzherbert (b. 1550), one of the Gilbert group, who had been a student at Oxford towards the end of Campion's time; he would thus have no difficulty in making use of the libraries at Oxford. Disturbing news reached Stonor when they were preparing to print the book. William Hartley had learned that Roland Jenks, a Catholic bookseller at Oxford, had been betrayed by his servant; this man had previously been employed by Parsons as a bookbinder at his house in Bridewell, which, as a consequence of this man's revelations, was at once raided and all its contents seized. Even more serious was the capture of Alexander Briant; he had been one of Parsons' pupils at Oxford, and had been trained at Douay; after his ordination, he returned to England in 1578 and had attached himself to his old tutor when Parsons arrived two years later. Briant was taken to the Tower after being kept a close prisoner in the Clink. He was barbarously tortured in the Tower but such was his fortitude in the faith, he revealed nothing of the whereabouts of Parsons and Campion.

Parsons had warned Campion not to put up at Catholic houses on his way south but to use inns. When he arrived at Stonor about the middle of May, they reviewed the situation, especially the implications of Briant's capture. 'For almost the whole of one night,' wrote Parsons, 'Campion and I sat up talking of what we should do were we taken, a fate that befell him soon after.' He added that Campion spent two days 'in almost continuous prayer.' While the printing of his book went on, Campion continued his preaching; he was the kind of man who could not sit still for long but must be up and doing. He and Parsons several times went to Uxenden Hall, near Harrow, the home of the Bellamys. Campion would go on to London and when he reached Tyburn at the southern end of the Edgware Road, he would walk bareheaded beneath the triple gallows in honour of the martyrs, and, as he told Parsons, because it would be the scene of his own tribulation. In London he stayed at Mrs Brideman's in Westminster, with a Mr Barnes in Tothill Street, or in the White Friars at the house of Lady Babington whose son Anthony was to give his name to the plot of 1586. Campion also visited her at her house in Twyford, as well as houses in Bledlow, Uxbridge (William Griffith), and Wynge.

The printing of Campion's small Latin book *Rationes Decem* was a slow business. Owing to the small amount of type it had to be printed by sections. It was ready by June 1582. It was a small book, $6\frac{1}{2}'' \times 4''$, and ran to something less than 20,000 words. The full title read:

> *Rationes Decem: quibus fretus, certamen adversariis obtulit in cause fidei, Edmundus Campianus, e Societate Nominis Iesu Presbyter: Allegatae Ad clarissimos viros, nostrates Academicos.*[3]

The next problem was how most effectively to distribute the book. It had been directed to the academic world and as Oxford was only twenty miles away from Stonor, it was the most obvious target; moreover, Campion's name still carried weight there especially among those who had known him in his university days. William Hartley undertook the task. He had been a fellow of St John's so was familiar with the ground and would know who would be sympathetic. Parsons described what happened.

> By most ingenious means – at one time mixing with such as he knew, at another with strangers, he was enabled to distribute more than four hundred copies, giving them partly to those who knew of the work or to those who were led by curiosity to see what it was, partly leaving copies in the Church of St Mary. Great was the consternation of the

university when the copies were found. There was at first a most unusual silence, and so furtively intent were many in perusing the book that never perhaps was discourse listened to with greater apathy than on this occasion. The professors and fellows, who knew not as yet what had occurred, wondered at the unusual silence. When the meeting came to a close and the whole affair was noised abroad, men's minds were swayed according as devotion or hatred moved them.

St Mary's was chosen as the 'Act' was held there towards the end of June. This was the public disputation when suppliants for degrees had to defend their theses. It was there that Campion had disputed before Queen Elizabeth fifteen years earlier. Such an important occasion meant that many students were present who had completed their studies as well as others who came to see what many regarded as good sport; friends and notables would also be there. It was a bold action to infiltrate copies of the *Rationes* into such a gathering; it could only have been done by someone like William Hartley who was familiar with the routine. As there was still some cryto-Catholicism in the university, a fact that greatly troubled the Chancellor, the Earl of Leicester, the little book was probably welcomed in some quarters however outraged other fellows may have been. The book would soon be passed from hand to hand.

Edmund Campion began by referring to his 'Challenge', written but not printed (except in Hanmer's confutation), which had been ignored except by execration. He had hoped that he would have been invited to argue the Catholic case with his fellow scholars; as this offer had not been accepted, he now set down the main heads of the arguments he would have used in a public disputation. The ten topics he discussed were these:

1. Scripture and how Protestants had misused the Bible.
2. How Protestants passed over texts that told against them.
3. The nature of the Church, visible and invisible.
4. The authority of all general councils not only the first four which Protestants accepted.

5. The authority of the Early Fathers.
6. How the Fathers agreed in their interpretations of Scripture.
7. The history of the Church long before Protestantism had raised its voice.
8. 'Paradoxes', as he called them; this section was a catena of quotations from leading Protestants to show how obnoxious their tenets were to Catholics.
9. The weakness of Protestants in their confusion of meanings and their circular arguments.
10. A number of topics left over, so to speak, such as heaven and hell, the apostolic succession of the pope and the bishop, etc.

The book ended with an appeal to the queen.

Hearken, Elizabeth, most powerful Queen, it is to thee this great prophet [Isaiah] utters his prophecy [*Kings shall be thy fosterfathers, and queens thy nurses*, 49, 23] therein to teach thee thy part. I tell thee: one and the same heaven cannot hold Calvin and the Princes I have named. With these Princes [e.g. Charlemagne, the English Edwards, the French Louises, etc.] link thyself and be worthy of thy ancestors, worthy of thy genius, worthy of thy excellence in letters, worthy of thy praises, worthy of thy fortune. To this effect alone do I labour, about thy person, and will labour, whatever shall befall me, for whom these adversaries so often augur the gallows, as though I were the enemy of thy life. Hail, good Cross. The day will come, Elizabeth, the day will surely come, that will show thee clearly which of the two have loved thee, the Society of Jesus or the brood of Luther.
I proceed. I call to witness all the coasts and regions of the world, wherever the Gospel trumpet has sounded since the birth of Christ. Was this a little thing, to close the mouths of idols and carry the kingdom of God to the nations? Of Christ Luther speaks: we Catholics speak of Christ. *Is Christ divided?* (1. Cor. 1, 13). By no means. Either we speak of a false Christ or he does. What then? I will say. Let Him be Christ, and belong to them, at whose coming Dagon broke his neck.[4]

Needless to say, Campion's book provoked replies. The Bishop of London, John Aylmer, asked scholars at Oxford and Cambridge to refute Campion's arguments. The first in the field was William Whitaker, later master of St John's College, Cambridge. He published his *Ad decem rationes Edmundi Campiani* in 1581, by which time Campion was in the Tower. Laurence Humphrey, a determined Puritan and objector to vestments, later president of Magdalen College, Oxford, followed with *Jesuitismi pars prima*. He must have known Campion as he was one of the doctors who welcomed the queen at the university in 1566. Both divines were quickly answered by Fr John Drury, S.J., a Scot. His *Confutation* was published in Paris in 1582. He in turn was answered by Whitaker and Humphrey, the former with *Responsionis* (1583), and the latter with the second part of his *Jesuitismi* (1584).

Since *Rationes Decem* was written in Latin as were the replies and the counter replies, its impact was limited. It is impossible to assess the effect of any book, but there are indications that some of the younger men at Oxford were strongly attracted to Campion and this, as we shall see, contributed to the imminent catastrophe.

To us there may seem something naïve, even pathetic, in Campion's belief that a well-conducted disputation according to academic practice could gain a victory for Catholicism. It was, however, an age of argument and controversy; those concerned were scholars and divines; the ordinary folk were little affected. Between say 1550 and 1650 the amount of printed controversy was of terrifying proportions. Opponents would keep up the discussion for as long as printers would risk publication. Replies, Replications, and Responses were weighed down with learning, and the only relief the reader gets to-day, if he dares to turn the pages of these ponderous folios, is for the passages of vituperation in which opponents accused one another of the basest vices; they were masters of this kind of exchange. Yet there seems to be no record of any controversialist convincing or converting his opponent; each became more entrenched in his original position. The writers certainly enjoyed themselves; there was the zest of combat, the intellectual satisfaction of working out an argument, the joy of scoring points off one's opponents, and the eager anticipation of his

reply. One cannot help feeling that this vast output of controversy was largely sterile; it made no impact on the general
public. The pulpit was a far more powerful influence. Parsons
and Campion recognised this for they found that wherever
they went Catholics eagerly and tirelessly listened to sermons.
The sacraments were the greatest blessings the priests could
bring them, but their preaching was the next gift that was
welcomed. So it was that Parsons and Campion urged that
students at the seminaries should be trained not only to be
good apologists but also to be good preachers.

[1] The Duke of Tuscany had given Queen Elizabeth warning of the Ridolfi plot.

[2] Knox, op. cit.

[3] Only four copies are known. One belongs to the Marquess of Bute, the second is at
Campion Hall, Oxford, the third at Stonyhurst, and the fourth at St Peter's
Presbytery, Winchester. The cover of the last copy was – surely imprudently – a
parchment deed of the Bellamy family of Uxenden.

[4] This refers to 1. Sam. 5, 1–8; the Philistines brought the Ark of the Covenant into
the temple of Dagon, their idol-god. 'And when they rose early on the next morning,
behold, Dagon had fallen face downward on the ground before the ark of the Lord,
and the head of Dagon and both his hands were lying cut off upon the threshold.'

Chapter 12

The Act of 1581

The Proclamations against Catholics issued in July 1580 and January 1581 were followed by further and more stringent penal laws. Parliament met on the 16th January 1581. The tone of the debates is best shown by an extract from a speech made by Sir Walter Mildmay, chancellor of the exchequer since 1566; he was the brother-in-law of Walsingham, a puritan and the founder of Emmanuel College, Cambridge. It is said that the queen made the comment, 'Sir Walter, I hear you have erected a Puritan foundation.' 'No, Madam,' he replied, 'far be it from me to countenance anything contrary to your established laws, but I have set an acorn which, when it becomes an oak, God alone knows what will be the fruit thereof.'

On the 25th January Sir Walter outlined to the Commons the work that lay before them. Part of this was the need for further measures against Catholics.

The obstinate and stiff-necked Papist [he said] is so far from being reformed as he hath gotten stomach to go backwards and to show his disobedience, not only in arrogant words but also in contemptuous deeds. To confirm them therein, and to increase their numbers, you see how the Pope hath and doth comfort their hollow hearts with absolutions, dispensations, reconciliations, and such other things of Rome. You see how lately he hath sent hither a sort of hypocrites, naming themselves Jesuits, a rabble of vagrant friars [sic] newly sprung up and coming through the world to trouble the Church of God; whose principal errand is, by creeping into the houses and familiarities of men of behaviour and reputation, not only to corrupt the realm with false doctrine, but also, under that pretence, to stir sedition.

In pursuance of this purpose, a grand committee of the House was appointed to frame a Bill.[1] As the Lords were engaged on the same matter, it was agreed that a conference of the two Houses would be advantageous. The Lords' Bill was not as severe as the one drafted by the Commons, but it included compulsory attendance at Communion in spite of the opposition the queen had previously shown to such a proposal; it was again dropped no doubt at her behest. Both Houses were determined on a very much stricter and more thorough-searching law to keep down Catholics. The agreed Bill was passed quickly and received the royal assent when Parliament was prorogued on the 18th of March.

The bill as finally enacted falls broadly into two sections, the first concerned with the work of the Catholic missionaries, the second stiffening the penalties for ordinary recusancy or refusal to attend church. As historians have pointed out, it drew a statesmanlike distinction between being and becoming a Catholic: or, to express this more pungently in the language of the day, it directed its greater severities against recruitment for the fifth column.

By its main provisions, whoever withdrew the Queen's subjects from their natural obedience, or converted them *for that intent* to the Romish religion, were to be adjudged traitors, as were those who willingly allowed themselves to be thus withdrawn or converted. Those significant words, *for that intent*, made the approach political and secular.[2]

It seems probable that it was the queen herself who had the italicised words *for that intent* inserted; this was in keeping with her claim that she had no wish to force men's consciences provided they were loyal. This distinction between religion and politics was a crucial issue and it led to the tragedy of the martyrdoms of Catholic priests and laity. A few years later, Francis Bacon stated what he believed to be the queen's policy.

Her Majesty, not liking to make windows into men's hearts

and secret thoughts, except the abundance of them did over-flow into overt and express acts or affirmations, tempered her law so as it restraineth only manifest disobedience, in impugning and impeaching advisedly and manifestly her Majesty's supreme power, and maintaining and extolling a foreign jurisdiction.[3]

The other sections of the Act must be noted.

The fine for saying Mass was 200 marks (a mark was 13s.4d.) for the priest with imprisonment until the fine was paid, and a fine of 100 marks for hearing Mass or a year's imprisonment. This clause does not seem to have been regularly enforced, perhaps because the later provisions of the Act were more effective. The clause that most closely affected the Catholic layman read as follows:

Be it further enacted by the Authority aforesaid that every person above the age of sixteen years who shall not repair to some church, or chapel or usual place of common prayer, but forbear[4] the same contrary to the tenor of a statute made in the first year of her Majesty's reign for the uniformity of common prayer, and being thereof lawfully convicted, shall forfeit to the Queen's Majesty for every month after the end of this session of Parliament which he or she shall so forbear, twenty pounds of lawful English money.

It should be noted that this did not repeal the original fine of one shilling for every absence from the statutory service; this new provision was clearly directed at the gentry. These fines were to be forfeit to the Crown, and were thus of concern to the Exchequer; they were no longer the business of the church-wardens. Any attempt to circumvent the Act by the collusive conveyance of lands or other property was declared void. Those who did not pay the fines were imprisoned until they either did so or conformed; as a consequence many recusants were to spend years in prison and some died there; their numbers are not known, but recent research has revealed that they must have numbered many thousands over the years. The monthly fine of £20 was a crippling exaction and could only be levied on the well-to-do and rich.

This Act brought an important change in the administrative

machinery. Recusancy while still being cognizable by the ecclesiastical courts, now became primarily the concern of the civil courts and the local magistrates. A sinister provision was that informers who brought successful actions were rewarded with one-third of the forfeiture; another third went to the Exchequer, and the last third could be used for the local poor. Here was a method that led to all kinds of blackmail, bribery and chicanery.

The early receipts from these heavy fines were not impressive. In the first full year they amounted to just over £900, but ten years later the total was over six thousand pounds.[5]

This new and drastic law was enacted about the time Parsons was moving his press to Stonor. The two Jesuit priests were directly threatened by the clauses of the Act against anyone persuading another to be reconciled to the Church. The Act, in fact, became known as 'the Act of Persuasions.' In a letter to the pope dated June 1581[6] Parsons did not refer to this threat against priests, but he explained the plight of lay Catholics.

We are in daily expectation of a new and bitter storm of persecution: for two days ago an edict was issued by the royal council to every part of the realm, that inquisition be made for Recusant Catholics, as they call them, according to the letter of the new statute made at the last session of the upper Chamber. By this all above the age of sixteen years are condemned to pay eighty crowns a month if they refuse to attend a Protestant church. And since there are very few Catholics who are able to pay, most of them expect perpetual imprisonment. Yet they are most cheerful and not in the least anxious about the matter, for they hope it will be with them as it was with the Israelites – the greater the pressure put upon them, the sooner the hope of relief. They are publishing most threatening proclamations against us, as well as books, sermons, ballads, libels, fables, comedies; the people, however, are most eager to receive us, comfort us, and protect us. There is a marvellous increase in the number of believers; and among them those who were our bitterest enemies we have made an impression on many, and some we have converted. It is a bitter fight: God grant us humility, patience and strength. Every priest or other person whom they capture and suspect of having knowledge of our affairs, they torture on the rack or scaffold to make him betray us. One of them they tortured most cruelly the other day, but could get nothing out of him [Alexander Briant]. In the meantime we are living under their eyes with considerable safety, conversing, preaching, writing, and pursuing the courses that make for resistance, expecting torture of all kinds when we are captured, but meanwhile through the goodness of God sleeping with peaceful minds. We urgently request a supply of new recruits; that they come quickly also lest we be captured before they can relieve us.

Parsons' hopes of further help were fulfilled by the arrival shortly after this letter was written of two Jesuit priests; Jasper Heywood and William Holt. Jasper was the son of Merry John Heywood who had married a niece of St Thomas More. William Holt had been a fellow of Oriel College towards the end of Campion's Oxford days. They came to England just in time to take over the Jesuit mission after Parsons' withdrawal and while Campion was in prison.

This intensified persecution of Catholics must be seen in its political setting. England was still at peace in 1580 as it had been since the beginning of the reign twenty-two years earlier. This considerable achievement was largely due to Queen Elizabeth's tortuous policy that baffled her councillors as much as it did foreign rulers and statesmen. But by 1580 the clouds were gathering for a storm. An undeclared war with Spain had been carried on for more than a decade across the Atlantic by such seamen as Hawkins and Drake, who had made many profitable raids (out of which the queen had her pickings) of a piratical nature. This has antagonised Spain. Tales of how the Inquisition dealt with captured English sailors stirred up national animosity. The long drawn-out struggle of the Protestant Dutch and the Spanish Netherlands excited sympathy in Protestant England. The designs of the papacy for an invasion of England under Spanish leadership further aggravated anti-Catholic feeling. The enemy was Spain, and Douay, where the priests were being trained, was in Spanish territory and was patronised by King Philip. The

Fitzgerald–Sander Irish venture seemed a foretaste of what might follow. There was indeed a very real threat of invasion hanging over a country with no standing army. It was a period of rising suspicion and apprehension; and it was at this critical period that the two Jesuit priests arrived in England; they could not have come at a less propitious time. They were inevitably regarded as emissaries of the enemy intent on stirring up trouble from within to coincide with threats from without. We know that such was not their purpose, and in the letters and writings of Campion and Parsons during the mission there is not the slightest hint of any political intention. We cannot blame our ancestors for thinking otherwise, and for taking whatever counter-action seemed necessary. One obvious measure was to intensify the harassment of Catholics in the hope that they would be forced into conformity. Hence the new legislation and the incessant search for the two Jesuits.

We find it easy to keep religion and politics in separate departments as Queen Elizabeth vainly tried to do. Religion no longer plays a determinative part in the lives of the vast majority of people, but from, say, 1550 to 1650, it was part of men's thinking and was inevitably interlocked with national affairs.[7]

---

[1] J.E. Neale, *Elizabeth I and her Parliaments, I,* p. 383. The best account of the making of the 1581 Act is given on pp. 382–92 of this book.

[2] Quoted from Neale, op. cit., p. 388.

[3] Spedding, *Life and Letters of Bacon,* I, 97–8.

[4] In the sense of 'abstain or desist from.'

[5] For a study of the financial effects of the Act, see, Dom Hugh Bowler, O.S.B., Introduction to C.R.S., Vol LVII.

[6] C.R.S., Vol. XXXIX, pp. 64–7.

[7] Perhaps Northern Ireland should be excepted. Can we see there an anachronistic and disastrous survival of out-worn attitudes?

Chapter 13

Lyford

On the 11th July 1581, the two Jesuits rode out from Stonor; they had decided that it would be safer for them to resume their separate missions. Edmund Campion with Ralph Emerson were to go north to Lancashire to call at Hoghton Tower (between Preston and Blackburn) to collect some books and papers Campion had left there in the care of Richard Hoghton whose elder brother Thomas had died in Liège, an exile for the faith. From Lancashire Campion was to make his way to Norfolk, calling at Catholic houses on the way. Parsons had still got the press at Stonor to supervise, but he moved about the district visiting Catholics.

We have seen how they had talked over how they were to face future perils. Neither had any illusions of what lay ahead. They had been both marked down as the special quarry of the priest-hunters, and the arrests during the past few months of a number of priests and of their harbourers was evidence of a determined search. So the two Jesuits prepared themselves spiritually by making confession one to another and by renewing their vows. The rest was in God's hands. Parsons rode with Campion and Emerson until 'they reached a wide and open common'; this was probably Christmas Common about three miles from Stonor; the ride would have been through the woods until they reached this slope of the Chilterns. Here Campion and Emerson could take their way northwards. Parsons turned back but presently he heard Campion galloping after him. He begged Parsons' permission to turn off the northern route to visit Lyford Grange some

twenty miles to the west. This was in Berkshire and was the
home of Francis Yate, imprisoned as a recusant, who had
several times asked that one of the Jesuits should visit his wife
at Lyford. This was the kind of appeal that Campion found it
hard to resist. Parsons hesitated; he wanted to get his companion out of the home counties where the search for them was
closing in. Lyford was bound to be watched from time to time
and it was too near Oxford, about ten miles, where Campion's
name was in everyone's mouth since the distribution of *Rationes
Decem* and where many would know him by sight. Campion
pleaded to be allowed to go; he would stay only as long as
Parsons decided, and Ralph Emerson would be his surety.
Parsons at length gave way; it was as difficult to refuse
Campion anything as it was for Campion to say 'No' to an
appeal; Parsons laid down the condition that Campion was to
put himself under obedience to Brother Emerson who was
charged to see that there was no lingering at Lyford.

Lyford Grange had a special interest. The Bridgettine nuns
of Syon had left the country after the dissolution; some had
returned under Queen Mary, only to be forced again into exile
when Queen Elizabeth succeeded. Disturbances in the Low
Countries sent them back to England where they were committed to the custody of such of the gentry as would receive
them and be answerable for them. Eight of them were at Lyford
where they led a community life as far as possible. There were
two Douay priests at Lyford, Thomas Ford and John Colleton
(or Collington), so the spiritual needs of the household and of
the nuns were met. Both Thomas Ford and John Colleton had
been at Oxford in Campion's time, Ford at Trinity College, of
which he was a fellow, and Colleton probably at Lincoln but
he left for Douay before taking his degree. Both were converts.
It is difficult to justify the calling of Campion to Lyford, and
Parsons was rightly hesitant; the pity is that he did not insist
on Campion keeping to their original plan; not that this could
have made much difference in the long run; the odds were not
in their favour.

So Campion cheerfully turned westwards and probably

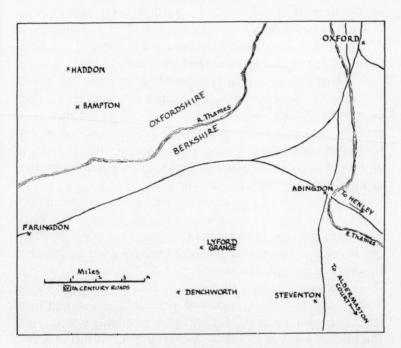

Lyford and district

crossed the Thames at Wallingford. His welcome at Lyford can be imagined. Confessions and conferences went on far into the night. Campion said Mass at dawn, then, after a meal, he and Ralph Emerson rode away with Fr Colleton as their companion.

That afternoon a party of Catholics called at the Grange to see the nuns. This may seem a hazardous proceeding, but the house was in an out-of-the-way situation and was unlikely to be bothered by unwanted callers unless a pursuivant happened to be in the neighbourhood, and this, unfortunately was the case. The visitors were upset to hear that they had just missed Fr Campion; they were told that he had left under instructions from his superior, but this did not satisfy them; couldn't he be brought back? Fr Ford undertook to ride after Campion and try to persuade him to return. He caught up with the party at an inn near Oxford where he found Campion in the company of a number of members of the university.

There are one or two unexplained aspects of this matter. What was Campion doing near Oxford? The obvious route north was through Burford and Chipping Campden. And how did it come about that a group of Oxonians was gathered at this particular inn? The records give no clue to the answers to these questions. It may be that a student from Oxford was at Lyford and had there suggested that Campion should meet some of his friends at this inn. Another possibility is that one of the priests, Ford or Colleton, had arranged this meeting soon after Campion's arrival for a few students who they knew were having doubts about Protestantism. This might explain why Colleton accompanied Campion from Lyford as he would know of the rendezvous; there was no need for him to act as a guide save in courtesy. Parsons was certainly right in fearing Campion's susceptibility to any Catholic appeal; he would go anywhere at any time, completely oblivious of his own safety if he could bring spiritual comfort to those in need. The Oxonians asked for a sermon, but this he refused to give as even he felt that proximity to the university was a serious risk. Fr Ford now urged Campion to return to Lyford for the week-end to

meet the new arrivals there; the Oxonions added their
entreaties; they too could go with him and, with those already
there, would give Campion a splendid opportunity for exercising his ministry. Campion pointed out that he had been put
under obedience to Ralph Emerson whose one thought was to
follow Parsons' instructions. Perhaps the Oxonians felt that
there was something absurd in such a famous scholar as
Campion being under the orders of a lay-brother. We know
nothing of Emerson's origins; there is no suggestion that he
had been to a university; he may have been of humble origin;
he was certainly not an impressive figure for a spy described
him as 'a very slender, brown, little fellow' and Campion sometimes referred to him affectionately as 'the little man.' The
company turned their fire on Emerson who was at a disadvantage; he seems to have withstood their arguments for a time
but it was difficult for a man of his lower social position (and
that meant much in those days) to resist the arguments of
university men especially when two of them, Thomas Ford
and John Colleton, were priests. At last Emerson agreed to the
proposal that he himself should go north to Hoghton Tower,
collect the books and papers, and then join Campion in
Norfolk who would go straight there from Lyford; thus there
would be no loss of time. So it was arranged. Parsons would
not have approved of this separation.

We must now look at George Eliot who was to be responsible
for Campion's capture. He was a Catholic who had been
employed as a steward by Thomas Roper (grandson of St
Thomas More) in Kent. Charles Basset, Thomas Roper's
nephew, said that he had known Eliot well at his uncle's house
and that he had been dismissed for misconduct with a maid,
and was also suspected of theft. The Roper's chaplain was
John Payne, and it was he who brought Eliot's wantonness to
light. Eliot had later entered the service of Anne, Lady Petre,
at Ingatestone, Essex. It is not known why he turned informer;
it was something more than cupidity, or spite, or a sense of
grievance, which were so often the cause of men becoming
government spies. He had been imprisoned for a grave offence,

perhaps rape or homicide, but there is no official record. The belief was that he was offered a pardon if he betrayed his former employers and their Catholic friends. It was from goal that he wrote letters to the Earl of Leicester giving him a list of Catholics, priests and layfolk, he had known. The list probably added nothing to the information already in the hands of the authorities. Eliot went further. He asserted that a plot to assassinate the queen involved old Lady Petre and her son Sir John as well as Thomas Roper. It is doubtful if such a cock-and-bull story deceived Leicester or Walsingham; the persons named were little likely to be concerned with such a wild plot. Lady Petre's husband, Sir William (d. 1572) had loyally served four sovereigns before he withdrew from public life in 1566. Their son John was knighted in 1576 and became a member of Parliament. Thomas Roper had succeeded his father, William, as protonotary of the Queen's bench, a post he held for twenty-four years; these were not the kind of people who went in for cloak and dagger plots. This part of Eliot's revelations led to nothing, but his knowledge of many Catholic families could be used. He seems to have been given a roving commission to search for priests and especially for Parsons and Campion. As a reputed Catholic he could gain admission to gentlemen's houses. He was not, however, given a free hand; the authorities were not too sure of him, so an experienced pursuivant, David Jenkins, was detailed to go with him. They were given the necessary warrants and also letters of credence from the Council to sheriffs and magistrates requiring them to give whatever help was needed.

Eliot heard Mass on the 3rd and 4th July at William Mo(o)re's at Haddon (Bampton) in Oxfordshire.[1] Here is the spy's report:

John Payne said mass at Mr William Moore his house at Haddon, Oxon., upon Sunday, being the 2nd July anno reg. 23. At which mass were, the said William Moore and his wife, one Mrs Tempas, one other gentlewoman daughter of the said William, Edward Moore and Mary Moore brother and sister to William Moore, two serving men-servants to the said William and myself.

Godsoffe said mass there on Tuesday, the fourth of the said month, at which mass were all the persons aforesaid, the said William Moore excepted. Signed, G.E.

The Mo(o)res of Haddon were not related to the family of St Thomas More, but William More's wife was Anne More, the only daughter of John and Anne (Cresacre) More and thus the granddaughter of St Thomas.

Two priests were seized at Haddon; their recorded names were Thompson and Godsalve, but nothing is known of their fates. Eliot's inclusion of John Payne was probably sheer vindictiveness. Payne·had got him dismissed by Thomas Roper, and when the priest followed Eliot to Ingatestone, he probably warned Lady Petre of Eliot's murky past. There is no confirmation of the claim that Payne was in Berkshire at this or any other period. He was taken at Ingatestone (not Haddon) in 1582 and Eliot was the chief witness at his trial; Haddon was not then mentioned. St John Payne was hanged at Chelmsford on the 2nd April 1582.

The pursuivant would not be present at the Masses at Haddon as he seems to have made no pretence of being a Catholic: he remained, as it were, at call. While there Eliot heard rumours of an assembly of Catholics at Lyford; he would probably have gone there in any case as it was a known Catholic centre with the nuns in residence.

Edmund Campion, the two priests and the Oxonians rode to Lyford where their arrival was warmly welcomed. As there is some variation in the records of those fateful days and they have been differently interpreted, it is difficult to establish an indubitable chronology. The following seems to fit the known facts.

Monday, 10th July	Campion and Emerson arrive at Lyford.
Tuesday, 11th July	At Lyford.
Wednesday, 12th July	They leave Lyford for an inn near Oxford.
Thursday, 13th July	?
Friday, 14th July	They return to Lyford.
Saturday, 15h July	At Lyford.

Sunday, 16th July	The search.
Monday, 17th July	Capture.
Tuesday, 18th July	Under arrest at Lyford.
Wdnesday, 19th July	Still at Lyford.
Thursday, 20th July	From Lyford to Abingdon and on to Henley.
Friday, 21st July.	To Colnbrook.
Saturday, 22nd July	Enter London. The Tower.

This time-table raises one problem; how long were they at the inn near Oxford? Parsons had given instructions that they were not to linger at Lyford, at most only for one night. The date[2] when the two Jesuits separated can be accepted as correct. As Lyford was not much more than twenty miles from Stonor, they would arrive there by the late afternoon. Assuming they stayed the night and left early they would reach the inn near Oxford mid-morning, a ride of only ten miles. Fr Ford might catch up with them in the afternoon. Time must be allowed for Campion's talk with the Oxonians followed by the argument when Fr Ford invited the Jesuit to return to Lyford. They could easily have done so that evening, say at dusk when their journeying would not be so noticeable. It looks as though they stayed at the inn or near-by for one night, if not two, as they do not seem to have got back to Lyford until the Friday. There seems to be a gap here that has not been accounted for.

Eliot and Jenkins came to Lyford early on the Sunday morning. They may not have known or even have suspected that Campion himself would be there; indeed, the rumour may have been that he had been there and had gone away. Eliot knew that a former fellow-servant at Thomas Roper's was now at Lyford as cook; his name was Thomas Cooper. This is but one example of how Catholics preferred to employ Catholics and recommended reliable servants to one another.

Eliot himself wrote an account of how he captured Campion; this was published immediately after the executions under the title, *A very true Report of the apprehension and taking of that arch-Papist Edmund Campion, the Pope his right hand: with three other lewd Jesuit Priests, and divers other Lay people, most seditious persons of like sort.* There is no reason to doubt the substantial accuracy of the narrative, though allowance must be made for Eliot's vaunting of his own share in the catastrophe.

When Eliot and Jenkins arrived at Lyford they found the gates closed and a servant on guard. Eliot asked him to tell Thomas Cooper that an old friend wanted to see him. The cook was delighted and invited the two men to come inside but Eliot demurred on the grounds that they were on their way to Derbyshire and could not stay, but the cook was insistent that they should at least have a drink and Eliot gave way with seeming reluctance. So the three went into the buttery and the cook drew some ale. Eliot's account reads:

> Presently after the said cook came and whispered to me, and asked whether my friend (meaning Jenkins) were within the Church or not? To which I answered, 'He was not; but yet,' said I, 'he is a very honest man, and one that wishes well that way.' Then said the cook, 'Will you go up?' By which speech I knew he would bring me to a Mass. And I assured him and said, 'Yes, for God's sake, that let me do; for seeing that I must needs tarry, let me take something with me for good.'

So the cook led Eliot through the hall and several rooms to a 'fair, large chamber' which was fitted up as a chapel. Eliot must have been startled to see Campion there; he may not have known him by sight but one of his neighbouring worshippers would no doubt tell him the priests' names. It must have been a great moment for Eliot when he saw the searched-for Jesuit there. Fr Ford was saying Mass. Frs Campion and Colleton were there and three of the nuns in their habits (an offence against the law); in addition there were thirty-seven laity. When Fr Ford had finished, Edmund Campion vested and said Mass, after which he distributed holy bread and asperged the congregation. Eliot received his portion of the holy bread. It should be explained that this was not the eucharistic bread or wafer. It was the custom in those days for the attenders at Mass to bring loaves of bread as oblations; if there were no wafers, some of the bread was consecrated, broken and distributed for communion. What remained was afterwards blessed and divided among those present; such holy bread was then given to the poor and the sick or taken home and given to Catholics who could not get to Mass. It was in no sense a communion.

Eliot's narrative continued:

> And then was there a chair set in the chamber something beneath the Altar, wherein the said Campion did sit down; and there made a Sermon very nigh an hour long; the effect of the text being, as I remember, 'That Christ wept over Jerusalem, etc.' And so applied the same to this our country of England for that the Pope his authority and doctrine did not so flourish here as the same Campion desired.

Campion's text was, 'O Jerusalem, Jerusalem, thou that killest the prophets,' (Mat. 23, 37.)

Eliot thought of the warrant in his pocket. It was desirable if practicable to make the arrest when the priest was saying, or had just said, Mass. With such a large congregation present, and without anyone to support him, Eliot realised that an attempt to serve the warrant there and then would be prevented. He therefore left immediately though he had been invited to stay for a meal. His abrupt departure made Mrs Yates somewhat suspicious, so she posted one of her men on a turret to watch for approaching strangers. Eliot had gone off to fetch the nearest magistrate, Edward Fettiplace of Denchworth, two miles away; when he saw the warrant the magistrate called together the *posse comitatus*.[3] By the time this armed force had been collected, most of the lay folk at the Mass had ridden home, but a few remained for dinner and some had arranged to spend the night at Lyford. While they were at dinner, the man on outlook broke in to say that a party of men was approaching. The house was soon surrounded and the magistrate demanded admittance; Eliot, to be known henceforth by Catholics as 'Judas Eliot,' was with him. Catholic households were well prepared for such emergencies; all signs of the Mass and of a chapel were quickly removed and concealed and the priests were taken to prepared hiding-places. Campion proposed that he should make an attempt to escape; his argu-

ment was that, if taken, as seemed likely, the magistrate would
not molest the household. He was overruled, and with Frs
Ford and Colleton he was taken to the prepared hiding-place,
a narrow room or cell over the gateway. Food and drink had
been put there in readiness. So the three priests stowed themselves away, waiting calmly for what might happen.

The magistrate with Eliot and Jenkins and the men were
admitted and they first made a quick search of all the rooms
without finding anyone who might be a priest. Mrs Yate, her
guests and the household were kept under guard. The magistrate apologised·to Mrs Yate and excused himself on the
grounds that he had to enforce a royal warrant. He must have
known that Lyford was a Catholic meeting-place; he was a
near neighbour but had preferred not to interfere; in a sense
the warrant was a rebuke to him for not having carried out his
duties in dealing with recusants. He was probably greatly
relieved when this preliminary search proved fruitless; he
began to withdraw his men, but Eliot was far from satisfied.
He had seen Campion with his own eyes; what he feared was
that the priests had slipped away while he was fetching the
magistrate. He insisted that the search should be renewed,
otherwise he would report Fettiplace to the Council for
negligence in obeying the warrant. No doubt the posse, all
local men, were as reluctant as the magistrate to push things
too far with a good neighbour; some may indeed have had
Catholic sympathies. It took some time to persuade the
magistrate to make a second search, but, in the end, he had to
admit that Eliot was acting under authority.

Meanwhile, the danger over as it was thought, the priests
had come out of their hiding-place and all were rejoicing at
their escape. When the magistrate returned and said they were
not yet satisfied, Mrs Yate remonstrated and finally broke
down. It was agreed that for the night she should use a room
where she would not be greatly disturbed by the noise, for it
was now evening and this second search would have to include
testing walls for hollow places and turning the whole place
upside down. As soon as the magistrate and Eliot had been

seen returning, the priests had slipped back into their cramped quarters which opened into a workshop that gave access to the room Mrs Yate had chosen for her night's rest. She no doubt played her part with skill in her expostulations. The men went through the house sounding the walls and breaking into suspected concealed parts. When they had finished and had still not found the priests, it was decided to remain in the house for the remainder of the night. Eliot took the precaution of posting guards in the passage ways; he had also sent an appeal for help to another magistrate; evidently he had lost confidence in Fettiplace's determination. The new magistrate was Edmund Wiseman of Steventon, five miles away. He arrived with some of his own men servants. By this time the place must have been swarming with searchers and watchers. Eliot had also sent a message to the High Sheriff, Humphrey Forster, of Aldermaston Court but that was twenty-five miles away.

The next occurrence in the house strains credulity as it seems so foolishly imprudent. When the intruders had settled down for the night after enjoying the refreshments provided by Mrs Yate, the three priests left their hiding-place and joined Mrs Yate in her temporary bedroom. Two or three others seem to have been present. One account, of later date, says that Mrs Yate insisted on Campion preaching a sermon; perhaps by a sermon is meant a few words of encouragement and comfort; she would surely not have been so incautious as to beg for a full-scale discourse. Exactly what roused the suspicions of the guard outside the door is not certain; one account says that one of the priests stumbled noisily, but the explanation may be simply that the guard thought the sound of several voices called for investigation. By the time Mrs Yate had been persuaded to open the door the three priests were once again hidden. The room was thoroughly searched but nothing suspicious was revealed.

There are two versions of the discovery of the hiding-place next morning. According to Eliot, he realised that the place over the stairs and behind the gateway had not been tested.

He himself seized a sledge-hammer and broke through the wall and found the priests. The second story is that the pursuivant Jenkins noticed a strip of light coming through a gap at the head of the stairs and it was he who had the wall broken down. Eliot's version was no doubt framed to boost his own share in the capture and so was Jenkins'; we can take our choice.

The priests offered no resistance. The others who were placed under arrest were Mrs Yate, her brother-in-law Edward, who had been found hiding with one of the servants in an out-house, John Cotton, an Oxford student of the Catholic Cottons of Warblington, Hampshire, three described as 'gentlemen', William Hildersley, Humphrey and James Keynes, as well as two yeomen named William Webley and John Mansfield. In another account the last two are described as serving-men. With Mrs Yate were three gentlewomen, probably her guests, Gilliam Harman, Katherine Kingsmill and Mrs Keynes.

Eliot sent off another messenger to the High Sheriff who does not seem to have done anything about the first message. This time he set off for Lyford at once. He had known Campion at Oxford and may have had Catholic sympathies; did he also know that Campion had been Leicester's protégé? If so he would be cautious how he acted. He sent up to the Council for instructions as to the disposal of the prisoners. While waiting for these, he took charge and treated the prisoners like a house-party and showed more respect to Campion than Eliot would approve. Two days after the arrest an order came for the prisoners to be brought up to London under a strong guard. Mrs Yate, however, was to be sent to the common gaol and no bail was to be allowed; her eventual fate is not known. The three gentlewomen were released under heavy sureties.

The prisoners and their escort made a first halt at Abingdon for a meal; they were still under the command of the High Sheriff who treated them with consideration. At Abingdon a number of Oxford scholars came to see Campion and have speech with him, but they were not allowed to stay long. At dinner Eliot said to Campion, 'Mr Campion, you look cheerfully upon everybody but me; I know you are angry with me for this work', a remark that suggests that even Judas Eliot was submitting to Campion's charms, though it is strange that he should have been surprised that the priest did not smile at him! To this remark, Campion replied, 'God forgive thee, Eliot, for so judging me; I forgive thee, and, in token thereof, I drink to thee; yea, and if thou wilt repent and come to confession, I will absolve thee; but large penance thou must have.'

The next halting place was Henley. Here a young priest, William Filby, was too demonstrative in his attentions to Campion, so he was at once arrested. He was a former Oxford student and had only recently come on the mission. Another version of his capture is that he had called at Lyford in the hope of seeing Campion and was then arrested, but the records give only three priests as being taken at Lyford. The news of Campion's arrest had reached Parsons who was still at Stonor or in the neighbourhood; he wanted to show himself to Campion as a gesture of comradeship but his friends persuaded him not to do anything so rash; instead he sent his servant, Robert Alfield, to Henley. Campion saw him in the crowd and, unobtrusively signalled that he was recognised.

At some stage of the journey, possibly at Henley where they crossed the river for the main London Road, the party was taken charge of by Sir Thomas Heneage, one of the most trusted and favoured of the queen's servants; at that time he was her treasurer and later became vice-chamberlain of the household. He was granted the sum of £33 'for bringing up one Edmund Campion, a Jesuit, three other priests and eight other persons.'[4] The entry referring to Eliot reads, 'A warrant to the Treasurer of Her Majesty's chamber [i.e. Heneage] to cause to be paid unto George Eliot, one of the Yeomen of Her Majesty's Guard, towards his charges and pains employed in the apprehension of Edmund Campion, the late Jesuit, and other Jesuits and Seminary Priests by their [*sic*] endeavour discovered in the county of Berkshire and Oxfordshire, the sum of ten pounds.' His appointment as a Yeoman may have been an additional award.

On the Friday they reached Colnbrook, fifteen miles from London. Here they stayed the night so that their entry into the City would be on a market day. While they were at Colnbrook, many Catholic gentlemen waited on Campion. Everyone was struck by his equanimity, even cheerfulness, and it was obvious that his guards were on easy terms with him. All that was changed the next morning. The prisoners had their hands bound behind their backs and their legs fastened with cords under the horses' bellies. A paper was stuck in Campion's hat with the inscription CAMPION THE SEDITIOUS JESUIT. He was put at the head of the procession.

Here Parsons' first account written to the General in Rome must be given.[5]

By letters from the Council of State orders were given for him to be led through all the length of London, a matter of two to three miles, and to pass through the open squares, and finally to be put in the fortress which we here call The Tower. The order of the cavalcade was as follows: in front of everybody came the Under-sheriff of the county of Berkshire for the reason that they were captured in that county, holding in his fist the white staff of justice. Immediately behind him came Fr Campion, on a very tall horse, without cloak on his back, his arms tied behind his loins and his feet fastened with a rope beneath his horse's belly. On each side of him were two guards close by his side lest he should speak to anyone or anyone to him. Around his head they encircled an inscription, written in great big capital letters: EDMUND CAMPION THE SEDITIOUS JESUIT. The others followed after him, all likewise bound, but without the title; Fr Campion was the only one to be honoured in that way. Behind them, in addition to the guard of fifty men who had accompanied him on the whole journey came a large crowd of other people, some on horseback, some on foot, who had come out to witness the spectacle and did not desert the Father until his entrance into the fortress. A good many of these related to me with how fearless and glad a countenance Fr Edmund and the others endured that ignomy. They wore at all times a look full of peace, and smiled also at times. It happened that they passed by the cross of Cheapside, that is to say the market place in the middle of which it was situated. It was the only one[6] in the whole kingdom which, on account of its great beauty, they had not thrown down; and as soon as Campion caught sight of it he made much account of it, inclining his head to it in sign of reverence, and, as well as he could with his hands tied behind him, he made the sign of the cross. And in the same way as he did, so likewise did his companions who came after him. This, being noticed by the populace, occasioned much wonder; nor were they on that account mocked at, except only by a few. Close to the gate of the fortress, which is likewise a prison, Fr Edmund turned round, thanked and said a polite farewell to those who had accompanied him.

On the 4th August the Council instructed Sir Henry Neville 'to search Lady Stonor's house for copies of the Latin books, which Campion has confessed to have printed there in a wood, and for other books of Parsons, and the press thought also to be there remaining, and to examine such persons as they shall find in the house as to what Masses have been said there, what reconciliations used, and of their conformity in religion.' The tale is taken up by Parsons who wrote, 'The house at Stonor was surrounded by Neville and his agents, and all those who had worked at the press were arrested on the spot, indeed they were busy in printing another Catholic work. From this house at Stonor, Sir Henry Neville hastened to that where Lady Stonor dwelt, and there John Stonor, the son of the widow lady, was taken on the charge of having received a priest into his house and was put with the prisoners.'

Edward Rishton, a priest, who was imprisoned in the Tower at the same time as Campion, gave some further details in an account of his imprisonment published in 1585.

William Hartley, priest, and with him John Stonor and Stephen Brinkley lay gentleman, and four servants, printers, John Harris, John Harvey, John Tucker and John Compton, were taken with the printing press in the house of the illustrious Lady Stonor and brought to the Tower. The last of these, being of a timorous nature, when the gaoler with a drawn sword threatened him with death if he would not promise to go to the heretical church, gave way and on that ground regained his liberty.

Parsons happened, fortunately, to be at Windsor at the time
of this raid; as it was impossible for him to return to Stonor, he
found a refuge at Michelgrove[7] in West Sussex, the home of
William Shelley (nephew of Sir Richard Shelley) who was
then in the Fleet prison. At Michelgrove, Parsons met a party
of Catholics, including priests, who were planning to leave the
country. One of the laymen was William Tresham, brother of
Sir Thomas and an associate of Gilbert. They urged him to
join them; it was a difficult decision to make. If he stayed in
England, he would almost certainly be captured; on the other
hand there was useful work he could do out of the country
while the hue-and-cry died down. In a letter to the General of
the Jesuits written in October 1581,[8] he explained why he had
left England. He wanted to report on the state of the mission to
William Allen and to consult with him as to future policy, and
he wanted to set up a press in the Low Countries for the
printing of books for Catholics and others. Experience had
proved that it was impossible to maintain continuous produc-
tion in England where it was necessary to move the heavy
equipment about from secret place to secret place, nor could
they manage to produce full-scale books. A third purpose he
had in mind was to see Archbishop John Leslie of Ross in Paris
where he represented the Queen of Scots, to urge him to send
missioners to Scotland.

Parsons had left his servant Robert Alfield behind in England
to forward letters to him and to keep him up-to-date with what
was happening. He wrote,

> To-day I have received two large bundles of letters sent
> from England by my servant and from them I learn that I
> am in great demand there by the Catholics; and for that
> reason I am impelled to hasten my return, chiefly because
> Fr Jasper [Heywood] and Fr William [Holt] who were the
> last to enter the country, are a long distance from London
> and are attending to other parts of the country where they
> are said to be gaining a very large harvest of souls.

That hope of a return to England did not die out for some
years; the fact was that the services Parsons could render out

of England were regarded by his superiors as more valuable than anything he could achieve in England in a ministry that might be speedily cut short. Even the rumour in later years that the Jesuit Parsons was again in England was sufficient to put the authorities on the alert.

[1] No trace of the house remains. A barn on a farm on the site may have been a chapel. The Moore's conformed by the end of the century.

[2] See C.R.S. XXXIX, p. 73n(3).

[3] Every adult able-bodied male had to be ready to support a magistrate in quelling a riot or making an arrest.

[4] *Acts of the P.C.* (new series), xiii, 136.

[5] C.R.S. XXXIX, p. 92.

[6] Parsons was at fault here. The Cheapside Cross was one of the Eleanor Crosses erected by Edward I in memory of his queen; this Cross stood opposite Wood Street; there was another at Charing Cross. Both were pulled down in the 1640s.

[7] On the Downs above Patching; I have walked all over the site but not a vestige of building remains; it is now woodland.

[8] C.R.S. XXXIX, p. 107.

Chapter 14

Interrogations and Conferences

Edmund Campion was made a close prisoner; this meant solitary confinement in the strictest conditions with no visitors and only a meagre diet. He was put in the cell in the White Tower known as 'Little Ease' since it was impossible to stand upright or to lie at full stretch. A bizarre episode came after four days. He was taken up the river to Leicester House[1] where he was received by the Earl of Leicester, the Earl of Bedford and other councillors. It must have been a poignant moment when Leicester met his former protégé in such changed conditions. They asked him why he had returned to England; to which he replied that it was for the defence of the Catholic faith and for the salvation of souls. He was taken into another room where the queen herself awaited him. On her asking him if he accepted her as the lawful queen of England, 'I answered,' he said at his trial, 'that I did acknowledge her Highness not only as my queen, but also as my most lawful governess.' The queen offered him his liberty and preferment if he could conform in religion, but this he refused to do. One outcome of this royal interview was that Leicester, perhaps shocked at Campion's bedraggled appearance, sent orders to the Lieutenant of the Tower that his prisoner was to receive more humane treatment. The physical conditions improved but, as Campion was kept incommunicado, we have no assured knowledge of all that happened to him.

Did he again meet Leicester? There is a reference in one of Burghley's memoranda to Campion's 'having been convented before my lord Chancellor and my lord of Leicester.' This may refer to the meeting with the queen though Burghley did not note her presence.

Campion was racked for the first time a few days after his return to the Tower. An order from the Council dated the 30th July gave a list of points on which he was to be questioned and, if he proved unwilling to answer them, then they were 'to deal with him by the rack.' This was addressed to Sir Owen Hopton, the Lieutenant, Dr John Hammond, chancellor of the diocese of London and a member of the court of high commission, Robert Beale, clerk to the Council, and to Thomas Norton who earned the nickname of 'Rackmaster-General', much to his annoyance. Fathers Ford and Colleton were also to be examined on their allegiance, threatened with torture, and then to be remanded to the Marshalsea. Webley and Mansfield, two of the other Lyford prisoners, had said they were willing to conform; they were to receive instruction from a minister, and, if they truly recanted, were to be discharged on bond.[2]

Careful preparation had been made for questioning Campion. Dr Hammond had collected allegedly treasonous passages from the books of Nicholas Sander, William Allen and Richard Bristow. The selected extracts referred to the rising of 1569, the Bull of excommunication, and the deaths of John Felton (1570) and Dr John Storey (1571). When asked if he agreed that these opinions were 'wicked on the whole or any part', Campion replied that 'he meddleth neither to nor fro and will give no further answer', and that the authors, not he, were the ones to deal with such questions. On the Bull of excommunication he said, 'That this question dependeth on the fact [action] of Pius V, whereof he is not to judge, and therefore refuseth to answer.' It is clear from these and other answers that Campion was unable in his own mind to resolve the dilemma of divided obedience. It cannot be doubted that his repeated professions of loyalty to the queen were genuine; he would not get involved in the political issues, nor would he judge others. His attitude was one of detachment; almost of unconcern.

At a second interrogation and racking he was questioned about the Fitzgerald–Sander rising in Ireland and in particular about a sum of £30,000 which, it was alleged, had been sent to Ireland by an Irishman believed to be named Rochfort. The Council knew of Campion's earlier residence in Ireland, and they wanted to discover if he had later connections with that country; was he, in fact, the mysterious Rochfort? If this link could be established, then he could be charged with conspiracy. However, they were unable to get anything to the purpose from him, so that line had to be abandoned.

After these interrogations, rumours were spread about, no doubt inspired by the authorities, that Campion was weakening and might be expected to recant, and, further, that he had revealed the names of Catholics who had sheltered him. Of one thing we can be sure; Campion would never have considered renouncing his faith. That part of the rumours can be dismissed as a fabrication. The second part, that of revealing names, cannot be dismissed. There seems little doubt that he did give some names, but, as far as the indications go, only of those people who had given him lodging; he does not seem to have named houses where he had said Mass. Under the strain of torture, he sought some mitigation of his pain by giving the minimum of information. At Tyburn he solemnly declared 'upon his soul' that he had not revealed anything about 'the saying of Mass, hearing confessions, preaching, and such like duties and functions of priesthood.' He must have suffered acutely; his sensitive nature shrank from physical pain and he had to endure more than the rack. Two ambassadors gave details in their despatches, and they would have no good reason for inventing tortures. The Venetian ambassador wrote on the 5th of August, 'They have inflicted torture on Campion, and not the ordinary torture; thrusting irons between his flesh and his nails, and have torn the nails off.'[3] A week later the Spanish ambassador reported in greater detail.

The priests they succeed in capturing are treated with a variety of terrible tortures: among others is one torment that people in Spain imagine to be that which will be worked by Anti-Christ, as the most dreadfully cruel of them all. This is to drive iron spikes between the nails and the quick; and two

priests in the Tower have been tortured in this way, one of
them being Campion, of the Society of Jesus, who with the
other, was recently captured. I am assured that when they
would not confess under this torture, the nails of their fingers
were turned back, all of which they suffered with great
patience and humility.[4]

These statements were confirmed by witnesses at Campion's
trial and execution; they noticed that his finger nails had been
torn out. The other priest referred to was probably Alexander
Briant.

Perhaps one should not dwell too much on the physical
sufferings the priests had to undergo for we can no longer, as
was done in the last century, palliate them as the expression of
sixteenth century barbarism; four centuries later more exquisite
ways of breaking men's wills have been devised, and no doubt
further technological progress [*sic.*] may be expected. The
twentieth century cannot afford to cast stones at the sixteenth.
We have, however, learned to suspect all extorted confessions
as well as much public propaganda. There was probably no
confession signed by Campion; the recording clerk would note
down the names Campion gave; that was sufficient, for the
time being, for the Council. Probably not one of the names
given by Campion was unknown to the authorities, but
Campion's list now gave them grounds for arrests and interrogations. Those brought up to London in August included Lord
Vaux, Sir Thomas Tresham, Sir William Catesby, Walter
Powdrell, Jane and Ambrose Griffin; they were committed to
the Fleet prison. They were brought to trial in the Star
Chamber on the 15th November, the day after Campion and
his companions had been brought before the Grand Jury of
Middlesex. One passage from Sir Thomas Tresham's defence
has already been quoted, but a more extended account will
bring out some points of importance.[5]

The Lord Chancellor, Sir Thomas Bromly, presided; he had
been a student at Oxford in Campion's time. As a judge he
had a reputation for fair-mindedness. The prosecution was led
by John Popham, the Attorney-General who was also Speaker

of the House of Commons and later became a chief justice. The evidence he brought forward was a confession by Campion that he had been at the houses of the prisoners; Popham did not claim that Campion had said Mass at any of them. In support the Attorney produced a letter from Campion to Thomas Pound who was then a prisoner at Wisbech. This letter is not extant but, as far as we know, Campion did not deny that he wrote it. Pound had written in dismay at hearing that Campion had disclosed the names of his hosts. In his reply Campion 'had confessed of some houses where he had been, which now he repented him, and desired Pound to beg him pardon of the Catholics therein, saying that in this he rejoiced that he had discovered no things of secret.' We have only this third person version.

Lord Vaux was the first to be questioned. He declared, 'As to the receiving of Mr Campion (albeit I confess he was school-master to some of my boys) yet I deny that he was at my house. I say he was not there to my knowledge, whereof disprove me.' Part of Tresham's answer has been already given. Walter Powdrell of Hadham, Derby, said, 'That I have received Mr Campion, I have confessed it, and I hope I have not offended therein for bestowing a night's lodging on him who sometime did read with me in the university, and by whom I did never know evil.' Sir William Catesby denied that Campion had been at his house.

Sir Thomas Tresham drafted what may have been intended at his defence speech, but it goes further than his recorded words at the trial. Some passages are worth quoting.

That Campion is a traitor is more than I know, and in matters doubtful I am bounden to judge the best. But admit he be so, it followeth not that he that is a traitor now always hath been so; no more than he that seemeth to be most godless now, happly hath not always been so deemed. . . . But admit Campion hath always been a traitor, and withal unknown to me. I say I am not bounden to accuse him in matters of conscience. Yet I grant that he who will not accuse a traitor in matters of treason against his prince or country is a traitor. But he that will not accuse a traitor for that he fasted thrice a week with bread and water, or that hath been occupied whole nights in prayer, or hath done alms-deeds, or in execution of those mysteries of religion which in my soul I think absolutely good; he I say that will not accuse as a traitor for these causes only or suchlike, is neither an offender nor a traitor at all. And for my part I have been always examined of Mr Campion concerning suchlike matters of religion, and not of state.

Tresham here gives us a glimpse of Campion's own asceticism. A later passage reads:

Mr Campion might have been in my company, might have been in my house, and also might have had conference with me, and notwithstanding pass from me unknown, he being one that I never had acquaintance withal nor did ever speak to him above once, if I did that, in the university before his departure beyond the seas, which as I take it, is ten or twelve years since. And especially your Lordships say how that he came disguised from his vocation, and coming in a contrary name; which being inferred against me, a disgraced man, that he being a priest and I a Catholic, and that he coming so far and such men being rare in this kingdom and most welcome to Catholics; therefore most likely will the jury find me to be perjured, chiefly if the jury were of those disposed people that hold with us for enemies of Christ, and none of their family or society, and who accounteth it a sacrifice to annoy us what lieth in them. . . . Your Lordships say that Campion hath accused me before your honours, his accusation is under his hand, of record and extant, wherein he saith he was at my house, he lodged there showing in what chamber he had conference with me and others, he said service, etc.: he was carried thence by my wife to Mrs Griffin's with other the like. That accusation is direct, this in the affirmative, this is for the queen; if he hath said it, likely he will again affirm it: if he does not his accusation is of record, which is sufficient. Against this what am I to pretend but a negative, which is a faint evidence though never so true.

The meaning does not come out quite clearly in that passage, possibly because Tresham was writing notes rather than a carefully worked out statement. It would appear that a written confession by Campion was not produced in court: 'your

Lordships say' was all that Tresham had to go upon. It has already been pointed out that there may not have been a written confession. He was also charged with possessing some of Campion's books; the reference in the following passage is to his account of Ireland which had been included in Holinshed's Chronicles in 1577.

> Campion is a native Englishman, was of great expectation in the university, and for his exercises there, and namely before her Majesty, he deserved among them great commendation. I have heard with my own ears of the Lords of her Majesty's council, well esteem of him. He departed beyond seas for his further increasing of his knowledge and learning, which is usual. He demeaned himself so there that he procured great and general opinion for his singularity and ability. I never then heard any ill of him, nor till this day did, but I have heard him well reputed of, and that by protestants of good account that returned from the emperor's court. Yea, such public commendation he merited here in England, that the book wherein the same is published is vendible in Paul's Churchyard, and extant in every man's custody, which in Holinshed is so often avouched and so singularly commended that even to one of her Majesty's most honourable privy council, in the epistle dedicatory, among many other his commendation, hath these words, in comparing him with Homer: that the realm might thirst for so rare a clerk as is Mr Campion.

Had Sir Philip Sidney told Tresham of his meeting with Campion at Prague? Sidney had been at the emperor's court. Tresham's 'in the epistle dedicatory' was a slip; the words he had in mind came in Richard Stanyhurst's introductory note to Campion's account of Ireland. The exact words were, '. . . how much more ought Ireland for to long and thirst after so rare a clerk as M. Campion.'

What Tresham said, or meant to have said, was a skilful defence of Campion; he warned the court that they were dealing with a man who had won wide esteem from men of standing as well as scholars. In his final appeal, Tresham asked that his accusers might be brought into court so that he could face them.

I take exceptions to Mr Campion's dispositions, that they all only be sufficient to convict me, and because they seem to be such not likely to pass from one of his calling, being a priest. I would not believe them to be his, but that in this honourable court they be produced. Notwithstanding I willingly would demand, if without offence I might, whether this his examination was in the time of his tortures or before or after, for if he hath confessed them through tortures, then may I take exceptions.

All this is what Tresham would have liked to say, but the report does not go so fully into his testimony; perhaps he was not allowed to speak his mind.

The prisoners were all found guilty; they were committed to the Fleet prison and fined sums ranging from a thousand pounds to five hundred marks apiece. They were kept in prison for well over a year and then put under house arrest or in designated places. Even though they were supposedly in close confinement they were able to hear a Mass said by Fr Edward Osborn; each one then present was fined another hundred marks.

Burghley, who seems to have been the prime mover in the pursuit and denigration of Campion, made some notes on those with whom the Jesuit had stayed during the first six months of 1581. On the 10th August, he wrote to Walsingham, who was in Paris, 'We have gotten from Campion knowledge of all his peregrination in England. . . . We have sent for his hosts in all counties.'[6] It is not clear whether Burghley's list includes only those named by Campion; some of the information could have come from such secret agents as George Eliot and Charles Sledd; this list begins 'Campion confesseth his being in these houses.' It will be noted, however, that Burghley did not write 'where he confesseth to saying Mass.'

All this was taking place while Campion was on trial and in the months following his hanging. We must now return to what happened while he was in the Tower.

It is not known who proposed that Campion's 'Challenge' should now be taken up in public conferences. The Bishop of London, John Aylmer, was opposed to the idea, but he was overruled and instructed to select competent divines who could dispute with Campion. Those who urged such conferences may have been alarmed at the widespread effect, especially in the universities, of *Rationes Decem*, and they may have felt that a public refutation would be salutary.

Campion was not informed of this fresh ordeal until an hour or so beforehand nor was he told of the topics that would be chosen for discussion. He was not allowed to have any books to which he could refer to support his arguments while his opponents had a small library at their disposal. Some of the other Catholic prisoners were taken to the first conference; they included Ralph Sherwin, James Bosgrave, and Thomas Pound. The last had been brought from Wisbech and lodged in the Tower. The place was the chapel of St Peter ad Vincula within the Tower.[7] It had been set out to provide seats for members of the Council and other notables, with standing room for any of the public who wished to attend. Two or three Catholics managed to get in, among whom was a printer, Stephen Vallenger, who kept notes which have been preserved.[8]

The conductors of the conference were Alexander Nowell, Dean of St Paul's, and William Day, Dean of Windsor. Both had Calvinist leanings. Nowell, a septuagenarian, was a leading preacher and was the author of the Anglican catechism that was in use for more than a century. Day was a younger man who eventually became Bishop of Winchester. William Charke and William Whitaker were there as notaries or reporters; we have noted the first as one of the respondents to Campion's 'Challenge', and the second to his *Rationes Decem*.

Dean Nowell opened the first conference by referring to Campion's objection in the preface to his book to the 'severe cruelty' of the government in the treatment of Catholics and to the bishops who preferred 'tortures rather than debate.' In reply Campion said he was glad his request for a discussion was now being met, but they had deprived him of a scholar's weapons, his books; even his notes had been taken away. Was it just to rack him first, and dispute with him after when his mind was far from clear: the Elizabethan racks were just as bad as the Marian ones; he had twice been racked and after that experience he would prefer hanging to racking. Sir Owen Hopton, the Lieutenant of the Tower, intervened. He declared that Campion had no cause to complain. 'For although you were put on the rack, yet notwithstanding you were so favourably used therein, as being taken off, you could and did presently go thence to your lodging without help, and use your hands, and all other parts of your body, which you could not have done if you had been put to that punishment with any such extremity as you speak of.'

Robert Beale, clerk to the Council, then asked Campion if he had been examined on any point of religion. Campion replied 'that he was not indeed directly examined of religion, but moved to confess in what places he had been conversant since his repair into the realm.' Beale said 'that this was required of him because many of his fellows, and by likelihood himself also, had reconciled divers of her Highness's subjects to the Romish Church.' To which Campion answered 'that forasmuch as the Christians in old time being commanded to deliver up the books of their religion to such as persecuted them, refused to do so, and misliked with them that did so, calling them *traditores*, he might not betray his Catholic brethren, which were, the temples of the Holy Ghost.' Had there been a written confession, it would surely have been produced at this point.

At the end of this exchange, Campion cried out, 'If any of you can prove me guilty of any crime except my religion, I will willingly agree to suffer the extremist torments you can inflict.'

The subject was then dropped, and Nowell and Day turned to one of the distinctive tenets of Protestantism, justification by faith alone. Here they were able to score two points: the first was when Campion failed to find a quotation he had used, and the second was a difficulty he had in dealing with a reference to the Greek New Testament. Such details were irrelevant but victory of this kind is dear to the heart of the pedant.

The conference went on until dusk with a break for a meal;

it would be interesting to know what kind of refreshment was given to the prisoners. At the end of the day, both sides were content. Such was, and is, the usual result of such confrontations; as has already been said, controversy, written or spoken generally serves to confirm each disputant in his own cherished opinions.

The second conference was on the 18th September. The authorities may have felt that the first had not been as conclusive as they had hoped. Campion had not been decisively confuted; indeed Catholics were openly giving him the victory but that was a prejudiced judgment. It was decided to have the second conference in the hall of the Lieutenant's lodging where there would be less room for the public. The Protestant conductors were also changed. Dr Goode, Provost of King's College, Cambridge, was assisted by William Fulke, Master of Pembroke College, Cambridge; he had been at Christ's Hospital with Campion and had failed to win the silver pen in the schools' contest. Fulke was a Radical Protestant and noted for his controversial powers; he had been, for instance, sent to Wisbech to dispute with the Catholic prisoners there, notably with Bishop Thomas Watson and Abbot John Feckenham, O.S.B. Now he was to cross swords with his old school-fellow. It must have been a strange meeting for both of them after a lapse of some thirty years. William Charke was again there as reporter but his colleague this time was John Field (or Feilde)[9] who had been imprisoned for his share in writing *An Admonition to Parliament* (1572) which advocated a Presbyterian form of church organisation. It may be noted that those chosen to dispute with Campion were what we should call left-wing Protestants.

The opening topic this time was the nature of the Church, whether it was visible or invisible. Campion maintained that he could speak only for the Church militant, that is the Church on earth warring against the powers of evil. The period of rest he had had since the first conference seems to have restored some of his mental resilience. Thus when Goode quoted St Jerome in support of his argument, Campion remarked, 'I would that you and I might shake hands with St Jerome's religion, that we might meet together with him in heaven.' 'No,' replied Goode, 'I will not be of man's religion further than he is of Christ's.'

Here is a specimen of their exchanges.

GOODE. Can you love God above all things and your neighbour as yourself? Can you love him with all your heart, with all your soul and with all your strength?

CAMPION. I can, for when I prefer God before all things and love him chiefly, I love him above all.

FULKE. Note that blasphemous absurdity.

GOODE. If a man may fulfil the law to justification, then Christ died in vain.

CAMPION. Why think you the law was given to no purpose? I am sure it was given to be fulfilled, and we are not bidden to keep it, if it were impossible.

FULKE. The law was given for another case, namely to show us our infirmity that we may be convicted of sin.

CAMPION. You will give me leave to declare my meaning.

FULKE. Belike you have an ill opionion of the audience that they can understand nothing except you tell them twenty times over. If you will not suffer me to proceed, I must desire Master Lieutenant to command you.

The subject of persecution kept slipping in; the point was that Catholics could hardly object to being persecuted themselves seeing they had persecuted Protestants when they had the power as under Queen Mary. Campion replied that, in the time of Queen Mary, Protestants could go to Germany to exercise their religion. It was an embarrassing topic as the Protestant answer was that Catholics could equally well go to Catholic countries. We must remind ourselves that we are talking of a period when the idea of toleration was remote from men's minds. In the afternoon the main topic was the administration of communion whether it should be in both kinds as with the Protestants, or in one kind (the bread) as with Catholics. Campion answered, 'I allow it may be so received [i.e. in both kinds] so that a man do it in humility and by license, for so I have seen myself [the Utraquists in Bohemia] and I confess that in the primitive Church it hath been used to be received sometimes under one kind and sometimes under both, and so may be received again, at the appointment and discretion of the Church.' That still holds good, as the manner of receiving the sacrament is not one of doctrine but of Church order. When Goode asserted that a general council had decreed that angels have bodies, Campion again drew the distinction between matters of faith and matters of allowable difference of opinion. He went on to object to some of the strange doctrines put forward by Protestants, such as that baptism does not take away original sin and that every temptation is itself a sin. It was Field's business to write the report of the conference; he did so with the comment, 'If Campion's answers be thought shorter than they were, thou must know that he had much waste of speech which, being impertinent, is now omitted.'

The third conference was staged on the 23rd September; like the previous one it was directed by Goode and Fulke. This time the discussion was on the Eucharist – the real presence and transubstantiation. The arguments followed established lines and need not be detailed here. Campion more than once pleaded to be allowed access to books to substantiate his arguments by quotations from the Fathers.

CAMPION. If you dare, let me show you Augustine and Chrysostom, if you dare.

FULKE. Whatever you can bring, I have answered already in writing against others of your side. And yet if you think you can add anything, put it in writing and I will answer it.

CAMPION. Provide me with ink and paper and I will write.

FULKE. I am not to provide you ink and paper.

CAMPION. I mean, procure me that I may have liberty to write.

FULKE. I know not for what cause you are restrained of that liberty, and therefore I will not take upon me to procure it.

CAMPION. Sue to the Queen that I may have liberty to oppose. I have now been thrice opposed. It is reason that I should oppose once.

FULKE. I will not become a suitor for you.

Four days later came the fourth and final conference. This time the direction was in the hands of Dr John Walker, a noted preacher of Radical Protestant opinions; with him was William Charke who had been reporter at the first two conferences. This time Thomas Norton[10] was the reporter. John Walker was in an aggressive mood.

> 'This man,' he declared, as if this were a trial and not a disputation, 'this man having departed the realm hath joined himself to the man of Rome, our common enemy, Antichrist, and now hath returned again into the realm, where he hath wandered from place to place through the greatest part thereof, and in the north country and Yorkshire he hath sown sedition that they now cry out at him and curse him; and now he hath proceeded further and hath charged us most impudently and falsely with mangling and cutting of the Scriptures.'

He further denounced Campion as 'an unnatural man to his country, degenerate from an Englishman, an apostate in religion, a fugitive from this realm, unloyal to his Prince', a man who had come 'to plant secretly the blasphemous Mass.'

The first subject was the canon and authority of the Scriptures. Campion argued that the Scriptures were 'subject to the interpretation of the Church.' To this Walker replied, 'I have been these two or three days turning and seeking books to prove that all things necessary to salvation are contained in the Scriptures, and now, by this subtle shift and distinction, he hath avoided all, for it is the practice of them to preach one thing, and when they come to defend it, to deny it, and maintain another thing.' Charke, for his part, took up a blustering attitude and declared that Campion had been routed by the arguments used against him. He grew tedious and some of the public attenders began to slip away, whereupon Charke had the doors locked so that they perforce had to listen to his diatribe. One report says that some ventured to hiss. Norton, who had warmly supported Charke, afterwards wrote to the Council that in his opinion the conference 'hath been both

fruitless and hurtful and subject to great harm by reports.'
The Bishop of London, who, it will be recalled, had been
against the conferences from the beginning, wrote to Burghley
after the fourth one, 'I wrote unto Master Lieutenant of my
misliking so many were admitted to it, whose authority is not
to be directed by me, but by her Majesty and your lordships.
And for that ill opinion that I had of it, I sent to stay it.' The
Council agreed, and a fifth conference that had been planned
for October was cancelled.

Norton was quite right about popular reports. Stephen
Vallenger and other Catholics who had managed to be present,
as well, perhaps some disillusioned Protestants, spread the
report that Campion, far from being discredited, had proved
the abler disputant. The Elizabethans were connoisseurs of
this kind of public debate which was almost a popular pastime.
Not much time passed before ballads were being sold on the
streets. Here are three specimens.

I

Campion is a champion,
Him once to overcome,
The rest be well drest
The sooner to mumm.

He looks for his life,
They say, to dispute,
And doubts not our doctrine
He brags to confute.

If instead of good argument,
We deal by the rack,
The Papists may think
That learning we lack.

Come forth, my fine darling,
And make him a dolt;
You have him full fast,
And that in strong holt.

That seems to be the composition of a disappointed Protestant
who thought that racking was not sound argument. Who 'my
fine darling' was among the Protestant divines is not known.

II

A Jesuit, a Jebusite? wherefore, I pray?
Because he doth teach you the only right way?
He professeth the same by learning to prove.
And shall we from learning to rack him remove?

His reasons were ready, his grounds were most sure,
The enemy cannot his force long endure;
Campion, in camping on spiritual field,
In God's cause his life is ready to yield.

Our preachers have preached in pastime and pleasure,
And now they be hated far passing all measure;
Their wives and their wealth have made them so mute,
They cannot nor dare not with Campion dispute.

This was clearly a Catholic effort. The reference to the Jebusites is not quite clear; they were a small Canaanite tribe allowed to remain in Jerusalem when it was captured by David.

III

Let reason rule, and racking cease,
Or else for ever hold your peace;
You cannot withstand God's power and His grace,
No, not with the Tower and the racking-place.

Several of those who dared to say in public that Campion had shown his learning to the disadvantage of his opponents, were imprisoned. Catholics also circulated accounts of the conferences. These were in manuscript; certainly no printed copies have survived. This method of passing on information was widely used; it was the method, for instance, by which Campion's 'Challenge' became so well known. In the nature of things, the extent of this written propaganda cannot be assessed; there must have been an army of Catholics willing to make copies of any record that would promote their cause or encourage their fellows.

On the 31st of October, Campion was once more put to the rack. What did they still hope to drag out of him? The Lieutenant had claimed that the previous rackings had been mild; he avoided mentioning the finger-nail torture; this time no mercy was shown. Afterwards Campion said that he thought they meant to kill him, and when he was asked how he felt he replied, 'Not ill, because not at all.' At his trial he was unable to raise his hand to take the oath. Dr Lawrence Humphrey wrote, 'It was his own fault because he would not use the ointment which the Lieutenant of the Tower, more charitable than others [sic], is wont to supply. These Papist prisoners in the Tower and elsewhere have all that is necessary, more than the Pope's prisoners at Rome would ever get.'

There is significance in the fact that in 1583, Robert Beale, who had witnessed at least the first racking, published a book entitled *A Book against Oaths ministered in the Courts of Ecclesiastical Commission from her Majesty, and in Courts Ecclesiastical* in which he condemned all racking as cruel, barbarous and contrary to the law and to English liberties, an opinion which the newly appointed Archbishop of Canterbury, John Whitgift, thought was atrocious.

It was also significant that it was not until 1584 that the official report of the conference was published under the editorship of John Field. Even three years after Campion's hanging it was thought necessary to combat the popular view, still current, that the conferences had failed in their purpose.

Parsons' report on the conferences reads:

The three [sic] disputations held with the heretics greatly stirred the souls of all here, such was the bearing of Fr Campion, accompanied by Sherwin. After the first disputations, however, the heretics would not tolerate the presence of Sherwin, because they said he was too choleric, and so Fr Campion had to conduct the disputation alone. And truly it can scarcely be told how much good these disputations have done, and are doing every day. And if he dies for that cause they will certainly do still more good. For they are the common talk and subject of conversation of everybody, not only of Catholics, but of our enemies also, and always to the great honour of Fr Campion.[11]

[1] Essex Street and Devereux Court mark the site west of the Middle Temple. At that time there was direct access from the river.

[2] The official report was not published until 1582 when it was still felt necessary to justify the treatment of Campion. The title was, *A particular Declaration or Testimony of the undutiful and traitorous affection borne against her Majesty by Edmund Campion, Jesuit, and other condemned priests witnessed by their own confessions.*

[3] P.R.O., Rome transcripts, 31st September 1978.

[4] Spanish Calendar, III, 153.

[5] See above p. 75, also Godfrey Anstruther, O.P., *Vaux of Harrowden* (1953), pp. 120–132.

[6] B. M. Lansdowne MSS., 30, No. 75.

[7] Was Campion aware at St Peter's, that beneath the floor, were the bones of John Fisher and Thomas More?

[8] They were seized by Richard Topcliffe, who was just beginning his career as a priest-torturer, and given to his friend John Foxe, the Martyrologist. Reports of the conferences by Catholics are as follows: First: H.M.C., iii; second, third and fourth: Harleian MSS., 422; second and fourth: Rawlinson, Miscellaneous, D., 353.

[9] For Field, see Neale, op. cit. I, pp. 295–7; also *D.N.B.* Supplement under 'Feilde'.

[10] For Norton see above p. 132, also Neale op. cit. Vol. I, *passim*. He was known as 'Master Norton the Parliament Man', a more creditable designation than 'Norton the scold' or 'Rackmaster General.' A man of varied abilities and complex character.

[11] C.R.S. XXXIX, p. 119.

Chapter 15

Priests and Informers

We must now say something of the other priests who were arraigned with Edmund Campion. It will be convenient to take them in alphabetical order and to record their fates though a few will again be mentioned in the account of the trial of Campion. Of some of them we know little; careful accounts, many by eye-witnesses of the deaths of those who were martyred, were written and published at the time, but these rarely give details of early years.

JAMES BOSGRAVE. In some way his story is the strangest. He was about the same age as Campion, that is forty or just over. Nothing is known of his origins save that he came of a gentle family of Dorsetshire and left England when very young. He entered the novitiate of the Society of Jesus in Rome in November 1564 and was ordained priest in 1572. His work lay in Moravia, Poland and Lithuania. As his health was poor, he was sent back to England in 1580 in the hope that his 'native air' would strengthen him. This belief in the recuperative effect of 'native air' was widely held and a number of seminarians were sent home for this purpose and some were arrested. Bosgrave landed on the Suffolk coast in the autumn of 1580 and was immediately arrested at Orford. It may be that after an interval of thirty years or so his English was rusty, and this would bring suspicion on him. He was first sent to the Marshalsea where he agreed to attend the Anglican services and was then released. This shocked the Catholics he met, but the fact was that he was unaware of the religious changes that

had taken place in England. When these were explained to
him, he at once wrote to the Council to declare his Catholicism.
So it was he found himself in the Tower with Campion and the
other priests. He was condemned with them but was reprieved
at the request of the king of Poland. He was banished with
other priests in January 1585. As some of the priests we are
considering were banished at the same time, the matter
deserves a note. During that year some seventy priests were
banished by batches. In the first group was Jasper Heywood
who had taken Parsons' place in England. When the priests
were assembled on the Tower Wharf in readiness to embark,
Heywood organised a kind of sit-down strike in protest at
being banished from their native land without proper trial.
However the priests were bundled on board and were later,
still protesting, put ashore in France. Bosgrave made his way
to Poland to resume his ministry there; he died in 1621. He
wrote an apology in 1583 for his initial error; this was published
with the title *The Satisfaction of M. James Bosgrave, the godly
confessor of Christ, concerning his going to the Church of the Protestants
at his first comming into England*; the title may not have been his.

ALEXANDER BRIANT. It has already been mentioned that Briant
had been a pupil of Robert Parsons at Oxford. At the university
he was known as 'the handsome boy of Oxford.' After conversion
he was trained at Douay and was ordained in 1578 and came
on the mission in the following year, going to his native county
of Somerset. There he reconciled Parsons' father. When
Parsons himself came to England, Briant was often with him
and, as we have seen, he was arrested at Parsons' house in
Bridewell. He was savagely tortured as it was hoped to wring
out of him the whereabouts of Parsons and Campion. He had
not only to endure racking but also the finger-nail torture and
what was known as the 'Scavenger's Daughter', a spiked iron
frame which clasped its victim. Briant revealed nothing. In a
letter to the rector of the English College in Rome, Parsons
wrote,

Fr Briant was quite a young man, and he excelled in patience above the ordinary, combined with an exceeding meekness; and so in the course of his tortures, which were extreme, he never uttered so much as a groan or cry. This the enemy admits and wonders at extremely, since he seemed to be very slender in build and of a very delicate constitution. They kept pressing him, when under torture, just to state where he had seen Fr Robert. He replied, 'You will never learn that from me, do whatever you can. I have seen him and lived with him, and yet I will never tell you where.' And although, as the torturers themselves declare,[1] they had stretched his body by force of the rack more than half a foot beyond its natural measure, he remained silent without a groan, as though he felt nothing, absorbed in prayer and meditation.[2]

While he was a prisoner he asked to be received into the Society of Jesus and this was granted. He was hanged on the 1st December 1581.

THOMAS COTTAM was born in 1549; he went to Brasenose College, Oxford during Campion's later years there. He was converted by Thomas Pound and went to Rome to enter the Society of Jesus; he was however unable to complete the training owing to ill-health. He then went to Douay-Reims where he was ordained. He came on the mission in June 1580 and landed at Dover where he was at once arrested at the instigation of Charles Sledd. He was sent up to London in the charge of Dr Humphrey Ely[3] (alias Havard) a Catholic professor of law who had been passed by the searchers. Ely allowed Cottam to slip away. Later Cottam had scruples lest Ely would get into trouble, so he gave himself up. Ely was imprisoned for a time but released when it was ascertained that he was not a priest. Cottam was sent to the Marshalsea on the 27th June and in December transferred to the Tower. He was hanged on the 30th May 1582.

JOHN COLLETON was one of the two Lyford priests. Born in 1548, he was at Oxford about 1565 but his college is not known. After conversion he went to Douay and was ordained in 1576. After his trial he was kept in the Tower until 1585 when he was banished with other priests. He returned to

England in 1587 and, for the rest of his life, ministered in London and Kent with one term of imprisonment in the Clink. He was a leader among the secular clergy and was vicar-general to Bishop William Bishop. Colleton died at the Ropers' house at Eltham in 1635 at the age of eighty-seven.

WILLIAM FILBY was born at Oxford and educated at Lincoln College. No dates are known, but, after conversion, he went to Douay-Reims and was ordained in 1581. The circumstances of his arrest at Henley while incautiously greeting Campion have been noted. He was hanged on the 30th May 1582.

THOMAS FORD, the other Lyford priest, was at Trinity College, Oxford where he took his degree in 1563. He was converted and went to Douay and was ordained in 1573. He was sent on the mission three years later. He was hanged on the 28th May 1582.

JOHN HART, a native of Oxford was at the university but his college is not recorded. He was no doubt a convert. He went to Douay and was ordained in 1578. He came on the mission in June 1580 and was at once arrested with Thomas Cottam. From the Marshalsea he was transferred to the Tower where he was tortured. He was tried and condemned but he recanted as he was being fastened to the hurdle to take him to Tyburn. He was allowed to go to Oxford to confer with John Rainolds (Reynolds) of Corpus Christi. Rainolds published an account of their conference in 1584 under the title, *The Summe of the Conference betweene John Rainolde and John Hart touching the Head and Faith of the Church. Penned by John Rainolde and allowed by John Hart for a faithful report*. It was several times reprinted. The upshot was far from what was expected for John Hart returned to the faith and was sent back to the Tower. Edward Rishton recorded that 'John Hart, priest under sentence of death, was punished for twenty days in irons for not yielding to one Reynolds, a minister.' Hart was received into the Society of Jesus while a prisoner. He was banished in 1585 with other priests and went to Rome. He died in Poland in 1594.

ROBERT JOHNSON, said to have been a servant in a gentleman's family in Shropshire, went to Rome where he was educated at the German College; from there he went to Douay and was ordained in 1576. He came to England in 1580. Two months later he and Henry Orton were arrested in the London streets at the instigation of Charles Sledd; they were first imprisoned in the Poultry Compter and transferred to the Tower in December 1580. He was hanged on the 28th May 1582.

LUKE KIRBY was a northerner and was at one of the universities but which is not known. After conversion he entered Douay in 1576 and was ordained a year later. After a brief ministry in England he went to the English College in Rome and returned as one of the 1580 party. He was arrested soon after his arrival in England; he was transferred from prison to the Tower in December 1580 and was tortured, being one of those who suffered the Scavenger's Daughter. Parsons recorded the following incident.[4]

> John Nichols, that minister who had apostatized, was led by repentance of his crimes to go to the prison to see Fr Kirby after the deaths of the other men. He confessed that he had acted most evilly and ungratefully and had told many lies; he begged forgiveness of his fault and offered to make satisfaction by going to the Secretary Walsingham and clearing them as far as was in his power of all suspicion of being traitors. When Kirby declined this offer, declaring that it would do no good now that they had been publicly condemned and sentenced. Nichols was evidently very much grieved, and he promised that he would publish a book in which he would expose the lives, morals, and crimes of Sledd and the other false witnesses. And on the following day he went off to Walsingham as he had promised, and began to rage and swear. Finally they sent the man away out of London.

Kirby was hanged on the 30th May 1582.

HENRY ORTON. Little is known of this young layman. He was at Rome though not, presumably, to be trained as a priest as Parsons referred to him as 'a student of jurisprudence.' He was arrested with Robert Johnson (see above), tried and condemned but kept in the Tower until his banishment with the 1585 party of priests.

LAURENCE RICHARDSON (*vere* Johnson), was a native of Lancashire and was at Brasenose College, Oxford of which he was a fellow. After conversion he entered Douay in 1573 and was ordained in 1577. His ministry in England was mostly in Lancashire. The circumstances of his arrest are not known; he was brought up to London and lodged in the Tower. He was hanged on the 30th May 1582.

EDWARD RISHTON (Rushton), a member of one of the old Lancashire families, was born in 1550. He went to Brasenose College, Oxford, where he took his degree in 1572. He went to Douay the following year. He was ordained in April 1577 and for the next three years was at the English College, Rome. He was one of the 1580 party of missioners. He was tried and condemned but kept in the Tower until he was banished in 1585 with others. His account of his imprisonment in the Tower has been quoted. Another work was his completion of Sander's *De Origine ac Progressu Schismatis Anglicani* (1588).

JOHN SHERT (Short), was born in Cheshire of a gentle family and went to Brasenose College, Oxford, taking his degree in 1566. For a time he was a schoolmaster in London, but, on conversion, he went to Douay in 1578 and on to the English College, Rome where he was ordained. He came on the mission in 1580 and was arrested in July 1581. He was hanged on the 28th May 1582.

RALPH SHERWIN was a native of Derbyshire and was at Exeter College, Oxford; he became a fellow of his college in 1568 and took his degree in 1571. After his conversion, he went to Douay and on to the English College, Rome, of which he was the first student and proto-martyr. He was ordained in March 1577. He was one of the 1580 mission. He worked in London until his arrest before November 1580 together with his host, a former fellow student at Oxford, Nicholas Roscarrock,[5] who was one of Gilbert's associates. Parsons' report is worth quoting.

> Sherwin, one of your men [i.e. of the English College], who in Rome used to burn with such zeal, has spent, with no less ardour of spirit, almost six whole months in preaching throughout various counties of the kingdom; and in this undertaking he has given graces and influence which were truly outstanding. And God in his Providence willed that in reward of such great labours he should be taken eventually in the act of preaching at the house of a certain noble youth named Roscarrock, who was committed to prison along with Sherwin, and it is said that he was afterwards tortured on the rack. When Sherwin had been brought to the inner court of the prison, they fastened very heavy fetters on him which he could hardly move; this done, the warders went away for the time being to see into what cell he was next to be thrust. He, however, when he had looked around everywhere and saw that he was alone, looked up to heaven with a countenance full of joy and gave thanks to God; again, however, he looked at his feet loaded with fetters and tried whether he could move them, and when, on moving them, he heard the sound of the chain, he could not contain himself, but with a loud laugh and shedding tears of joy as well, and raising his hands and eyes to heaven, he gave vent to his feeling of intense joy. The whole of this was witnessed by two heretics, members of the family of Love,[6] who were being held prisoners in a place hard by, and they were never able to cease from astonishment, and afterwards were in the habit of relating very often the whole sequence of what he had done. This same Sherwin had spent the night with me two days before he was taken, and on account of the extreme cold (for it was winter) had pushed himself in with difficulty between two or three others at the little fire which we had. In reference to this, when he had been six days, I think, in prison, he wrote to me thus: 'I have received the alms you sent me yesterday; may God repay you. I had had a small sum, too, before, that; when it is finished, I shall go down to my brother robbers in the pit so as to live from the common basket of alms, and I shall go down assuredly much more willingly than I have ever gone to any feast before. For the bread out of that basket will represent the cause of my God, sweeter than all honey, and than banquets of every kind. I have now some little bells on my feet and legs to remind me

who I am and whose I am; I have never experienced such sweet harmony elsewhere. If I were with you now, they would win me a place when I approached to the fire, and you would not press me out. Pray for me that I may complete my course bravely and faithfully.'[7]

Sherwin was hanged on the 1st December 1581.

To the above may be added a note on 'the little man', RALPH EMERSON who was Campion's companion until they parted at the inn outside Oxford, Campion returning to Lyford, and Emerson going north. After Campion's capture, Emerson made his way to the Low Countries and rejoined Parsons. In February 1582 he accompanied William Crichton, S.J., to Scotland, and made several later journeys to and fro the Low Countries, escorting priests on the mission and illegally importing some eight hundred books. He was with William Weston, S.J., in September 1584 when they landed on the coast between Yarmouth and Lowestoft and after arranging for their stock of books to be taken by carrier to London, they set off on horseback. When Ralph went to collect the books he was arrested and committed to the Poultry Compter for bringing in Catholic books. He was moved to the Counter as Parsons reported in December.

Ralph keeps well and has a more commodious prison called the Counter in which respectable persons are confined for debt, and his patience, serenity and zeal afford the highest edification to all. A fellow prisoner was here with us lately who makes no end of praising him.[8]

Ralph was moved from prison to prison, a proceeding used with long-term prisoners to foil escape plots. By the summer of 1594 he was in the Clink and in the next cell to John Gerard who in his *Autobiography* wrote,[9]

Had I been given a choice I would have chosen just the neighbour I had. Next door to me was Ralph Emerson, the Brother, who was referred to by Father Campion in a letter to Father General as 'My little man and I'. He was a very little man in build, but in endurance and sturdiness of spirit he was as great as you could wish anyone to be. Through many long years of imprisonment, he was always the same devout and good man, a true son of the Society. He stayed on in the Clink six or seven years after my arrival there, and was finally taken off to Wisbech Castle with the other confessors. There he was attacked by paralysis, losing control of half of his body, and he could not move about or do the smallest thing to help himself. But he lived on and heaped up great merit by his patience. Eventually, with the same priest companions, he was sent into exile and came to St Omers where he died [in March 1604].

Of the fourteen priests here noted, at least ten were converts. They were also at Oxford during the years Campion was in residence; indeed the reader must have noticed the number of priests and laymen mentioned in these pages who were contemporaries of Campion at the university. It is not possible to say how far their turning to the Church was due to his influence even though he himself at that period was still feeling his way, but the number is impressive.

Something should also be said, by way of contrast, of the informers who were to give evidence, true and false, at the trials. To what has been said of GEORGE ELIOT can be added a record of a conversation he had in the Tower with Campion after his condemnation.

ELIOT. If I had thought that you would have had to suffer aught but imprisonment through my accusing of you, I would never have done it, however I might have lost by it.

CAMPION. If that is the case, I beseech you in God's name, to do penance, and confess your crime, to God's glory and your own salvation.

Eliot expressed his fears that, in revenge, he might be murdered by Catholics.

CAMPION. You are much deceived if you think the Catholics push their detestation and wraths so far as revenge; yet to make you quite safe, I will, if you please, recommend you to a Catholic duke in Germany where you may live in perfect security.

It is a curious incident; it supports the impression made by the dinner at Henley that Eliot had become spellbound by the very man he had betrayed. So 'Judas Eliot' passes off the scene.

CHARLES SLEDD made full use of his service at the English College, Rome, and became one of the most active and successful of betrayers of priests. What is believed to be one of his reports, or partly his, is among the Yelverton Papers in the British Museum;[10] these were the papers of Robert Beale, the clerk to the Council. It is very detailed and must have been of considerable use to the Council.

Little is known of CADDY beyond the fact that, like Sledd, he had gathered his information in Rome. He may have been the Laurence Caddy who was dismissed from the English College.[11] We know a great deal, however of ANTHONY MUNDAY[12] since he made a reputation in another walk of life – as poet and dramatist. He was born in 1553, the son of a London draper. After a brief spell as apprentice to a stationer and as an actor, he set out 'to see the world' and early in 1579 he reached Rome. He entered the English College, under the name of Antonius Auleus; this was probably simply a way of getting more inside information. Munday left a few months later and no doubt at once passed on his information to the Council. He published an account of Campion's arrest to which Eliot's narrative was a corrective and is more reliable. Munday later wrote what was in effect the official justification for the executions of 1581, and part of this was read aloud when Campion was on the scaffold. Munday also wrote *The English Romayne Lyfe* (1582), a mixture of fact and fiction. In 1582 he became an assistant to Richard Topcliffe and two years later was appointed 'one of the messengers of Her Majesty's chamber.' It is not known how long he kept up his trade as informer and professional witness but it was probably not for long as he soon became a prolific writer as well as dramatist, work with which we are not here concerned. He died in 1633 at the age of eighty.

[1] Thomas Norton, Rackmaster General, made this boast.

[2] C.R.S. XXXIX, p. 134.

[3] See above, p. 66.

[4] C.R.S. XXXIX, p. 132.

[5] For Roscarrock, see A. L. Rowse, *Tudor Cornwall* (1941), pp. 368–9.

[6] The Familists originated in the Netherlands; religion, they held, consisted in love, and that obedience was to be given to all established governments.

[7] C.R.S. XXXIX, p. 90.

[8] Op. cit., p. 267.

[9] See *John Gerard: the Autobiography of an Elizabethan*, trans. Philip Caraman, S.J. (1951), pp. 78–9.

[10] It is printed in C.R.S. Vol. LIII, pp. 186–245.

[11] See, C.R.S. XXXIX, p. 116n.

[12] See, C. Turner, *Anthony Munday* (1928). Anthony Kenny, *Antony Munday in Rome*, Recusant History, Vol. 6, No. 4.

Chapter 16

The Indictments[1]

At first it was proposed to bring Edmund Campion to trial by himself before dealing with the other imprisoned priests in the Tower. The preliminary draft of an indictment read as follows:

PRELIMINARY INDICTMENT.

On the — day of June in the 23rd year of the Queen, at — in Oxfordshire.

He [Edmund Campion] *did traitorously pretend to have power to absolve the subjects of the said Queen from their natural obedience to her majesty, and with the intention to withdraw the said subjects of the said Queen from the religion now by her supreme authority established within this realm of England to the Roman religion, and to move the same subjects of the said Queen to promise obedience to the pretensed authority of the Roman See to be used within the dominions of the said Queen. Also, that the same Edmund Campion did, with the intention of withdrawing a certain —, being a subject of the said Queen, and born within this realm of England, from his natural obedience, then and there wickedly, falsely, and traitorously persuade the same — from the religion now established; and did then and there wickedly, falsely, and traitorously move the same — to promise obedience to the pretensed authority, etc., against the form of a statute in this case made and provided, and to the evil example of all other subjects in such wise offending.*

The gaps were to be filled in later; unless 'Oxfordshire' was a slip, Campion's ministry at Lyford (Berkshire) was not the basis of the charge against him, but some occurrence elsewhere; nor can we fill in the name of the 'subject.'

This indictment, based on the 1581 Act of Persuasions, was put aside and a new one drawn up. It calls for careful study, though its legal phraseology makes hard reading. It is here given in full.

THE INDICTMENT AS PRESENTED TO THE GRAND JURY.

The Jury present in behalf of the Queen, that William Allen, D.D., Nicholas Morton, D.D., Robert Parsons, clerk, and Edmund Campion, clerk. . . .

[Originally it was decided to proceed against these four alone though two of them were out of the country and the third was believed to be at large in England; then it was decided to inlude the other imprisoned priests, so the following names were added in the margin to be included in the fair copy – James Bosgrave, William Filby, Thomas Ford, Thomas Cottam, Lawrence Richardson, John Collyton, Ralf Sherwin, Luke Kirby, Robert Johnson, Edward Rishton, Alexander Briant, Henry Orton, a civilian, and — Short.].

The indictment continues:

. . . that being traitors against the Queen, not having the fear of God in their hearts, nor weighing their due allegiance, but led astray by the devil, intending altogether to withdraw, blot out, and extinguish the hearty love and true and due obedience which true and faithful subjects should bear and are bound to bear towards the Queen, did, on the last day of March, Anno 22nd, at Rome in Italy, in parts beyond the sea, and on the last day of April in the same year at Rheims in Champagne, and on divers other days and occasions before and after, both at Rome and at Rheims, and in divers other places in parts beyond the seas, falsely, maliciously, and traitorously conspire, imagine, contrive and compass, not only to deprive, cast down, and disinherit the said Queen from her royal state, title, power, and rule of her realm of England, but also to bring and put the same Queen to death and final destruction, and to excite, raise and make sedition in the said realm, and also to beget and cause miserable slaughter among the subjects of the said Queen throughout the realm, and to procure and set up insurrection and rebellion against the said Queen, their supreme and natural lady, and to change and alter according to their will and pleasure the government of the said realm, and the pure religion there rightly and religiously established, and totally to subvert and destroy the state of the whole commonwealth of the realm, and to invite, procure, and induce divers strangers and aliens, not being subjects of the said Queen, to invade the realm, and to raise, carry on, and make

war against the said Queen; and in order to bring to pass the said wicked and traitorous designs, the said Allen, Morton, Parsons and Campion did, on the last day of March at Rome, and on the last day of April at Rheims, and on other days, falsely and traitorously conspire, treat, and debate by what ways and means they could compass the death of the said Queen and raise a sedition in the realm; and with the said intent and purpose the said Allen, Morton, Parsons and Campion did afterwards on the 20th March 1581, at Rome aforesaid, and on divers other days before and after, both by persuasions and letters, move, exhort and comfort divers strangers and aliens to invade the realm and raise war against the Queen. And further, that the same Allen, Morton, Parsons and Campion did, on the 20th day of May at Rome, and on the last of the same month at Rheims, traitorously agree that the said Parsons and Campion should go into England, there to move and persuade such subjects of the Queen as they could come at to aid and assist such strangers and aliens as they should traitorously bring into the realm to make war and rebellion against the Queen, and to change and alter the religion established. And that the said Parsons and Campion did after, to wit on the first of June 1580, by the treason, procurance, comfort and command of Allen and Morton at Rheims, set out to come to England to perform their aforesaid treasonable intents against their due allegiance and against the peace of the said Queen, her crown and dignity, and in manifest contempt of the laws of this realm, and against the form of divers statutes in this case made and provided.

The question arises, Why was the preliminary indictment set aside? It was based upon the 1581 Act of Persuasions which made reconciliation to the Romish religion 'by any ways or means' treason as it withdrew subjects from 'their natural obedience' to the queen. The emphasis was on religion. A conviction on these grounds was almost certain; the alternative chosen was difficult, almost impossible to establish.

The second indictment was based on an alleged plot to overthrow and kill the queen. The emphasis here was on political action.

It has been argued[2] that this change from religion to politics was due to the presence in the country of the Duke of Alençon and Anjou, the youngest son of Catherine de Médicis as a suitor for the hand of the queen. This affair had been blowing hot and cold for five or six years. By the time of his visit in

November 1581, this strange courtship had worn threadbare. As far as the records tell us, religion was not a serious consideration, though in the popular view it raised difficulties. There is no reason to think that Alençon was disturbed by the fact that England had become a Protestant country. He himself had fought with the Huguenots and at the time of his visit he was actively supporting the cause of the Netherlands against Spain and was looking for a crown. It may be hazarded that he was far more anxious to get support, both money and men, for his campaigns than to win the queen's hand. An authority has written, 'With Alençon the religious difficulty . . . was as slight as it possibly could be with a Catholic husband.'[3] Moreover, when Alençon was approached by some Catholics in the hope that he could get the condemned priests reprieved, he refused to be interested.

A more likely explanation is that the queen wished to keep religious differences as far in the background as possible and therefore decided that the trial should be one of treasonous conspiracy, thus putting the emphasis on political considerations. The 1581 Act made 'reconciling' a treasonous activity but a trial on that count would inevitably have been about religion. The second indictment was based on the Edward III Act of Treason of 1351. Henry VIII's monstrous Act of 1534 in which even speech could be made treasonous, was repealed in the first year of his son's reign; in its place there was a reversion to the Edward III Act with a few additions. This was in turn repealed in the first year of Queen Mary's reign and nothing was put in its place. The chief grounds under the Edward III Act were compassing the king's death, levying war against him and adhering to his enemies. It will have been noticed that the indictment of the priests emphasised the first two of these. To make the accusation stick it was necessary to have a plot. The movements of the four principals in the Low Countries and Rome had been reported by spies so it was an easy matter to claim that their meetings were conspiracies against the realm even though there was no clear evidence of what they talked about.

A trial for treason at that period was a political act, and, though it had all the trappings of judicial procedure, it bore little resemblance to what we should consider an equitable trial; there was no nonsense about assuming a defendant to be innocent until proved guilty. The prisoner was not given a copy of the indictment until he came before the Grand Jury, nor was he allowed counsel to defend him except to argue a point of law, nor could he call witnesses in his support; the prisoner had in fact to defend himself as best he could, and the trial really resolved itself into a verbal duel between him and the prosecutor. He could challange the jurors but this right was of small value as he was not given a list of them before he came into court. Juries were not the independent bodies we know today; they were often packed and were not incorruptible. They lacked the careful guidance of the judge in weighing up the evidence. Unless, as was usual, they gave their verdict at once in open court, and it was tacitly assumed they would find for the Crown, they were locked up without food, drink or heating, until they 'came to their senses,' as a judge of the time might have said. The verdict had to be unanimous. After the verdict, the prisoner was allowed to argue why sentence should not be passed upon him; this was seldom effective in gaining any mitigation but it gave the prisoner a chance to speak his mind, as Sir Thomas More did at his trial. Execution usually followed as soon as possible after the death sentence had been passed.

The Grand Jury and the subsequent court were held in Westminster Hall. Where the broad flight of steps now leads into St Stephen's Hall, there were two courts side by side – the Chancery on the right and the Queen's Bench on the left. There was not much space in which to pack the counsel, the prisoners and the witnesses. The body of the Hall was used for lawyers to meet their clients and the public could be there as well but they could not have heard much of what was going on beyond the barrier that separated the main Hall from the courts. This lack of space would explain why the priests had to be tried in two groups; in the first was Campion with six priests and one layman; in the second group were seven priests.

The presiding judge at the Grand Jury and at the trial was Sir Christopher Wray, chief justice of the Queen's Bench since 1572, who, according to the legal standards of the day, was considered to be a fair judge who maintained the decorum of the court. As a member of an old northern family, he may have had Catholic sympathies, but he kept to the *via media*.

The Grand Jury met on the 14th of November when Campion and his companions were arraigned. According to a contemporary record Campion said, after the indictment had been read, 'I protest, before God and His holy angels, before heaven and earth, before the world and this bar whereat I stand, which is but a small resemblance of the terrible judgement of the next life, that I am not guilty of the treason contained in the indictment, or of any other treason whatever.' When the jury for the trial was being empanelled, he said, 'Is it possible to find twelve men so wicked and void of all conscience in this city or land that will find us guilty together or this one crime, divers of us never meeting or knowing one the other before bringing to this bar?' Ralph Sherwin declared, 'The plain reason of our standing here is religion and not treason.' The chief justice then said, 'The time is not yet come wherein you shall be tried, and therefore you must now spare speech, and reserve it till then, at which time you shall have full liberty of defence, and me to sit indifferent between her Majesty and yourself; wherefore now plead to the indictment whether you be guilty or not.'

The report continues: 'They were then commanded, as the custom is, to hold up their hands, but both Campion's arms were pitifully benumbed by his often cruel racking before, and he having them wrapped in a furred cuff, he was not able to lift his hand so high as the rest did and was required of him, but one of his companions, kissing his hand so abused for the confession of Christ, took off his cuff, and so he lifted up his arm as high as he could, and pleaded "Not guilty" as all the rest did.'

On the following day the second group of priests was

similarly arraigned. The Grand Jury brought in true bills on both days.

[1] B. M. Lansdowne MSS. 33, Arts. 64, 65.

[2] By Richard Simpson and Evelyn Waugh. Until his elder brother, Henry, Duke of Anjou, become Henry III in 1574, he was Duke of Alençon, but he then added his brother's former title. It is simpler to call him Alençon.

[3] J.E. Neale, *Queen Elizabeth* (1934), p. 228.

Chapter 17

The Trial[1]

On the 20th November Edmund Campion and his fellow prisoners[2] were taken up river from the Tower to Westminster Hall for their trial. With Sir Christopher Wray were three other judges – John Southcote, Thomas Gawdy and William Ayloff. The prosecution was led by Edmund Anderson, the queen's serjeant-at-law, later chief justice of the Common Pleas; he was assisted by John Popham, the attorney-general and later chief justice of the Queen's Bench, and Thomas Egerton, the solicitor-general who was to be Lord Chancellor under James I.

The appointment of three such leading lawyers showed the importance the Council attached to the trial of Campion for he was the main target of the prosecution. Anderson was to show some animus, but under Wray's direction, the trial was conducted as fairly as was possible in the circumstances. The counsel had to make the best of a poor case; they knew that, for want of hard evidence, it was impossible to prove there had been a conspiracy abroad; it would have been far easier if the trial had been under the Act of Persuasions.

One interesting point may be noted. The protonotary or clerk of the Queen's Bench was Thomas Roper, the son of William Roper. Like his father, Thomas did not conceal the fact that he was a Catholic, but he was too useful in his official position to be discarded, so he paid his fines for not attending his parish church and was not otherwise molested. Was he present at Campion's trial? Perhaps he evaded being present just as his father had absented himself from the trial of his father-in-law, St Thomas More.

After the indictment had been read, CAMPION was the first to speak.

'My lord,' he said, 'forasmuch as our surmised offences are several so that the one is not to be tainted with the crime of the other, the offence of one not being the offence of all, I could have wished likewise, for the avoidance of confusion, we might also have been severally indicted, and that our accusations carrying so great importance, and so nearly unto us as our lives, each one might have had one day for his trial. For albeit I acknowledge the jurors to be wise men and much experienced in such cases, yet all evidence being given or rather handled at once, must needs breed a confusion in the jury, and such a misprision of matters, as they may take evidence against one to be against all, and consequently the crime of the one for the crime of the other, and finally the guilty to be saved and the guiltless to be condemned; wherefore I would it had pleased your lordship that the indictments had been several, and that we might have several days of trial.

HUDSON.[3] It seemeth well, Campion, that you have had your counsel.

CAMPION. No counsel but a pure conscience.

LORD CHIEF JUSTICE. Although, if many be indicted at once, the indictment in respect of them all containing all their names be joint, yet in itself being framed against several persons, it cannot be but several at the trial, whereof evidence shall be particularly given against every one, and to the matters objected every one shall have his particular answer, so that the jury shall have all things orderly; notwithstanding I could have wished also that every one should have had his special day assigned him, had the time so permitted, but since it cannot be otherwise, we must take it as it is.

ANDERSON. With how good and gracious a prince the Almighty has blessed this island, continuing the space of twenty-three years; the peace, the tranquillity, the riches and abundant supplies, especially the light and success of the

Gospel, wherewith since her Majesty's first reign this realm hath flourished above all other, most evidently doth manifest; the which, notwithstanding they ought to have stirred us up into a most dutiful affection and zealous love unto her crown, for whose sake and by whose means, next under God, we enjoy these prosperities, yet hath there not, from time to time, been wanting amongst us mischievous and evil-disposed enemies of her felicity, which, either by insolent and open denouncing of war, or by secret and privy practices of sinister devices, have ambitiously and most disloyally attempted to spoil her of her right, and us of these blessings. Yet such hath been God's incomparable puissance against them, so tender his care over her, so favourable his mercy towards us, that neither they thereby have been bettered, nor her state impaired, nor our quiet diminished. For who knoweth not of the rebellions and uproars in the North, who remembereth not the tragical pageant of Storey,[4] who still seeth not the traitorous practices of Felton?[5] Prevailed they against her? Was not their strength vanquished? Were not their policies frustrated? And did not God detect them and protect her to her safety and their perdition? The matter is fresh in remembrance. Their quarters are yet scarcely consumed; they were discovered, they were convicted, they sufferered; we saw it. If you ask from whence these treasons and seditious conspiracies had their first offspring, I ask from whence they could have it but from the well itself – the Pope? For if we inspect the northern seditions, he it was that was not only the encouragement, but also, being put to flight, was their refuge. If we mean Storey, he it was that was the sworn liege and lord of so perjured a subject; if we look to Felton, he it was that excommunicated the Queen and all the commonalty that did her obedience. Finally, if we recount all the treasons and rebellions that have been conspired since the first hour of her coronation, he it was, and principally he, that suborned them. What then are we to think these latest and present conspiracies to have been done either unwitting or unwilling the Pope? Shall we deny either Campion or his companions, without the Pope's assent or consent, to have conspired these matters beyond the seas themselves? Why? Had they no entertainment at his hands? Did he bestow nothing upon them for their maintenance? Was there no cause why he should either do for them or they for him – they Papists, he Pope; they flying their country, he receiving them; they Jesuits, he their founder; he supreme head, they sworn members; he their chief provost, they his dearest subjects; how can it be but he was privy? Privy!, nay the author and onsetter? We see that other treasons have been squared to his platforms and yielded he no direction in this? Came all the rest unto him, and came not this near him? It is impossible. An enemy of the Crown, a professed scourge to the Gospel, envying the tranquillity of the one, impatient of the success of the other, what would he not do to subvert them? He hath been always like to himself – never liker in aught than in this. He knew well enough no foreign hostility was convenient. The Spaniard would be discovered; the Frenchman would be suspected; the Roman not believed. How then? Forsooth, men bred and born in our own nation, perfect in our own tongue and languages, instructed in our own universities, they, and only they, must endeavour our overthrow. In what order? They must come secretly into the realm; they must change their habit and names; they must dissemble their vocation, they must wander unknown. To what ends? To dissuade the people from their allegiance to their prince, to reconcile them to the pope, to plant Romish religion, to supplant both prince and province. By what means? By saying of Mass, by administering the Sacrament, by hearing confessions. When all these things were purposed, endeavoured, and practised by them, whether they were guilty of these treasons or no? If not, then add this further; and they were privy and parties to the rebellion in the North, they were instruments to the practices of Storey, they were ministers to execute the Bull sent from Pius Quintus against her Majesty. How appeareth that? How? How should it appear better than by your own speeches and examinations? They highly commended the rebellion in the North; they greatly rejoiced in the constancy of Storey; divers of their counsel and conferences was required for the Bull. Yea, and which is more, and yet sticketh in our stomachs, they afforded so large commendations to Sander, liking and extolling his late proceedings in Ireland, that it cannot be otherwise intended but that thereof they also have been partakers. To conclude: what loyalty may we hope for from the Pope; what fidelity from the hands that have bowed themselves unto him; what trust may the country repose in them that have fled and renounced their country? How can their return be without danger, whose departure was so perilous? Note all the circumstances, note all probabilities, not one amongst all but notes them for traitorous; and so being, it is reason they should have the law and the due punishment ordained for traitors, the which, in her Majesty's behalf, we pray that they may have, and that the jury, upon our allegation, may pass[6] for the trial.

This speech, very vehemently pronounced and gestured, with a grim and austere countenance, dismayed them [the prisoners] all, and made them very impatient and troublesome affected; for it seemed by their temperature that it sounded very grievously to their trial, and therefore, utterly denying all that was alleged, they protested themselves true and faithful subjects; only Campion bear it out best, and yet, somewhat amazed, demanded of Mr Anderson whether he came as an orator to accuse them, or as a pleader to give evidence.

LORD CHIEF JUSTICE. You must have patience with him, and the rest likewise; for, they being of the Queen's Council, they speak of no other intent than of duty to her Majesty; and I cannot but marvel that men of your profession should upon any such occasion be so much distempered; for as concerning the matters which my brother Anderson hath alleged, they be but inducements [preliminary statements] to the point itself, and thereto everyone shall have his several answer.

Whereupon Campion, for himself and his companions, answered unto Mr Anderson's speech as followeth:

CAMPION. The wisdom and providence of the laws of England, as I take it, is such as proceedeth not to the trial of any man for life and death by shifts of probabilities and conjectural surmises, without proof of the crime sufficient evidence and substantial witness; for otherwise it had been very unequally provided that upon the descant and flourishes of affected speeches a man's life should be brought into danger and extremity, or that upon the persuasion of any orator or vehement pleader, without witness *viva voce* testifying the same, a man's offence should be judged or reputed mortal. If so, I see not to what end Mr Serjeant's oration tended, or if I see an end, I see it but frustrate; for be the crimes but in trifles, the law hath his passage [procedure];

be the theft but of a halfpenny, witnesses are produced; so that probabilities, aggravations, invectives, are not the balance wherein justice must be weighed, but witnesses, oaths, and apparent guiltiness. Whereto, then, appertaineth these objections of treason? He barely affirmeth; we flatly deny them. But let us examine them; how will they urge us? We fled our country; what of that? The Pope gave us entertainment; how then? We are Catholics; what is that to the purpose? We persuaded people; what followeth? We are therefore traitors. We deny the sequel; this is no more necessary than if a sheep had been stolen, and to accuse me you should frame this reason: my parents are thieves, my companions suspected persons, myself an evil liver, and one that loveth mutton; therefore I stole the sheep. Who seeth not but these odious circumstances to bring a man in hatred with the jury, and no necessary matter to conclude him guilty? Yes, but we seduced the Queen's subjects from their allegiance to her Majesty! What can be more unlikely? We are dead men[7] to the world, we only travelled for souls; we touched neither state nor policy, we had no such commission. Where was, then, our seducing? Nay, but we reconciled them to the Pope. Nay, then, what reconciliation can there be to him, since reconciliation is only due to God? This word soundeth not to a lawyer's usage, and therefore is wrested against us unaptly. The reconciliation that we endeavoured was only to God, and, as Peter saith, *reconciliamini Domino*. What resteth then against us? That we were privy to the rebellion in the North, instruments to Storey, ministers to Felton, partakers with Sander. How so? Forsooth, it must be presumed. Why, because we commended some, some we rejoiced at, concerning some we gave counsel and conference. How appeareth that? By our own speeches, nothing less. God is our witness we never meant it, we dreamed it not. These matters ought to be proved and not urged, declared by evidence and not surmised by fancy. Notwithstanding it ought to be so, yet must all circumstances note us for traitors. Indeed, all yet that is laid against us be but bare circumstances and no sufficient arguments to prove us traitors, insomuch that we think ourselves somewhat hardly dealt with that for want of proof we must answer to circumstances. Well, circumstances or other, as I remember, this was all; and this were all, all this were nothing. Wherefore, in God's behalf, we pray that better proof may be used, and that our lives be not brought in prejudice by conjectures.

QUEEN'S COUNSEL. It is the use of seminary men,[8] at the first entrance into their seminaries, to make two personal oaths, the one unto a book called Bristow's Motives,[9] for the fulfilling of all matters therein contained; the other unto the Pope to be true to him and to his successors, of the which oaths there is neither but is traitorous, for how can a man be faithful to our state and swear performance to those motives; a true liege to his sovereign and swear fealty to the Pope, forasmuch as the one is quite contrary to our laws and government, the other the most mortal enemy her majesty hath?

CAMPION. What oaths seminary men do take at their first entrance, or whether Bristow's Motives be repugnant to our laws or no, is not anything material to our indictment, for that we are neither seminary men nor sworn at our entrance to any such Motives. But were it so that any seminary men stood here for trial this matter could prove no great evidence against them, for that none are sworn to such articles as Bristow's but young striplings that be under tuition; whereas unto men of riper years and better grounded in points of religion (as most of England are before they pass the seas) that oath is never administered; and then many a study else flourished in Rome, wherein both seminary men and others are far better employed than they otherwise could be in reading English Pamphlets.

KIRBY. I think of my conscience there be not four books of those Bristow's Motives in all the seminaries.

Thereupon they all cried that whereas they were indicted for treason, they feared lest under the vizard [mask] of that, they should be condemned of religion; and to prove that Campion framed a reason in manner following:

CAMPION. There was offer made unto us, that if we would come to the church and hear sermons and the word preached, we should be set at large and at liberty; so Paschall[10] and Nicolls,[11] otherwise as culpable in all offences as we, upon coming to the church and acceptance of that offer, were received to grace and had their pardon granted; whereas, if they had been so happy as to have persevered to the end, they had been partakers of our calamities. Wherefore, if liberty were offered to us on condition to come to church and hear sermons – and that could we not do by professing our religion – then, to change our religion and to become

Protestants, that, forsooth, was that that should purchase us liberty. So that our religion was cause of our imprisonment, and, *ex consequenti*, of our condemnation.

ATTORNEY-GENERAL POPHAM. All these matters at the time of Nichol's enlargement were altogether unknown, and not once suspected; neither can we now conjecture that he was guilty of any such drift or purpose, in that he stood not, as you do, stubbornly in that religion which might be any cloak or colour for such treasons.

QUEEN'S COUNSEL. All you jointly and severally have received money of the Pope to spend in your journeys. Some two hundred crowns, some more, some less, according to your degrees and conditions. Was such liberality of the Pope's without cause? No, it had an end; and what end should that be but by your privy inveighings and persuasions to set on foot his devices and treacheries?

CAMPION. We have received of him according to the rate he thought best to bestow it. We saw neither cause why to refuse it, nor means how to come hither penniless; it was his liberality, it supplied our need. What would you have us do? We took it, was that treason? But it was to an end: I grant, had it been to no end, it had been in vain; and what end should that be? Marry, to preach the Gospel; no treachery, no such end was intended.

There was a witness produced named H. CADDY or H. Caddocke, who deposed, generally against them all, that being beyond the seas he heard of the holy vow made between the Pope and the English priests for the restoring and establishing of religion in England; for the which purpose two hundred priests should come into the realm, the which matter was declared to Sir Ralph Shelley,[12] an English knight, and captain to the Pope, and that he should conduct an army into England for the subduing of the realm unto the Pope, and the destroying the heretics. Whereunto Sir Ralph made answer that he would be rather drink poison with Themistocles than see the overthrow of his country; and added further, that he thought the Catholics in England would first stand in arms against the Pope before they would join in such an enterprise.

QUEEN'S COUNSEL. The matter is flat [plain]; the holy vow

was made, two hundred priests had their charge appointed, the captain-general was mentioned, our destruction purposed. If, then, we confer all likelihoods together, what is more apparent than that of those two hundred priests you made up a number, and, therefore be parties and privy to the treason?

CAMPION. Two hundred priests made a holy vow to labour for the restoring of religion. It seemeth, by all likelihood, that we made up the number, and therefore privy and parties to the treason; here is a conclusion without any jot of affinity to the premises; first an holy vow, then an establishing of religion. What colour is there here left for treason? All the treason rehearsed was reputed to Sir Ralph Shelley; not one syllable was referred to the priests. But granting, and which the witnesses have not deposed, and namely, that we are some of the two hundred priests, you see Sir Ralph Shelley, a Catholic, a Pope's captain, a layman, would rather drink poison than agree to such treason; it is like that the priests, devotaries and dead men to the world, would in any wise consent unto it. This deposition is more for us than against us.

Then was order taken that every man's evidence should be particularly read against himself, and everyone to have his several answer, and first against Campion.

QUEEN'S COUNSEL. About ten years since, you, Campion, were received into conference with the Cardinal [Jesualdi] of St Cecilia concerning the Bull wherein Pius Quintus did excommunicate the queen, the nobility, and the commonalty of this realm; discharging such of them as were Papists from their obedience to her Majesty, the which conference cannot otherwise be referred than to the putting in execution of the Bull; so that the Bull containing manifest treason, whereto you were privy, doth flat prove you a traitor.

CAMPION. You, men of the jury, I pray you listen. This concerneth me only, and thereto must I answer. True it is that at my first arrival into Rome (which is now about ten years past) it was my hap to have access to the said Cardinal, who, having some liking of me, would have been the means to prefer me to any place of service whereunto I should have most fancy; but I, being resolved what course to take, answered that I meant not to serve any man, but to enter the Society of Jesus, thereof to vow and be professed. Then being demanded further what opinion I had conceived of the Bull, I said it procured much severity in England, and the heavy hand of her Majesty against the Catholics. Whereunto the Cardinal replied that he doubted not it should be mitigated in such sort as the Catholics should acknowledge her highness as their queen without danger of excommunication. And this was all the speech I had with the Cardinal, which can in no wise be construed as an offence, much less as the least point of treason.

QUEEN'S COUNSEL. We can impute no more by your words than a mitigation of the Bull against the Catholics only; so that the principal, which was the excommunication of her Majesty, was still left in force, not detected by you, and therefore your privity thereto concludeth you a traitor.

CAMPION. My privity thereto enforceth not my consenting; rather, it proved my disagreement, in that I said it procured much severity; and therefore, being here published before I could detect it (for who knew that the Queen of England was excommunicated?), it excused my privity and exempted me from treason.

QUEEN'S COUNSEL. You had conference with the Bishop of Ross,[13] a professed papist and a mortal enemy to the state and crown of England; and to what end should any such communication be had, but for the practising of such treasons as had been conspired?

CAMPION. What the Bishop of Ross is, either for religion of affection, I think little pertinent to me, much less to this purpose; but as for the conference passed between him and me, I utterly deny that ever there was any, and therefore let that be proved.

The clerk of the Crown[14] read a letter sent from Dr Allen to Dr Sander[15] in Ireland wherein Allen showeth why the insurrection in the north prevailed not, was in two respects: either that God reserved England for a greater plague, or for that the Catholics in other places had not intelligence for the purpose for otherwise that could not so badly have succeeded. In this letter moreover was contained that ———— feared the war as a child doth the rod, and that ———— at all times will be ready with 2000 [men] to aid him.

QUEEN'S COUNSEL. What an army and host of men the pope,

by the aid of the King of Spain and the Duke of Florence,[16] had levied for the overthrow of this king-realm, the destruction of her Majesty and the placing of the Scottish Queen as governess in England, could not any ways have escaped your knowledge; for being sent from Prague, where your abode was, to Rome, and then being by the Pope charged presently towards England, what other drift could this sudden ambassage pretend than the practising and execution of such a conspiracy? Whereof you are also the more to be suspected forasmuch as in your coming from Rome towards England you entered into a certain privy conference with Dr Allen at Reims, to whose letters above mentioned, touching the estate, it cannot but by means of that conference you were privy, for the furtherance of which platforms and devices yourself came as procurator from the Pope and Dr Allen to break these matters to the English papists, to withdraw the people from their due allegiance and to prepare men ready to receive those foreign powers.

CAMPION. When I was first received into the Order of Jesuits, I vowed three things incident to my calling – chastity, poverty and obedience: chastity in abstaining from all fleshly appetites and concupiscences; poverty, in despising all worldly wealth, living upon the devotion of others; obedience, in dutifully executing the commandments of my superiors. In respect of which vow enjoining obedience, I came, being sent for, from Prague to Rome, having not so much as the smallest inkling of those supposed armies, nor the least inclination to put any such thing in practice; but there rested for eight days attending the pleasure of my provost, who at last, according to my vow (which, by the grace of God, I will in no case violate) appointed me to undertake this journey into England, the which I accordingly I enterprised, being commanded thereto, not as a traitor to conspire the subversion of my country, but as a priest to minister the sacraments and to hear confessions; the which ambassage I protest before God I would as gladly have executed and was as ready and willing to discharge, had I been sent to the Indians or uttermost regions of the world, as I was being sent into my native country. In the which voyage I cannot deny but that I dined with Dr Allen at Reims, with whom also after dinner I walked in his garden, spending a time in speeches referred to our old familiarity and acquaintance; during the whole course thereof (I take God to witness) not one jot of our talk glanced to the crown or state of England; neither had I the least notice of any letters sent to Sander, nor the smallest glimmering of these objected platforms. Then, as for being procurator from the Pope to Dr Allen, I must needs say there could be no one thing have been inferred more contrary; for as concerning the one, he flatly with charge and commandment excused me from matters of state and regiment; the other I owed no such duty and obedience unto as to execute matters repugnant to my charge. But admitting (as I protest he did not) that Dr Allen had communicated such affairs unto me, yet for that he was not my superior, it would have been apostasy in me to obey him. Dr Allen, for his learning and good religion, I reverence, but neither was I his subject or inferior, nor he the man at whose commandment I rested.

QUEEN'S COUNSEL. Were it not that your dealings afterwards had fully betrayed you, your present speech had been more credible; but all afterclaps [17] make those excuses but shadows and your deeds and actions prove your words but forged; for what meaning had that changing of your name? Whereto belonged your disguising in apparel? Can these alterations be wrought without suspicion? Your name being Campion, why were you called Hastings? You a priest and dead to the world, what pleasure had you to roist it? A velvet hat and a feather, a buff leather jerkin, velvet venetians [hose or breeches] are they weeds for dead men? Can that beseem a professed man of religion which hardly becometh a layman of gravity? No, there was a further matter intended; your lurking and lying hid in secret places concludeth with the rest a mischievous meaning. Had you come hither for love of your country, you would never have wrought a hugger-mugger [concealment], had your intent been to have done well, you would never have hated the light; and therefore this budging [sneaking] deciphereth your treason.

CAMPION. At what time the primitive church was persecuted, and that Paul laboured in the propagation and increase of the Gospel, it is not unknown to what straits and pinches he and his fellows were diversely driven; wherein, though in purpose he were already resolved rather to yield himself to martyrdom than to shrink an inch from truth which he preached, yet if any hope or means appeared to escape and that living he might benefit the Church more than dying, we read of sundry shifts whereto he betook himself to increase God's number and to shun persecution; but especially the changing of his name was very oft and familiar, whereby, as opportunity and occasion was ministered, he termed himself Paul, now Saul;[18] neither was he of opinion always to be known, but sometimes thought it expedient to be hidden, lest being discovered, persecution should ensue, and thereby the Gospel greatly forestalled. Such was his meaning, so was his purpose, when, being in durance for points of religion, he secretly stole out of prison in a basket. If these shifts were then approved by Paul, why are they not approved in me, he, an Apostle, I a Jesuit? Were they commended in him, are they condemned in me? The same cause was common to us both; and shall the effect be peculiar to the one? I wished earnestly the planting of the Gospel; I knew a contrary religion professed; I saw if I were known I should be apprehended; I changed my name; I kept secretly; I imitated Paul. Was I therein a traitor? But the wearing of a buff jerkin, a velvet hat, and such like, is much forced against me, as though the wearing of any apparel were treason, or that I in so doing were ever the more a traitor. I am not indicted upon the Statute of Apparel,[19] neither is it any part of this present argument; indeed, I acknowledge an offence to Godwards for so doing, and thereof it did grievously repent me, and therefore do now penance as you see me.

(He was newly shaven, in a rug-gown [coarse woollen] and a great black nightcap covering half his face.)

The clerk of the Crown read a letter sent from Campion unto one Pound,[20] a Catholic, part of the contents whereof was this: 'It grieveth me much to have offended the Catholic cause so highly as to confess the names of some gentlemen and friends in whose houses I have been entertained; yet in this I greatly cherish and comfort myself that I never discovered any secrets there declared, and that I will not, come rack, come rope.'

QUEEN'S COUNSEL. What can sound more suspicious or nearer treason than this letter? It grieveth him to have betrayed his favourers the Catholics, and therein he thinketh to have wrought prejudice to religion. What, then, may we think of that he concealeth? It must needs be some grievous matter, and very pernicious, that neither the rack nor the rope can wring it from him. For his conscience being not called in question, nor shifted in any point of religion, no doubt if there had not been further devices intended, and affairs of the state and the commonwealth attempted, we should as well have discovered the matter as the person, wherefore it were well these hidden secrets were revealed, and then would appear the very face of these treasons.

CAMPION. As I am by profession and calling a priest, so I have singly vowed all conditions and covenants to such a charge and vocation belonging, whereby I sustain one office and duty of priesthood that consisteth in shriving and hearing confessions, in respect whereof, at my first consecration (as all other priests so accepted must do) I solemnly took and vowed to God never to disclose any secrets confessed; the force and effect of which vow is such as whereby every priest is bound and endangered under pain of perpetual curse and damnation never to disclose any offence opened nor infirmity whatsoever committed to his hearing. By virtue of this profession and due execution of my priesthood, I was occasioned to be privy unto divers men's secrets, and those not such as concerned state or commonwealth, whereunto my authority was not extended, but such as surcharged the grieved soul and conscience, whereof I had power to pray for absolution. These were the hidden matters, these were the secrets, in concealing of which I so greatly rejoiced, to the revealing whereof I cannot nor will not be brought, come rack, come rope.

Thereupon the clerk of the Crown read certain papers containing in them oaths[21] to be administered to the people for the renouncing their obedience to her Majesty, and the swearing of allegiance to the Pope, acknowledging him for their supreme head and governor; the which papers were found in divers houses where Campion had lurked, and for religion been entertained.

QUEEN'S COUNSEL. What can be more apparent than this? These oaths, if we went no further, are of themselves sufficient to convince you of treason; for what may be imagined more traitorous than to alien the hearts of the subjects from her Majesty, renouncing their obedience to her and swearing their subjection to the Pope? And therefore these papers thus found in houses where you were, do clearly prove that for ministering such oaths you are a traitor.

CAMPION. Neither is there, neither can there be anything imagined more directly contrary or repugnant to my calling than upon any occasion to minister an oath; neither had I any power or authority so to do; neither would I commit an offence so thwart to my profession for all the substance and treasure in the world. But, admit that I were authorised, what necessity importeth that reason, that neither being set down by my handwriting nor otherwise derived by any proof from myself, but only found in places where I resorted, therefore I should be he by whom they were administered? This is but a naked presumption – who seeth it not? – and nothing vehement nor of force against me.

ANDERSON. It could not otherwise be intended but that you ministered these oaths, and that being found behind you, it was you that left them. For if a poor man and a rich man come both to one house, and that after their departure a bag of gold be found hidden, forasmuch as the poor man had no such plenty, and therefore could not leave no such bag behind him, by common presumption it is to be intended that the rich man only, and no other, did hide the bag. So you, a professed Papist, coming to a house, and then such reliques found after your departure how can it otherwise be implied but that you did both bring them and leave them there? So it is flat they came there by means of a Papist, *ergo* by your means.

CAMPION. Your conclusion had been necessary if you had also showed that none came into the house of my profession but I; but there you urge your conclusion before you frame the minor, whereby your reason is imperfect; *ergo* it proveth not.

ANDERSON. If here, as you do in schools, you bring your minor and your conclusion, you will prove yourself but a fool: but minor or conclusion, I will bring it to purpose anon.

QUEEN'S COUNSEL. You refuse to swear to the supremacy a notorious token of an evil willer to the Crown, insomuch as, being demanded by the commissioners whether the Bull wherein Pius Quintus had excommunicated her Majesty were in your opinion of force, and the excommunication of effect or no, you would answer nothing but that these were bloody questions,[22] and that they which sought these sought your life, also resembling the commissioners unto the Pharisees who to entrap Christ propounded a dilemma, whether tribute were to be paid to Caesar or no; so that in your examination you would come to no issue, but sought your evasions and made answers aloof, which vehemently argueth a guiltiness of conscience, in that the truth would never have sought corners [concealment].

The two commissioners, Mr Thomas Norton and Dr John Hammond were present and verified the matter as the Queen's Counsel had urged.

CAMPION. Not long since[23] it pleased her Majesty to demand of me whether I did acknowledge her highness to be my queen or not. I answered that I did acknowledge her Highness not only as my queen, but also as my most lawful governess; and being further required by her Majesty whether I thought the Pope might lawfully excommunicate her or no, I answered, I confess myself an insufficient umpire between her Majesty and the Pope for so high a controversy, whereof neither the certainty is as yet known, nor the best divines in Christendom stand fully resolved. Albeit I thought that if the Pope should do it, yet it might be insufficient; for it is agreed, *clavis errare potest*; but the divines of the Catholic Church do distinguish of the pope's authority, attributing to him *ordinatam et inordinatam potestatem: ordinatam*, whereby he proceedeth in matters merely spiritual and pertinent to the Church, and by that he cannot excommunicate any prince or potentate; *inordinatam*, when he passeth by order of law, as by appeals and such like, and so some think, he may excommunicate and depose princes. The self-same articles were required of me by the commissioners, but much more urged to the point of supremacy, and to further supposals than I could think of. I said, indeed they were bloody questions, and very pharasaical, undermining of my life; whereunto I answered as Christ did to the dilemma, 'Give unto Caesar that which is due to Caesar, and to God that to God belongeth.' I acknowledge her Highness as my governess and sovereign; I acknowledge her Majesty both *facto et jure* to be queen; I confessed an obedience due to the Crown as my temporal head and primate. This I said then, so I say now. If then I failed in aught, I am now ready to supply it. What would you more? I will willingly pay to her Majesty what is hers, yet I must pay to God what is his. Then, as for excommunicating her Majesty, it was exacted of me – admitting that excommunication were of effect, and that the Pope had sufficient authority so to do – whether then I thought myself discharged of my allegiance or no? I said this was a dangerous question, and they that demanded this demanded my blood. Admitting – why admitting? *ex admissis et concessis quid non sequitur* – if I would admit his authority, and then he should excommunicate her, I would then do as God should give me grace; but I never admitted any such matter, neither ought I to be wrested with any such suppositions. What they, say they, because I would not answer flatly to that which I could not, forsooth I sought corners; mine answers were aloof. Well, since once more it must needs be answered, I say generally that these matters be merely spiritual points of doctrine and disputable in schools, no part of mine indictment, not to be given in evidence, and unfit to be discussed at the Queen's Bench. To conclude: they are no matters of fact; they be not in trial of the country; the jury ought not to take any notice of them; for although I doubt not they are very discreet men and trained up in great use and experience of controversies and debates pertinent to their callings, yet are they laymen, they are temporal, and unfit judges to decide so deep a question.

ELIOT, a witness, deposed against Campion that he made a sermon in Berkshire, his text being of Christ weeping over Jerusalem, wherein Campion showed many vices and enormities here abounding in England, and namely heresies, wherewith he was sorry that his countrymen were so blinded; but hoped shortly there would hap a day of change comfortable to Catholics, now shaken and dispersed, and terrible to the heretics here flourishing in the land. Eliot added that in his sermon Campion had persuaded his audience to obedience to the Pope; but on being urged by Campion he confessed that he did not remember the Pope being named once in the sermon.

QUEEN'S COUNSEL. Lo, what would you wish more manifest? The great day is threatened, comfortable to them, and terrible to us; and what day should that be but that wherein the Pope, the King of Spain, and the Duke of Florence have appointed to invade this realm?

CAMPION. O Judas, Judas! No other day was in my mind, I protest, than that wherein it should please God to make a restitution of faith and religion. For as in all other Christian commonwealths, so in England, many vices and iniquities do abound, neither is there any realm so godly, no people so devout, nowhere so religious, but that in the same places many enormities do flourish, and evil men bear sway and regiment. Whereupon, as in every pulpit every Protestant doth, I pronounced a great day, not wherein any temporal potentate should minister, but wherein the terrible Judge should reveal all men's consciences and try every man of each kind of religion. This is the day of change, this is the great day which I threatened; comfortable to the well-believing, and terrible to all heretics. Any other day than this, God he knows I meant not.

MUNDAY, a witness, deposed that he heard the Englishmen, as the doctors and others talk and conspire of these treasons against England, and that Campion and others afterwards had conference with Dr Allen.

CAMPION. Here is nothing deposed against me directly; and as for my conference with Dr Allen, it hath appeared when and what it was.

Evidence was next given against Sherwin, who before the comissioners had refused to swear to the supremacy, neither would answer plainly what he thought of the Pope's Bull, but confessed that his coming into England was to persuade the people to the Catholic religion.

QUEEN'S COUNSEL. You well knew that it was not lawful for you to persuade the Queen's subjects to any other religion than by her Highness's injunctions is already professed; and therefore, if there had not been a further matter in your meaning, you would have kept your conscience to yourself, and yourself where you were.

SHERWIN. We read that the Apostles and Fathers in the primitive Church have taught and preached in the dominions and empires of ethnic [pagan] and heathen rulers and yet not deemed worthy of death. The sufferance, and perhaps the like toleration, I will hope for in such a commonwealth as where open Christianity and godliness is pretended; and albeit in such a diversity of religion it was to be feared lest I might not discharge my conscience without fear of danger, yet ought I not therefore to surcease in my functions, although that conscience is very wavering and unsteady, which with fear of danger draweth from duty.

ONE OF THE JUSTICES. But your case differeth from theirs in the primitive Church, for that those Apostles and preachers never conspired the death of those emperors and rulers in whose dominions they so taught and preached.

The clerk of the Crown read a letter which showed that by the fireside in the English seminary beyond the seas, Sherwin should say that if he were in England he could compass many things, and that there was one Arundell in Cornwall who at an instant could levy a great power, and that if an army were to be sent into England, the best landing would be at St Michael's Mount.

SHERWIN. I never spake any such matter, God is my record; neither was it ever the least part of my meaning.

BOSGRAVE'S opinion was read wherein he had denied the supremacy, and staggered [hesitated] without any perfect answer to the Bull, but said that he came into England to persuade and teach, acknowledging her Majesty his queen and temporal head. In the which examination he confessed that beyond the seas he heard it reported how the Pope, the King of Spain and the Duke of Florence, would send a great army into England to deprive the Queen's Majesty both of life and dignity, for the restitution of the Catholic religion.

QUEEN'S COUNSEL. The keeping close and not detecting of treason maketh the hearer of it become a traitor; and therefore, inasmuch as you concealed what you heard, and made not information of it to her Majesty, the Council, nor the commonwealth of this realm, you became thereby privy and party unto it, and therefore in these respect you are a traitor.

BOSGRAVE. What! Am I a traitor because I heard it spoken?

But Campion perceiving Bosgrave merely daunted with the matter, spake to excuse him in manner as followeth.

CAMPION. My lord, it is not unknown to your honour how brittle and slippery ground fame and reports are wont to built on; the which, as for the most part they are more false than credible, so ought they always to make men wary and fearful to deal with them, insomuch as the broacher of rumours and news is he that getteth commonly least credit or thanks for his labour. The cause is the property and

nature of fame, which is never but uncertain and sometimes
but forged, for who findeth it not by daily experience, how
that in every city, every village, yea, in most barber's shops,
in all England, many speeches, both of states and commonwealths be tossed, which were never meant nor determined
of in the court. If it be so in England, shall we not look for
the like in Italy, Flanders, France and Spain? Yes, truly, for
though the countries do differ yet the nature of man remaineth
the same, namely, always desirous and greedy of news. Many
things there be diversely reported and diversely canvassed
by the common sort, which were never intended by the
bearers of rule and principality. Were it not, then, a great
point of credulity for a man divided from England with a
many seas and lands, upon a matter only blazed among the
vulgar people, either by a journey or letter to certify the
Queen's Council or commonalty of things never purposed
much less put in practice? I rather think Mr Bosgrave's
discretion to have been greater in passing [over] such
dangerous occasions with themselves, than otherwise it had
been in using means of bewray them. But, supposing he had
done as you would have had him, and what he heard he had
signified here, what had come of it? Marry, then, greater
danger for slandering the realm and how little thanks for his
false information! So that if he would deal either wisely or
safely, how could he deal better than to do as he did?

ATTORNEY-GENERAL. There is no cloth so coarse but Campion
can cast a colour upon it. But what, was it not Bosgrave's
own confession that he arrived in England to teach and
persuade the people, and what persuasions should they be
but to prepare a readiness for these wars?

CAMPION. These be but faint and bare implications, which
move but urge not, affirm but prove not; whereas you ought
not to amplify and gather upon words when a matter
concerneth and toucheth a man's life.

COTTAM, in his examination, would neither agree to the
supremacy, nor answer directly concerning the Pope's
authority.

QUEEN'S COUNSEL. You came into England at or near the
time that the rest came, so that it must needs be intended a
match made between you, for the furtherance of those affairs
which were then a-brewing; and how answer you thereunto?

COTTAM. It was neither my purpose nor my message to

come into England; neither would I have come had not God otherwise driven me; for my journey was appointed to the Indians, and thither had I gone had my health been thereto answerable but in the meanwhiles it pleased God to visit me with sickness and being counselled by the physicians for my health's sake to come into England – for otherways, as they said, either remaining there or going elsewhere I should not recover it – I came upon that occasion, and upon no other, into this realm.

CAMPION. Indeed, the physicians in Rome do hold for a certainty that, if an Englishman shall fall sick amongst them, there is no better nor scant any other way for his health than to repair to England, there to take his natural air, which agreeth best with his complexion.

COTTAM. And that only was the cause of my coming, and not any determinate intent either to persuade or dissuade, being otherwise by my provost charged to the Indians. Neither, after my arrival here, did I hide myself, nor dealt otherwise than might beseem any man that meddled no more than I did. I lay for the most part in Southwark; I walked daily in Paul's; I refrained no place which betokened my innocency.

QUEEN'S COUNSEL. Did you neither persuade nor dissuade? Was there not a book found in your budget the contents whereof tended to no other purpose? The which was made by one D'Espignata[24] entitled *Tractatus Conscientiae*, containing certain answers to the supremacy and how sophistically to frustrate any kinds of demands; with a further method how you ought to demean yourself in every sort of company, whether it were of Protestants or Puritans, and what speeches you should use to convert them both; as unto the Protestants highly commending them and showing that they are far nearer the right way than Puritans, and whom you should utterly dispraise unto the Puritans; likewise in commending the Protestants and persuading them to the obedience of the Pope. To what end, then, should you carry this book with you, if you were not purposed to do as it prescribeth?

COTTAM. I protest before God I knew nothing of that book neither how nor where it came to me.

Then Campion seeing him driven to so narrow an exigent

[need] as to deny which was manifest, answered for him to this effect following.

CAMPION. Many casualties and events may happen whereby a man may be endangered ere he be ware by the carrying of a thing he knoweth not, as either the malice of others that privily convey it amongst other his provisions, or his own negligence or oversight which marked no attentively what he took with him; whereof both are to be judged errors, yet not deemed an offence; and therefore this cannot be maintained to be done by Mr Cottam on purpose which we see flatly to be out of his knowledge. But suppose that purposely he brought the book with him, yet what can that make against him for treason? It treateth of conscience; it toucheth good demeanour; it showeth how to make the unbelieving faithful; matters wholly spiritual, points of edification, preparing to Godwards, where is, then the treason? But were these reasons impertinent yet it is a custom with all students beyond the seas, when any man learned or well thought of draweth a treatise touching either conscience or behaviour, to copy it out and to carry it about with them, not thereby aiming at any faction or conspiracy, but for their own proper knowledge and private instruction.

JOHNSON would neither grant to the supremacy neither yield any resolute opinion of the Pope's authority in his Bull and excommunication.

ELIOT, a witness, deposed against Johnson, that at Christ's Nativity come two years, being at my Lady Petre's house, he fell into acqaintance with one Payne [Paine] a priest that exercised the office of a steward in the house,[25] who by reason that he was appointed to be his bedfellow grew into a further familiarity with him, insomuch that at length he ventured to dissuade him from his allegiance to her Majesty and to become the subject of the Pope; affirming that her Highness could not live for ever, and that shortly after her days the Catholic religion should be restored; for the furtherance whereof the Catholics beyond seas had already devised a practice, which is this: that fifty of them, whereof either should know other, should come to the court with privy coats, poggets, daggs,[26] and two-handed swords, attending until her Majesty should take the air or go on some pretty progress, and then some of them should set upon her Majesty, some upon the lord-treasurer [Burghley], some upon the Earl of Leicester, some upon Sir Francis Walsingham, and others upon others the favourers of this heretical religion, there to kill her Majesty and to tie her by the hair of her head unto a horse, to be lugged and haled up and down to the joy of all Catholics and distress of all heretics: of the which so Payne offered this deponent, if he would he should be one, adding further, that if he had place and opportunity convenient, he should stab her Majesty with a dagger himself, for he thought it no more unlawful to kill her than to kill a horned beast.[27] After which communication, Payne, finding this deponent not so conformable unto him as he hoped, and receiving a bitter and flat refusal of his ungracious offer, conveyed himself away, and was no more heard of. Whereupon this Johnson, now arrived, came to the deponent and inquired what was become of Payne to whom he answered that he knew not. Then said Johnson, 'He is gone beyond the seas, fearing lest you would discover his secrets, and therefore I forewarn you and conjure you not to disclose anything that Payne hath told you, for if you do you stand in state of damnation.'

JOHNSON. I never in my life had any such talk with him nor uttered any such speeches tending to any such matter.

Bristow's[28] examination was read, wherein he had acknowledged her Majesty his lawful queen and governess, and notwithstanding aught that the Pope had done or could do, she was his supreme head.

QUEEN'S COUNSEL. What was, then, the cause of your coming into this realm? For it seemeth by your sudden arrival and journeying with the rest that you were also a party and furtherer of their purpose.

BRISTOW(?) I have to my mother a poor widow, who besides had one other son, with the company of whom during this life she was well appayed; but it pleased God afterwards to dispose him at His mercy, and to deprive my mother of his further succour. She, taking the matter very heavily, used what means she could possibly for my return. She sent letters after letters, and those so importunate, that, will I nill I, I must needs come home; the which was the only cause of my arrival, and not any other, God is my witness.

ANTHONY MUNDAY deposed against Bristow, that he should say he was cunning in fireworks, and that shortly he would make a confection of wildfire, wherewith he would burn her Majesty when she were on the Thames in her barge; and the deponent swore further, that he heard it spoken beyond seas that whosoever had not the watchword, which was 'Jesus Maria' should be slain.

BRISTOW(?) I call God to witness I never suffered such thoughts, nor never had any such cunning in fireworks, and therefore he sweareth the greatest untruth that may be.

KIRBY, in his examination for the supremacy and the Pope's authority, was of no other opinion than was Campion.

SLEDD, a witness, deposed that Kirby, that being sick beyond the seas, this Kirby came unto his bedside and counselled him to beware how he dealt with any matters in England, for there would come a great day wherein the Pope, the King of Spain, and the Duke of Florence should make as great an alteration as ever was. He deposed that Kirby was at a sermon of Dr Allen's who then persuaded the priests and seminary men to take their journey into England, to remove the Englishmen from their obedience to her Highness and to persuade them to aid the Pope and his confederates. He deposed, moreover, that beyond the seas he spoke with one Tedder,[29] a familiar friend of Kirby's, of whom he, the deponent, demanded whether he were of kin to her Majesty, for that his name was Tedder; whereunto he answered that if he knew himself to be kin to that Whore of Babylon, that Jezebel of England, he would think the worse of himself as long as he lived, but one day he would make a journey into England, and, if it were possible, despatch her out of the way.

KIRBY. As I hope to be saved at the last doom, there is not one word of this deposition that concerneth me either true or credible; neither at any time made I the least mention of that alleged day; neither was I present at any sermon so preached; but I always bore as true and faithful heart to her Majesty as any subject whatsoever in England, insomuch that I never heard her Majesty evil spoken of but I defended her cause, and always spake the best of her Highness. It is not unknown that I saved the English mariners from hanging only for the duty I bore to her Majesty, with the love and goodwill which I bore to my country.[30] But you that have thus deposed, when was then this sermon that you talk of so preached? At what time of the day?

The witness answered that the same day there were three philosophical disputations after the which the sermon was preached.

ORTON would neither agree to the supremacy, or openly affirm what authority the Pope had, nor whether he thought the excommunication of Pope Pius V to be of force or no.

ANTHONY MUNDAY deposed against Orton that he being at Lyons in France said unto this deponent that her Majesty was not lawful queen of England, and that he owed her no kind of obedience. The deponent said further that this Orton made suit unto Dr Allen that he might be one of the Pope's pensioners, whereunto Dr Allen would not agree unless Orton would become a priest or seminary man, which he refused.

ORTON. I utterly deny that I ever had any speech with the witness, either at Lyons or elsewhere; but he manifestly forsweareth himself, as one that having neither honesty nor religion, careth for neither.

The same all the parties did affirm, and that he was an atheist; for that beyond the seas he goeth on pilgrimage and receiveth the sacrament, and here taketh a new face and playeth the Protestant; and therefore is unfit and unworthy witness to give in evidence or to depose against life.

MUNDAY, the witness, answered, that in France and other places he seemed to favour their religion because he might thereby undermine them and sift out their purposes. The prisoners took exceptions to another of the witnesses,[31] which of them I know not, for that he was a murderer and had slain two men, already well known by his own confession and acknowledgement; for the which reason he was no sufficient nor allowable witness.

These matter thus sifted, and that the jury should pass, one of the justices said to the jurors, All the matter resteth in that, either to believe the prisoners that speak for their lives, or the witnesses that come freely to depose as they are demanded: the witnesses affirm sufficient proof against them; they deny whatsoever is alleged.

LORD CHIEF JUSTICE. You that are here indicted, you see what is alleged against you. In discharge thereof, if you have any more to say, speak, and we will hear you till to-morrow morning. We would be loth you should have any occasion to complain on the court; and therefore, if aught rest behind that is untold, that is available for you, speak, and you shall be heard with indifference.

They all thanked his lordship, and said they could not otherwise affirm but that they found of the court both indifference and justice. Whereupon Campion made this speech to the jurors.

CAMPION. What charge this day you sustain, and what accompt you are to render at the dreadful Day of Judgment, whereof I could wish this also were a mirror, I trust there is not one of you but knoweth. I doubt not but in like manner you forecast how dear the innocent is to God and at what price he holdeth man's blood. Here we are accused and impleaded to the death; here you do receive our lives into your custody; here must be your choice, either to restore them or condemn them. We have no whither to appeal but to your consciences; we have no friends to make there but your heeds and discretions. Take heed, I beseech you, let no colours nor inducements deceive you; let your ground be substantial for your building is weighty. All this you may do sufficiently, we doubt not, if you will mark intentively what things have been treated, in three distinct and several points. The speech and discourse of this whole day consisteth, first in presumptions and probabilities; secondly in matters of religion; lastly, in oaths and testimonies of witnesses. The weak and forceless proof that proceedeth from conjectures is neither worthy to carry the verdict of so many, nor sufficient evidence for trial of man's life. The constitutions of the realm exact a necessity, and will that no man should totter upon the hazard of likelihoods; and albeit the strongest reasons of our accusers have been but in bare and naked probabilities, yet are they no matters for you to rely upon, who ought only to regard what is apparent. Set circumstances aside, set presumptions apart, set that reason for your rule which is warranted for certainty. But probabilities were not the only matters which impertinently have been discussed; there were also points of doctrine and religion, as excommunications, books and pamphlets wherein a great part of the day hath been so unfitly consumed. Insomuch as this very day you have heard not only us, but also the Pope, the King of Spain, the Duke of Florence, Allen, Sander, Bristow, Espignata, and many more arraigned. What force excommunications be of, what authority is due to the Bishop of

Rome, how men's consciences must be instructed, are no matters of fact, nor triable by juries, but points yet disputed and not resolved in schools; how then can they be determined by you, though wise, laymen otherwise experienced, yet herein ignorant? Yet were it so, that for your knowledge and skill in divinity ye might seem approved censurers of so high a controversey, yet are they no part of all our indictments, and therefore not to be respected by the jury. You perchance would ask me, If these prove naught against us, what then should you inquire of, for these set aside, the rest is almost nothing! Pardon me, I pray you, our innocency is such that if all were cut off that have been objected either weakly or truly against us, there would indeed rest nothing that might prove us guilty; but I answer unto you, that what remaineth be oaths, and those not to rest as proofs unto you, but to be duly examined and fully considered whether they be true and their deposers of credit. In common matters we often see witnesses impealed, and if at any time their credit be little, it ought then to be less when they swear against life. Call, I pray you, to your remembrance how faintly some have deposed, how coldly others, how untruly the rest; especially two who have testified most. What truth may you expect from their mouths? The one hath confessed himself a murderer, the other well known a detestable atheist – a profane heathen – a destroyer of two men already. On your consciences, would you believe them – they that have betrayed both God and man, nay, that have left nothing to swear by, neither in religion nor honesty? Though you would believe them, can you? I know your wisdom is greater, your consciences uprighter; esteem of them as they be. Examine the other two, you shall find neither of them precisely to affirm that we or any of us have practised aught that might be prejudicial to this estate, or dangerous to this commonwealth. God give you grace to weigh our causes aright, and have respect to your own consciences; and so I will keep the jury no longer. I commit the rest to God, and our convictions to your good discretions.

The pleadings had taken about three hours, and the jury consulted for nearly an hour before they agreed on their verdict. In this interval someone brought Campion a glass of beer to refresh him after his labours. The greater part of the lawyers and gentlemen present thought an acquittal was certain, at least for Campion, but judges and jury had all been bought and the desire to gratify Caesar prevailed, Mr Popham, the Attorney General, having plainly signified to them what the Queen's will was. Edmund Plowden,[32] the famous lawyer, himself a Catholic, had come with the rest to see the trial, but one of the judges, not liking that he should report it, or even witness it, sent word to him to leave the court. As he was himself in question for religion, he thought it prudent to obey.

When the verdict was given, Anderson said, 'Forasmuch as these prisoners here indicted and arraigned undertook to be tried by God and their country, and by the verdict of a whole jury, directly and by most sufficient evidence, are found guilty of the said treasons and conspiracies, we pray your lordships to accept the verdict and in her Majesty's behalf to give judgment against them as traitors.'

LORD CHIEF JUSTICE. Campion and the rest, what can you say why you should not die?

CAMPION. It was not our deaths that ever we feared. But we knew that we were not lords of our own lives, and therefore for want of answer would not be guilty of our own deaths. The only thing that we have now to say is, that if our religion do make us traitors, we are worthy to be condemned; but otherwise are and have been as true subjects as ever the Queen had. In condemning us, you condemn all your own ancestors – all the ancient priests, bishops and kings – all that was once the glory of England, the island of saints, and the most devoted child of the See of Peter. For what have we taught, however you may qualify it with the odious name of treason, that they did not uniformly teach? To be condemned with these old lights – not of England only, but of the world[33] – by their degenerate descendants, is both gladness and glory to us. God lives; posterity will live: their judgment is not so liable to corruption as that of those who are now going to sentence us to death.

LORD CHIEF JUSTICE. You must go to the place from whence you came, there to remain until ye be drawn through the open city of London upon hurdles to the place of execution, and there be hanged and let down alive, and your privy parts cut off, and your entrails taken out and burnt in your sight; then your heads to be cut off, and your bodies to be divided in four parts, to be disposed of at her Majesty's pleasure. And God have mercy on your souls.

All the prisoners after this judgement stormed in countenance, crying they were as true and faithful subjects as ever the Queen had any. Only Campion suppressed his affection, and cried aloud, 'Te Deum laudamus, Te Deum laudamus.' Sherwin took up the song, 'Haec est dies quam fecit Dominus, exultemus et laetemur in illa' and the rest expressed their contentment and joy, some in one phrase of Scripture, some in another, whereby the multitudes in the Hall were visibly astonished and affected. Campion was taken to the barge and rowed back to the Tower; and the rest were sent back to their own prisons, where, being laid up in irons for the rest of their time, they expected God's mercy and the Queen's pleasure.

The next day, the remaining priests – Colleton, Richardson, Hart, Ford, Filby, Briant and Shoet — were similarly condemned. But on this occasion, after the verdict was given, one Mr Lancaster witnessed that he was in company with Colleton in Gray's Inn the very day that he was charged with plotting at Reims, where indeed he had never been in his life, as he had been sent to Douay. He was afterwards banished. Among the spectators there was a priest named Nicholson, who, seeing the success of Lancaster's testimony about Colleton, and being able to give similar witness about Ford, offered his evidence, but he was apprehended by the judge's order and sent to prison, where he was well-nigh starved to death.

Even the least legal-minded reader must have felt there was something wrong about this trial. The Crown did not produce any convincing form of evidence of treason. The case was based on such considerations as these:

(1) The Pope had paid the expenses of some priests –
    therefore they were traitors.
(2) Campion and Allen had met and talked at Reims –
    therefore they were traitors.
(3) Campion was alleged to have met the Bishop of Ross –
    therefore Campion was a traitor.

(4) Campion had used an alias and had dressed as a layman
    therefore Campion was a traitor.

(5) Copies of an oath renouncing allegiance were found
    where Campion had been –
        therefore he was a traitor.

(6) Cottam had a book on how to deal with Protestants –
    therefore he was a traitor.

(7) Bristow (Rishton?) was alleged to be skilled in fireworks –
    therefore he was a traitor.

And so on.

Each informer-witness told his tale but brought no cor-
roborative evidence. It was his word against the prisoners'
denials. All the prisoners declared their loyalty to the queen,
but refused to give opinions on the supremacy and the authority
of the Pope, neither of which was a treasonous matter under
the 1351 Statute.

The term 'judicious murder' is not one to be used lightly but
it is the only one applicable to the fates of these thirteen priests
and one layman. According to the court, all were equally
guilty, though, had they been tried separately, as Campion
asked, several of them, such as Thomas Cottam, would surely
have been acquitted by any jury. Their after-treatment was
anomalous. Why were five of them kept in prison and later
banished? Nor is it clear why the hanging of seven was post-
poned for five months after the executions of Campion, Sherwin
and Briant on the 1st December 1581.

Campion's speeches at the trial give us a measure of his
intellectual quality. There were no rhetorical flourishes and no
long-drawn out arguments. All was logical and pertinent. He
kept closely to the prosecutor's case. Time and again he urged
that irrelevant matters should be ignored and that what was
needed was solid proof not 'presumptions and probabilities.'
The lawyers present must have felt that had Campion been
one of them, he would soon have risen to eminence. Certainly
as we read the record of the trial, we see that it was dominated
by Edmund Campion, and one feels almost sorry for the

counsel who had to make bricks without straw in what was a
mockery of justice.

[1] This account of the trial follows Richard Simpson's excellent recension in chapter
XV of his biography of Campion. See also *State Trials* (Cobbett's).

[2] Ralph Sherwin, Luke Kirby, James Bosgrave, Thomas Cottam, Robert Johnson,
Henry Orton, Edward Rishton.

[3] Hudson was probably the Queen's Counsel mentioned later. He evidently thought
that Campion had been advised by a lawyer. The point made by Campion was a good
one, as the L.C.J. admitted, but he had had his marching orders, and 'it cannot be
otherwise.'

[4] See above pp. 26, 132.

[5] See above pp. 47, 132.

[6] Pass = give a verdict. So Shakespeare, 'The Jury, passing on the prisoner's life'
(Meas. 2.1, 19).

[7] It will be noticed that this was a favourite figure with Campion.

[8] Students not yet ordained.

[9] This refers to Richard Bristow's *A Briefe Teatise of diuerse plaine and sure waves to finde
out the truthe in this doubtful and dangerous time of Heresies: conteyning sundry worthie Motiues
unto the Catholike faith, or Considerations to moue a man to beleue the Catholcikes, and not the
Heretickes.* It was printed in Antwerp in 1574. See, Southern, op. cit. pp. 146, 390–1,
and Ap. I.

[10] See above pp. 34, 64, 94.

[11] See above pp. 90f, 153.

[12] This should be Sir Richard Shelley, last grand prior of the Knights of St John in
England. He was established at Venice and kept in touch with the English Government in the hope of winning better treatment for Catholics. He had been in Rome
when Campion and Parsons set out for England. For his newphew William, see above
p. 00.

[13] John Leslie (1528–96), Bishop of Ross, was among the most consistent supporters
of the Queen of Scots. He was involved in the Ridolfi plot and was imprisoned in the
Tower but was allowed to leave the country in 1574 when he went to Paris and Rome,
where he represented the interests of the Queen of Scots.

[14] Thomas Roper ?

[15] The letter was from Sander to Allen; Nov. 1577. From this the gaps in the record
can be filled; it was the King of Spain who feared the war, the Pope who was ready
with men.

[16] See above p. 25 for this non-existent alliance. The Duke had sent a warning of
the Ridolfi plot to Queen Elizabeth, and of another plot against King James of
Scotland just before he became King of England; the messenger was Henry Wotton.

[17] Something that happens after an affair is thought to be ended.

[18] This explanation of Paul/Saul is not now accepted.

[19] The Statute of Apparel was passed at Wolsey's suggestion in 1515; additions
were made to it under Elizabeth to curb, e.g. Italian fashions.

[20] See above p. 69.

[21] It should be noted that these documents were not produced at the trials of Vaux
and others in whose houses they were supposedly found. See above pp. 134f.

[22] Was this the first use of this term?

[23] See above p. 131.

[24] The recorder's version of Azpilcuseta (Martin) who was known as Navarrus. Another record of the trial gives 'Dr Navarre.' The book may have been his 'Enchiridion' or 'Manuele.' The title used in the report is not known.

[25] See above pp. 117ff.

[26] An expert suggests that there should be no comma between 'poggets' and 'daggs.' The probable meaning would then be 'pocket dags (pistols).' The term 'pogget' by itself is not known. A two-handed sword was at least five feet long, and anyone with such a weapon would have come under suspicion, as anyone carrying a machine-gun would if he entered the House of Commons.

[27] It is difficult to believe that anyone in the court could take this inept tale seriously. Payne did not go abroad.

[28] There is some confusion here. Richard Bristow came to England in September 1581 to recover his health in 'his native air.' He stayed with the Bellamy family at Uxenden, near Harrow, and there died on the 14th October. He was not apprehended. The only one of the prisoners not otherwise questioned at the trial was Edward Rishton; so perhaps for 'Bristow' we should read 'Rishton.'

[29] William Tedder, an apostate priest, though he did not make his public recantation at Paul's Cross until the end of 1588. The linking of 'Tedder' with 'Tudor' seems far-fetched but it may have been a matter of pronunciation.

[30] Nothing is known of this incident. It will be noted that Stedd carefully refrained from giving dates and times.

[31] Probably Eliot.

[32] Edmund Plowden (1518–85). 'By his contemporaries he was acknowledged to be the greatest and most honest lawyer of his age.' *D.N.B.* It is said that the queen offered him the Lord Chancellorship if he would conform; his Catholicism kept him from advancement in his profession. His law reports became authoritative; they were continued by Edmund Anderson, the leader of the prosecution in this trial.

[33] St Thomas More had made the same point at his trial.

Chapter 18

Tyburn

The prisoners had been condemned on the 20th and 21st November; it was usual for executions to be carried out within a few days of sentences being given, but there was some delay in deciding when the priests should be hanged. It was for the Council to give the order; divisions of opinion among the Councillors caused some hesitation. Perhaps some of them may have felt that the trial, which had been public and was soon the cause of adverse comment, did not reflect much credit on the government. Campion's astonishing prestige had also to be taken into account; what would the reaction be to his hanging? It has already been argued that Alençon's presence in England was not a decisive factor but it may have influenced some of the Councillors. Eventually the execution was fixed for the 25th November, but there was yet another and inexplicable change; the final date was to be the 1st December. It was also decided that Ralph Sherwin and Alexander Briant should be hanged at the same time as Campion.

We have already noted two visits paid to Campion during this waiting period. One was from his sister, who, it is said, was empowered to offer him preferment and a pension if he conformed. The second visitor was George Eliot. No doubt Protestant divines were also, as was usual, sent to attempt the prisoner's conversion. One of the keepers, we are told, was so affected by Campion's demeanour and talk that he became a Catholic.

It seems best to use here an eye-witness account of the hanging, rather than attempt a fresh narrative. The observer was almost certainly Thomas Alfield, a Douay priest who had just come on the mission. He was the brother of Parsons' servant Robert. A law student of Gray's Inn, named Dolmen, was with Alfield and he also took notes.

On the morning of the 1st December, Edmund Campion was led from his cell to the Coleharbour prison[1] where he was joined by Ralph Sherwin and Alexander Briant.

'They were drawn from the Tower to Tyburn there to be martyred for the Catholic faith and religion. Father Campion was alone on one hurdle, and the other two together on another, all molested by ministers and others calling upon them by the way for their subversion, and by some others also, as opportunity served, comforted, and Father Campion especially consulted by some in cases of conscience and religion, the mire wherewith he was all spattered most courteously wiped off his face.

'When they were come to the place of execution, where divers of her Majesty's honourable Council, with many other persons of honour, besides an infinite multitude of people, attended their coming. Father Campion was first brought up into the cart, where after some small pause he began to speak upon that text of St Paul "We are made a spectacle to the world and to angels and men" (I.Cor.4.9), but was interrupted by Sir Francis Knollys[2] and the Sheriffs urging him to confess his treason against her Majesty, and to acknowledge himself guilty; to whom he answered, "For the treasons which have been laid to my charge and I am come here to suffer for, I desire you all to bear witness with me that thereof I am altogether innocent."

'Whereupon answer was made to him by one of the Council, that he might not seem to deny the objections against him, having been proved by sufficient evidence. "Well, my lord," said he, "I am a Catholic man and a priest. In that faith have I lived, and in that faith do I intend to die; and if you esteem my religion treason, then am I guilty. As for any other treason, I never committed, God is my judge; but you have now what you desire. I beseech you to have patience, and suffer me to speak a word or two for discharge of my conscience." But not being suffered to go forward, he was forced to speak only to that point which they most urged, protesting, that he was innocent of all treason and conspiracy, desiring credit to be given to his answers as to the last answer made upon his death and soul; adding, that the jury might easily be deceived, but that he forgave all as he desired to be forgiven, desiring all them to forgive him whose names he had confessed upon the rack, for, upon the Commissioners' oaths that no harm should come unto them, he uttered some persons with whom he had been.

'Further he declared the meaning of a letter sent by himself in time of his imprisonment to Mr Pound, a prisoner then also in the Tower, in which he wrote that he would not disclose the secrets of some houses where he had been entertained, affirming upon his soul, that the secrets he meant in that letter were not, as it was misconstrued by the enemy, treason or conspiracy, or any matter else against her Majesty or the State but saying of Mass, hearing confessions, preaching and such like duties and functions of priesthood. This he protested to be true as he would answer before God.

'They pressed him to declare his opinion of Pius Quintus his Bull concerning the excommunication of the Queen; to which demand he made no answer. Then they asked whether he renounced the Pope. He answered, he was a Catholic; where-upon one inferred saying, "In your Catholicism (I noted the term) all treasons are contained." In fine preparing himself to drink his last draught of Christ's cup, he was interrupted in his prayer by a minister, willing him to say some prayer with him; unto whom, looking back with a mild countenance, he meekly replied, "You and I are not one in religion, wherefore I pray you content yourself. I bar none of prayer, only I desire them of the household of the faith to pray with me, and in my agony to say one Creed," for a signification that he died for the confession of the Catholic Faith therein contained.

'Some also called to him to pray in English, to whom he

answered that he would pray in a language he well understood. At the upshot of this conflict he was willed to ask the Queen's forgiveness, and to pray for her; he meekly answered, "Wherein have I offended her? In this I am innocent; this is my last speech; in this give me credit; I have and do pray for her." Then Lord Charles Howard[3] asked of him for which Queen he prayed, whether for Elizabeth the Queen? To whom he answered, "Yes, for Elizabeth, your Queen and my Queen."

'And the cart being drawn away, he meekly and sweetly yielded his soul unto his Saviour, protesting that he died a perfect Catholic.

'After Mr Campion was executed and the butchery finished, the hangman taking hold of Mr Sherwin with his hands all bloody, said to him, thinking to terrify him, "Come, Sherwin, take thou also thy wages." But the holy man, nothing dismayed, embraced him with a cheerful countenance, and reverently kissed the blood that stuck to his hands; at which the people were very much moved. Then getting into the cart, he employed some time in prayer and contemplation having his eyes shut and his hands lifted up to heaven. After which he asked if the people looked for any speech from him. Many of the people, and some also of the more honourable sort, answering "Yes," he began with manly courage and a loud voice first to render thanks to each of the three Persons of the eternal Trinity for the mercies and blessings bestowed upon him, and then was going on to give an account of his faith when Sir Francis Knollys interrupted him and bade him confess his treason against the Queen. Mr Sherwin with great constancy replied, "I am innocent of any such crime." And when he was still further pressed to acknowledge himself guilty, he said, "I have no occasion to tell a lie; 'tis a case where my soul is at stake," and so still persisted to maintain his innocence, adding, that although in this short time of mortal life he was to undergo the infamy and punishment of a traitor, he made no doubt of his future happiness through Jesus Christ, in whose death, passion, and blood he only trusted.

'Then he made a sweet prayer to our Lord Jesus acknowledging the imperfection, misery and sinful wretchedness of his own nature, still protesting his innocence from all treasons and traitorous practices, and that his going out of this realm beyond the seas was only for his soul's health, to learn to save his soul. And being again tempted by Sir Francis Knollys, he answered in this wise, "Tush, tush! you and I shall answer this before another Judge, where my innocence shall be known, and you will see that I am guiltless of this." Whereupon Sir Francis said, "We know you are no contriver or doer of this treason, for you are no man of arms, but you are a traitor by consequence." But Mr Sherwin boldly answered, "If to be a Catholic, if to be a perfect Catholic, be to be a traitor, then am I a traitor."

'After which words, being by authority debarred from further speech, he said, "I forgive all who, either by general presumption or particular error, have procured my death"; and so devoutly prayed to his Saviour Jesus. After which prayer he was pressed to speak his opinion touching Pope Pius his Bull: to which point he gave no answer. Then being willed to pray for the Queen, he answered, "I have and do." At which words Lord Howard again asked which Queen he meant, whether Elizabeth Queen? To whom, somewhat smiling, he said, "Yea, for Elizabeth Queen I now at this instant pray my Lord God to make her His servant in this life, and after this life coheir with Jesus Christ."

'When he had thus prayed, there were some that said openly that he meant to make her a Papist; to whom he boldly replied, "God forbid otherwise." And so recollecting himself in prayer, he died patiently, constantly, and mildly, crying, "Jesu, Jesu, Jesu, be to me a Jesus."'

'After Mr Campion and Mr Sherwin had finished their course, Mr Briant was ordered up into the cart. Being there prepared to death, he began first to declare his bringing up in the Catholic faith and religion, and his being at Oxford; upon which word he was cut short by one saying, "What have we to

do with Oxford? Come to thy purpose, and confess thy treason."
Whereupon he answered, "I am not guilty of any such thing; I
was never at Rome nor at Reims at that time when Dr Sander
came into Ireland." To this end he spoke and protested, as he
would answer before God.

'He spake not much, but whereas he was urged more than
the other two to speak what he thought of the Bull of Pius
Quintus, he said he did believe it, as all Catholics did, and the
Catholic Faith doth, and thereupon protesting himself to die a
true Catholic, as he was saying "Miserere mei Deus", he was
delivered from the cart, with more pain, by negligence of the
hangman, than either of the others.'

---

[1] This was on the west side of the White Tower connected by a wall running
southwards to the Wakefield Tower; it was demolished many years ago. 'Coldharbour
Tower' preserves the name.

[2] Sir Francis Knollys (d. 1596) served the queen in many capacities but did not
reach high office because of his extreme Puritanism. He was, with Lord Scrope, the
earliest guardian of Mary of Scots when she took refuge in England.

[3] Lord Charles Howard of Effingham, of Armada fame. He was then Lord
Chamberlain. His question, 'Which queen?' was to make sure that Campion (and
later Sherwin) did not mean Mary, Queen of Scots.

Chapter 19

Aftermath

A young law student of Gray's Inn named Henry Walpole was one of the 'multitude of people' at the hanging of the three priests at Tyburn. When Campion's body was being dissevered some of the blood bespattered the young student. He had been at the conferences in the Tower and also at the trial in Westminster Hall. The blood of the martyr was a sign to him that the moment had come to take a step that had probably been in his mind for some time. He crossed to France and entered the seminary at Reims in July 1582; he later went to Rome and was admitted to the Society of Jesus. He was ordained priest in 1588 and came on the mission in 1593; he was at once captured, and, after cruel torturing, was hanged at York on the 7th April 1595.

Before he left England, Henry Walpole composed some verses in honour of his hero; these, with some by other hands, were included in a volume containing Thomas Alfield's account of the martyrdom; one of the poems was circulated in manuscript separately with the title *An Epitaphe of the lyfe and deathe of the most famouse clerke and vertuous priest Edmund Campion.* This poem has been ascribed with strong probability to Henry Walpole.[1]

The book containing Alfield's account was entitled, *A true report of the death and martyrdom of M. Campion Iesuite and preiste, & M. Sherwin, & M. Bryan preistes, at Tiborne the first of December 1581. Observid and written by a Catholike preist, which was present thereat. Whereunto is annexid certayne verses made by sundrie persons.*[2] This was a reply to a four-leaved pamphlet probably written by Anthony Munday at the Council's request. It was entitled: *An Aduertisement and defence for truth against her backbyters, and especially against the whispering fauvorers and colorers of Campions, and the rest of his confederates treasons.* This was published in November 1581 before the hangings.

Alfield's account was also a rebuttal of Anthony Munday's *A Discoverie of Edmund Campion and his Confederates, their most Horrible and Traiterous Practises against her Majesties most royall Person and the Realm. Wherein may be seene how thorowe the whole Course of their Araignement, they were notably convicted in every Cause. Whereto is added the Execution of Edmund Campion, Ralphe Sherwin and Alexander Brian, executed at Tiburn, the 1 of December. Published by A. M., sometime the Pope's scholar, allowed in the Seminarie at Rome amongst them.*

The Council took action to suppress the 'true report'. The printer, Stephen Vallenger was arrested and accused of being responsible for the writing and printing; he admitted that he had written the manuscript copy found in his possession, but denied that he was the author. He was brought before the Star Chamber court on the 16th May 1582, and condemned to the pillory, one day at Westminster and one day in Cheapside and at each place to lose an ear, and then to be imprisoned for life. He was associated in the printing with Richard Verstegan,[3] an Oxford scholar, who had a secret press in Smithfield where he printed under a family name of Rowlande; the press was seized when Vallenger was arrested, but Verstegan managed to escape abroad. Vallenger was imprisoned in the Fleet and died there about 1590.

A French publication of 1582, *L'Histoire de la Mort que le R. P. Edmunde Campion . . . et autres ont souffert en Angleterre*, was based on English materials. In the same year other accounts were published in Rome, Ingoldstadt, Milan, Turin, Venice and Louvain.

Anthony Munday replied to Alfield's account and the French version in his *A breefe Aunswer made unto two seditious Pamphlets, the one printed in French, and the other in English. Contayning a defence of Edmund Campion and his complices, their moste horrible and vnnatural Treasons, against her Maiestie and the Realme.* By A. M. London, 1582.

The Council decided that an authoritative justification was necessary, and this was published as a twenty-eight page pamphlet under the title *A particular Declaration or Testimony of the undutiful and traitorous affection borne against her Majestie by Edmund Campion, Iesuite, and other condemned Priests, witnessed by their own Confessions; in reproof of those slanderous books and libels delivered out to the contrary by such as are maliciously affected towards her Majestie and the State.*

The most important record was edited by William Allen in a book published in Reims; this included the substance of Alfield's narrative with other eye-witness accounts and some material provided by Parsons and others. The title was: *A Briefe Historie of the Glorious Martyrdom of XII Reuerend Priests, executed vvithin these tvvelue-monethes for confession and defence of the Catholike Faith. But vnder the false pretence of Treason. VVith a note of sundrie things that befel them in their life and imprisonment: and a preface declaring their innocencie. Set furth by such as were much conuersant vvith them in their life, and present at their arraignement and death.*[4] The book was published in September 1582; Latin, Italian and Spanish translations followed.

Burghley was provoked by all this eulogy of Campion and the other priests who had been hanged as traitors to issue at the end of 1583 a twenty-page pamphlet entitled, *The Execution of Justice in England for the maintenance of publique and Christian peace, against certeine stirrers of sedition, and adherents to the traytors and enemies of the Realme, without any persecution of them for questions of Religion, as is falsely reported and published by fautors and fosterers of their treasons. xvii. Decemb. 1583.* To this Allen replied in a two-hundred paged book: *A Trve Sincere and Modest Defence of English Catholiques that svffer for their Faith both at home and abrode: against a false, seditious and slaunderous Libel intitled; The Execvtion of Ivstice in England. VVherin is declared, hovv vniustlie the Protestants doe charge Catholiques with treason; hovv they deny their persecution for Religion; and hovv deceitfullie they seeke to abuse strangers about the cause, greatnes, and maner of their sufferings, vvith diuers other matters perteining to this purpose.* Rouen. 1584.[5]

It is not necessary to go into the details of the arguments used in this controversy; the titles have been given in full becaue they summarise so well the authors' intentions. The official justification was also expressed by Sir Walter Mildmay at the opening of Parliament in November 1584.

'Divers other malicious and secret practisers' were dependent upon the Pope; 'the most pernicious those that are called Jesuits and seminary priests a rabble of vagrant runagates that creep . . . into sundry parts of the realm and are occupied to stir sedition . . . under pretence of reforming men's consciences.' As for the public trials of the Jesuit Campion and his fellows these men, said Mildmay, were prosecuted 'not for the superstitious ceremonies of Rome but for the most high and capital offences and conspiracies – the deposing of our most gracious Queen, advancing of another in her place, alteration and subversion of this whole state and government.' 'Being asked openly whether the Pope had authority to depose the Queen and whether her Majesty was a lawful and rightful Queen, notwithstanding anything that the Pope hath or might do,' they had answered, 'It is a question of divinity: we pray you demand no such thing of us.'[6]

This tragic dilemma of conflicting loyalties was never resolved. Priests continued to enter the country from the English seminaries abroad, and the grim fates of their predecessors did not daunt them. Except for one or two aberrants, they were in no way involved in political policy; they were, first and foremost, missioners intent on fortifying the faithful and winning souls to Christ. This separation of the spiritual from the temporal was, at that period, impossible for those who had to govern the country. As the menace of a Spanish invasion came nearer with the threat of the country's subjection to a foreign power, so anti-Papist feeling in the country was exacerbated. It was the duty of the government to safeguard the realm and so the priests were inevitably regarded as emissaries of the enemy, as what we should call a fifth column.

When they were caught, they had to suffer the penalty of treason. Hanging, drawing, and quartering was not a specially devised cruel death for priests; all traitors had to suffer in the same way. During the reign of Elizabeth, 125 priests were hanged.[7]

Something should be said, however briefly, of Robert Parsons' career after leaving England in the summer of 1581. One of his purposes was to establish a printing press that could issue books for Catholics in England; there was a great demand for such aids to devotion. His experience with his secret press had proved that this was too uncertain a method of producing books in any quantity or of any length in England. At Rouen he found a printer named George L'Oyselst who could work for him; this arrangement lasted until 1585 when Parsons once more employed Stephen Brinkley, his former printer at Greenstreet. Another successful project was the foundation of a school for boys at Eu (near Le Tréport); this was later transferred to St Omer and is now at Stonyhurst.

Parsons' next concern was the mission to Scotland under William Crichton. s.j. Catholics wanted Mary, Queen of Scots, reinstated, and there was the lesser hope that her son James could be brought under the influence of his mother's religion. This was a complicated affair and its details cannot be set out here, but it brought Parsons into association with Philip II of Spain whose confidence he gained; an immediate outcome was an annual pension for the support of the badly-off seminary at Reims.

It is not known at what stage Robert Parsons and William Allen came to the conclusion that, valuable and essential as the mission to England was, there was no hope of widespread conversion. Parsons' own experience probably showed to him what an impossible task it was under the existing regime. The mission could not be more than a holding operation, and time was to show that this was to weaken gradually. So Allen and Parsons turned to a political solution which was in keeping with the contemporary theories of the state and religion. A change, they felt, could only come about by force of arms, and the prime mover must be Spain. The Pope could not possibly raise an army and navy for such a purpose. Philip was sympathetic, but it should be noted that his final attack in Armada year was not primarily for the cause of religion; it was for the cause of Spain. Here we meet the problem of treason. We must recall that we are talking of a period when religious changes could be effected by war; the principle of *cuius regio, eius religio* of the so-called religious peace of Augsburg (1555) was operative. Allen and Parsons maintained that there was no intention of submitting England to a foreign power, but a foreign power must intervene to secure the re-establishment of the Catholic religion by a change of sovereign. They shared the exiles' delusion that they had only to land an army and supporters would flock to their standard. Parsons has always been regarded as the chief intriguer, but, a study of the records (and much was not recorded) suggests that Allen was the real manager but, of course, with the whole-hearted collaboration of Parsons.

It is easy to condemn them and the many English exiles who thought as they did. Perhaps we can gain a less prejudiced attitude if we consider an historical parallel. In June 1688 a letter signed by, among others, Bishop Compton of London, was sent to William of Orange asking him to intervene to protect the Protestant religion and succession. William landed on Guy Fawkes' Day with an army of which two-thirds were foreign mercenaries. He succeeded in forcing James II to leave the country and the Glorious Revolution was over. Were Bishop Compton and the other signatories traitors when they signed that letter? Perhaps the answer may be found in one of the epigrams of Sir John Harrington, the godson of Queen Elizabeth.[8]

> Treason doth never prosper: what's the reason?
> For if it prosper, none dare call it treason.

Political planning was not Parsons' main work. His pen was seldom idle for long. In 1582 he published at Rouen what was to be the most influential of his writings. He may have begun work on it while in England. This was: *The First Booke of the Christian Exercise, appertayning to resolution. VVherein are layed downe the causes & reasons that should moue a man to resolue hym selfe to the seruice of God: And all the impedimentes remoued, which may lett* [prevent] *the same.* Rouen.[9] 1582. The book became known as *The Christian Directory* and was frequently reprinted for two centuries. It was indeed among the most influential books of devotion in English right into the nineteenth century not only among Catholics, but in an adaptation among Protestants. Edmund Bunny, an Anglican clergyman, adapted the book for Protestant use with the title *The Booke of Christian Exercise appertaining to Resolution.* Like its prototype it had a long popularity. Thus Richard Baxter (1615–91) wrote in his autobiography, 'A poor day-labourer had an old torn book which he lent my father, which was called *Bunny's Resolution* being written by Parsons the Jesuit and corrected [*sic*] by Edmund Bunny. And in the reading of this book, it pleased God to awaken my soul.' In addition to this *Christian Directory,* Parsons wrote twenty other books after leaving England.[10]

A bare summary must suffice for the rest of Parsons' activities. In 1587 William Allen was created a cardinal and, in the following year, Parsons took charge of the English College at Rome, but his services were soon needed in Spain and there in 1592 he established and for a time directed English seminaries at Valladolid, Seville and Madrid.

A book was published in Antwerp in 1594 that caused a stir. Its title was *A Conference about the next Succession to the Crowne of Ingland,* but it was usually known as *The Book of the Succession,* and was blamed on Parsons.[11] The book was originally drafted by a group of English exiles of whom the leader was probably Sir Francis Englefield. Its purport was, and still is, grossly misrepresented; it was said to advocate the Infanta of Spain as Queen Elizabeth's successor. On no subject was the queen so sensitive as the succession and no one dared to raise the question with her. When Parliament risked her displeasure by pleading the importance of the matter, she told the members to mind their own business. Yet it was a problem that became more and more urgent as she aged. The succession of James I seems to us to have been inevitable but it was far from being so even in the last decade of Elizabeth's reign. Indeed Sir Robert Cecil, Burghley's son, took out an insurance policy by getting into touch with King Philip as well as King James. The first part of *The Book of the Succession* was an almost academic discussion on what principles the succession to a crown could be determined; the second part discussed the claims of a dozen possible descendants of English kings but without favouring one of them. Parsons and Allen read the manuscript but how far they were responsible for its final form is not known; it is certainly inaccurate to blame Parsons for the whole work or even for its conception.

When William Allen died in October 1594, some urged that Robert Parsons should receive the red hat; he himself did not stir in the matter, and his opponents were successful in blocking the proposal. In 1587 he became rector of the English College, Rome, a post he held until his death on the 15th April 1610. At his desire he was buried beside William Allen in the College chapel. Their tombs were among those violated when French Revolutionary soldiers occupied Rome in 1798.

Thirty years had passed since Robert Parsons and Edmund Campion had parted on the open heath near Stonor. During that time Parsons had borne on his person a piece of the rope that had bound Campion on the scaffold; it had been bought from the executioner. After Parson's death this relic was kept at the English College, and is now at Stonyhurst.

Some words Parsons wrote soon after Campion's condemnation may fittingly end this record.

> I call him brother for that once God made me worthy of so great preferment, now I take him rather for my patron than for my brother, whose steps I beseech Christ I may be worthy to follow.[12]

¹ See Appendix.

² Southern, op. cit., pp. 279–283, 376–9.

³ For Verstegan, see C.R.S., Vol. LII.

⁴ Southern, op. cit., pp. 383–5.

⁵ Southern, op. cit., pp. 386–7.

⁶ Quoted from Neale, op. cit., II, p. 29.

⁷ It is of interest to note that at least fifty-two of them were converts.

⁸ The queen once referred to him as 'that saucy poet, my godson.' He vainly tried to enliven her in her last illness.

⁹ Southern, op. cit., pp. 467–9.

¹⁰ See Southern, pp. 467–478. None of these had any policitcal implications. See also the essay by Joseph Crehan, S.J., in *English Spiritual Writers* (1961).

¹¹ For a full discussion, see, Leo Hicks, S.J., in *Recusant History*, Vol. 4, No. 3.

¹² C.R.S., XXIX, p. 120.

Appendix

Verses said to have been composed by St Henry Walpole. The original is in the Bodleian Library.

The spelling has been modernised.

JESUS MARIA

An Epitaph of the life and death of the most famous clerk and virtuous priest EDMUND CAMPION, and reverend father of the meek Society of the blessed name of Jesus.

Why do I use my paper, ink and pen?
  Or call my wits to counsel what to say?
Such memories were made for mortal man,
  I speak of saints, whose names cannot decay.
An angel's trump were meeter far to sound
  Their glorious deaths, if such on earth were found.

Pardon my wants. I offer naught but will.
  Their register remaineth safe above,
Campion exceeds the compass of my skill.
  Yet let me use the measure of my love,
And give me leave in low and homely verse,
  This high attempt in England to rehearse.

He came by vow. The cause, to conquer sin,
  His armour prayer. The word his targe and shield,
His comfort heaven, his spoil our souls to win.
  The devil his foe, the wicked world his field.
His triumph joy. His wage eternal bliss,
  His captain Christ, which ever during is.

From ease to pain, from honour to disgrace,
  From love to hate, to danger, being well.
From safe abroad, to fears in every place.
  Contempting death, to save our souls from hell.
Our new apostle coming to restore
  The faith which Austin planted here before.

His native flowers were mixed with herb of grace.
   His mild behaviour tempered well with skill.
A lowly mind possessed a learned place.
   A sugared speech, a rare and virtuous will.
A saint like man was set in earth below
   The seed of truth in hearing hearts to sow.

With tongue and pen the truth he taught and wrote,
   By force whereof they came to Christ apace,
But when it pleased God it was his lot
   He should be thrall, he lent him so much grace,
His patience there did work so much nor more,
   As had his heavenly speeches done before.

His fare was hard, yet mild and sweet his cheer.
   His prison close, yet free and loose his mind.
His torture great, yet scant or none his fear.
   His offers large, yet no thing could him blind.
O constant man, O mind, O virtue strange,
   Whom want, nor woe, nor fear, nor hope could change.

From rack in Tower they brought him to dispute,
   Bookless, alone, to answer all that came,
Yet Christ gave grace, he did them all confute
   So sweetly there in glory of his name
That even the adverse part are forced to say
   That Campion's cause did bear the bell away.

This foil enraged the minds of some so far
   They thought it best to take his life away,
Because they saw he would their matter marr,
   And leave them shortly naught at all to say.
Traitor he was with many a seely slight
   Yet was a jury packed, that cried guilt straight.

Religion there was treason to the queen,
   Preaching of penance were against the land,
Priests were such dangerous men, as hath not been,
   Prayers and beeds were fight and force of hand.
Cases of conscience bane unto the State.
   So blind is error, so false a witness hate.

And yet behold these lambs are drawn to die,
    Treasons proclaimed, the queen is put in fear,
Out upon Spain, fie malice, fie.
    Speakest thou to them that did the guiltless hear?
Can humble souls departing now to Christ,
    Protest untrue? Avaunt foul fiend, thou liest!

My sovereign liege, behold you subjects' end,
    Your secret foes do misinform your grace.
Who in your cause their holy lives would spend,
    As traitors die? A rare and monstrous case.
The bloody wolf condemns the harmless sheep,
    Before the dog, the while the shepherds sleep.

England look up. This soil is stained with blood,
    Thou hast made martyrs many of thine own,
If thou hadst grace, their deaths would do thee good.
    The seed will take, which in such blood is sown,
And Campion's learning fertile as before,
    Thus watered too, must needs of force be more.

Repent thee ELIOT, of this Judas kiss,
    I wish thy penance, not thy desperate end.
Let NORTON[1] think, which now in prison is,
    To whom was said, he was not Caesar's friend,
And let the judge consider well in fear,
    That Pilate washed his hands and was not clear.

The witness false, SLEDD, MUNDAY, and the rest
    Which had your slanders noted in your books,
Confess your fault beforehand, it were best,
    Lest God do find it written, when he looks
In dreadful doom upon the souls of men,
    It will be late, alas, to mend it then.

You bloody jury, LEE,[2] and all the 'leven,
    Take heed, your verdict which was given in haste
Do not exclude you from the joys of heaven,
    And cause you rue it, when the time is passed,
And everyone whose malice caused him say
    Crucify, let him dread the terror of that day.

Fond ELDERTON[3] call in this foolish rhyme,
  Thy scurril ballads are too bad to sell.
Let good men rest, and mend thyself in time.
  Confess in prose, thou hast not metred well.
Or if this folly cannot choose but fain
  Write alehouse joys, blaspheme thou not in vain.

Remember you that would oppress the cause,
  The Church is Christ, his honour cannot die,
Though hell itself wrest her grizzly jaws,
  And join in league with schism and heresy,
Though craft devise and cruel rage oppress,
  Yet skill will write, and martyrdom confess.

You thought perhaps when learned Campion dies,
  His pen must cease, his sugared tongue be still.
But you forget how loud his death it cries,
  How far beyond the sound of tongue and guile.
You did not know how rare and great and good
  It was to write his precious gifts in blood.

Living he spoke to them which present were,
  His writing took the censure of the view.
Now fame reports his learning far and near,
  And now his death confirms his doctrine true.
His virtues now are written in the skies,
  And often read with holy watered eyes.

All Europe wonders at so rare a man,
  England is filled with rumour of his end.
London must needs, for it was present then
  When constantly four saints their lives did spend,
The streets, the stones, the steps, they hail them by
  Proclaim the cause, for which these martyrs died.

The Tower says the truth he did defend,
  The bar bears witness of his guiltless mind.
Tyburn doth tell, he made a patient end.
  In every gate his martyrdom we find
In vain you wrought, that would obscure his name,
  For heaven and earth will still record the same.

Your sentence wrong pronounced of him here
    Exempts him from the judgment for to come.
O happy he that is not judged there!
    God grant me too, to have an earthly doom.
Your witness false and lewdly taken in,
    Doth cause he is not now accused of sin.

His prison now, the city of the king,
    His rack and torture joys and heavenly bliss,
For men's reproach with angels he doth sing
    A sacred song, which everlasting is.
For shame but short, and loss of small renown,
    He purchased hath an ever during crown.

His quartered limbs shall join with joy again,
    And rise a body brighter than the sun
Your bloody malice tormented him in vain,
    For every wrench some glory hath him won,
And every drop of blood which he did spend
    Hath reaped a joy which never shall have end.

Can dreary death then daunt our faith or pain,
    Lest lingering life we fear to lose our ease?
No. No. Such death procureth life again.
    'Tis only God we tremble to displease.
Who kills but once, and ever since we die,
    Whose whole revenge torments eternally.

We cannot fear a mortal torment, we.
    These martyrs' blood hath moistened all our hearts,
Whose parted quarters when we chance to see
    We learn to play the constant Christian parts.
His head doth speak, and heavenly precepts give
    How we that look should frame ourselves to live.

His youth instructs us how to spend our days.
    His fleeing bids us learn to banish sin.
His straight profession shows the narrow ways
    Which they must walk that look to enter in.
His home return by danger and distress
    Embolden us our conscience to profess.

His hurdle draws us with him to the cross,
  His speeches there provokes us for to die.
His death doth say, this life is but a loss.
  His martyred blood from heaven to us doth cry.
His first and last and all conspire in this
  To show the way that leadeth us to bliss.

Blessed be God, which lent him so much grace,
  Thanked be Christ which blessed his martyr so,
Happy is he, which seeth his master's face,
  Cursed all they that thought to work him woe,
Bounden be we, to give eternal praise,
  To Jesus name which such a man did raise.

NOTE

William Byrd (1540–1623) composed a madrigal on the first verse of this poem. A leading authority, E. H. Fellowes, has called it 'perhaps the finest of Byrd's serious madrigals.' Byrd, of the Chapel Royal, was a Catholic, but he was protected by his eminence as a musician in the service of Queen Elizabeth and King James; he was presented as 'a papistical recusant' from time to time and paid his fines, but was not otherwise harassed.

[1] He was imprisoned in the Tower at the end of 1581 for speaking against the Alençon courtship but was soon released. This reference dates these verses.

[2] William Lee, foreman of the jury; nothing more is known of him.

[3] William Elderton, a prolific ballad writer, but nothing of his about Campion has survived, unless they are the verses in Anthony Munday's *A Brief Answer* (1582).

Index of Personal Names

Index of Personal Names